The First Austrian Republic
1918–1938

The First Austrian Republic 1918–1938

A Study based on British and
Austrian Documents

F. L. CARSTEN

Gower/Maurice Temple Smith

Published by
Gower Publishing Company Limited
Gower House
Croft Road
Aldershot
Hants GU11 3HR
England

Gower Publishing Company
Old Post Road
Brookfield
Vermont 05036
USA

British Library Cataloguing in Publication Data
Carsten, F.L.
    The first Austrian Republic 1918–1938.
    1. Austria — 1918–1938
    I. Title
    943.6'051   DB96

ISBN 0 566 05162 1

Printed in Great Britain at the
University Press, Cambridge

Contents

Preface

Since Charles Gulick published his *Austria from Habsburg to Hitler* in 1948, many books have appeared dealing with the history of the First Austrian Republic or with the forcible incorporation of Austria into Hitler's Third Reich. The present book is to a large extent based on the voluminous British records in the Public Record Office, which follow developments in Austria from day to day and provide a vivid commentary on these events, whether written in Vienna or in London. Very fortunately, this study could be written using not only the records of the Cabinet, the War Office and the Foreign Office, but also those of the British Legation in Vienna, which are virtually complete for this period: according to the staff of the Public Record Office, a very exceptional case.

Austrian and German documents, as well as British newspapers, have been used to supplement these sources, but the voluminous literature on the subject has been used very sparingly, mainly to check these accounts. Many Austrian ministers and officials had the habit of talking confidentially to British diplomats in Vienna. A picture thus emerges which in many respects sheds new light on the events of these years. Apart from that, the very detailed records of the Society of Friends tell us much about the terrible social conditions in Vienna and other Austrian towns after the end of the First World War. They make the general picture more intimate and add a new dimension to the official reports and minutes.

My thanks are due to the staff of the Public Record Office and of the Society of Friends for their help and, above all, to my wife for her patient advice and assistance.

London
February 1986
F.L.C.

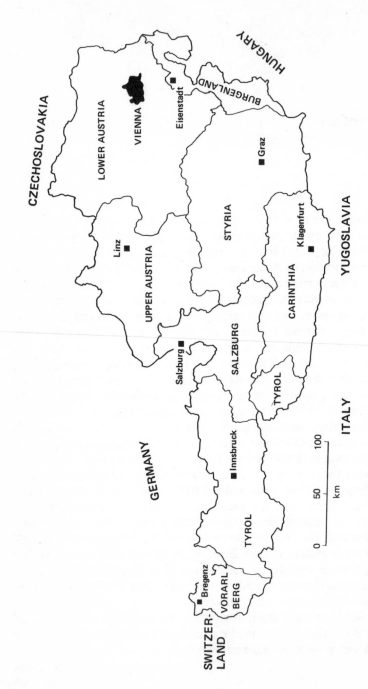

Austria, showing provinces and principal towns.

1 Collapse of the Old Order – the Revolution, 1918–19

After more than four years of savage fighting on many fronts and tremendous losses in men and material, the Habsburg Monarchy which had dominated Central Europe for more than four centuries, collapsed. During the last days of October 1918 national committees, hastily formed from the leading political parties, took over power in Vienna, Budapest and Prague, and the imperial order disappeared. The last Austro-Hungarian government, in a note to the American President, Woodrow Wilson, declared its acceptance of the peace conditions of the Entente, and on 3 November an armistice was concluded with the Entente powers, a week before the Kaiser's government in Germany did the same. Two weeks before the armistice, the Deputies of the German-speaking areas of the Monarchy constituted themselves a 'Provisional National Assembly of the Independent German–Austrian State' and elected an Executive Committee to take over the powers of government. A few days later, the Czechs, the Hungarians, the Poles and the southern Slavs followed suit and formed their own governments. Nationalism, and the principle of national self-determination, thus triumphed in Central Europe. However, its different nationalities did not live in separate areas, but coexisted throughout the former Empire. Wherever the frontiers of the new states were to be drawn, national minorities were bound to be created who would fall under the sway of the majority nationalities which constituted themselves the rulers of the new states and paid scant regard to the rights of the minorities: neither the South Tyrolese nor the Sudeten Germans, for example, were to be permitted to join the new German–Austrian Republic, which was officially proclaimed on 12 November, and which itself contained sizeable Slav minorities.

The signs of the coming dissolution of the Habsburg Monarchy had been carefully noted in London. A memorandum of August 1918, prepared by the General Staff at the War Office, described the mutinies and desertions from the Austro-Hungarian army which had reached formidable proportions. It also commented on the strikes which had broken out in Vienna and elsewhere in January and again in June, due to economic as well as political causes. In January

> the negotiations at Brest Litovsk [between the victorious Germans and Austrians and the new Bolshevik government] had just come to a standstill and the masses of the people were determined that peace with Russia should not, as they feared, be sacrificed to Imperialism; economic anxiety was forgotten for the moment in the political aim.

From Wiener Neustadt and Vienna the strike movement of January had quickly spread to Upper Austria and Styria. Five months later, however, it was largely confined to Vienna and Lower Austria, caused by a severe cut in the bread ration which had

> increased the excitement and led to the despair of the workpeople. Strikes became inevitable; and they were postponed rather than prevented by an appeal from the conference [of the Social Democratic Party] which declared that, in view of the general situation in Europe, the moment was inopportune for strikes, and asked them [the workers] to avoid any rash course of action, warning them at the same time against over-rating their strength.

This appeal was supported by the Workers' Council, which had been constituted during the January strike 'and issued another appeal against any extension of the strike'. In June, therefore, 'the strike movement was not comparable with that of last January', but it secured 'certain economic concessions'; and 'it did much to make the re-assembly of the *Reichsrat* [the Austrian Parliament] inevitable.' In conclusion, the memorandum found that, in contrast to the January strikes, 'this time all political aims were subordinated to anxiety for the daily bread.'[1] The meeting of the Workers' Council on 18 June was mentioned briefly, but no special importance was attached to it, and no comparison was made with the far more important Russian soviets which had helped the Bolsheviks seize power.

At the end of October the British Minister, Lord Acton, wired from Bern that he had been visited by Father Anton Korošec, the leader of the Yugo-Slav group in the Austrian Parliament, who informed him that 'authority in Vienna no longer exists. Governing classes are much more anxious to save their personal property than to save the State.' With the people of Vienna 'all hinges on question of food. Socialist leaders have working classes well in hand and they realise that promiscuous [sic] Bolshevism will not bring people bread.' The food supplies 'are running dangerously low and there might be popular uprising at any moment.' Yet there was 'no likelihood of a political revolution among Austro-Germans' who were 'content to leave political status of their country to general Peace Congress'; the threat of joining the German Empire need not be taken seriously.[2]

The hatred of the masses was, of course, directed against the Germany of the Kaiser, and not against the new German Republic which was born on 9 November 1918. A few weeks later Lord Acton sent a note on a conversation with the Bishop of Feldkirch, who stated that the Italian army had 'occupied the southern part of German Tyrol, namely, the region from a point north of Trent, where the languages divide, to a point beyond and including the Brenner Pass.' If this should be confirmed by the peace treaty (as it was nine months later) North Tyrol 'will have no option but to join Bavaria, for which there is no desire among the Tyrolese. ... The Bishop ... says that there is no wish in German Tyrol for incorporation either in the German Austrian Republic or in Germany.' The British Minister rightly claimed that 'the principle of self-determination has gone by the board.'[3] Not only in the Tyrol, but also in Carinthia in the south, in the Burgenland in the east, and in Bohemia in the north, the new Austria was soon confronted with the conflicting claims of the nationalities and of the national minorities which had bedevilled the history of the Habsburg Monarchy since the nineteenth century.

Meanwhile another, and at first more terrifying, problem had more or less solved itself – that of the demobilisation and return of the multinational Austrian army. At the time of the armistice chaos threatened. As an English businessman who had been interned in Austria during the war reported:

The breakdown of the Austrian army was an entire one and

surpassed the expectations of the greatest pessimists in Austria. Soldiers simply left the front and their officers. ... Soldiers rushed the trains, broke the windows to get in, the roofs of the railway-carriages were packed with men.... Most of the soldiers on the roofs, however, were knocked down and killed passing the tunnels, the rails being lined with dead all along.

Yet he also mentioned the orderly functioning of the railways, especially of the Trieste–Vienna line: 'from Laibach [Ljubljana], where all the various armies had to meet, a train left about every 20 minutes carrying off 70,000 to 100,000 men a day. Thus the demobilization, which was expected to last about two years, was done in about three weeks.' As to the population of Styria, through which the retreating armies had to pass, it 'was very pleased the armies used the railways for their retreat, for it was in great anxiety that the soldiers retreating and moving back would use the main roads and not having anything to eat would rob, plunder and burn their properties.' The soldiers' return also caused grave anxiety in Vienna, but the city remained quiet: 'many rich, aristocrats and archdukes left Vienna', escaping to Switzerland, Bohemia or their estates, and all the soldiers thought of was to get home as quickly as possible.[4]

The same report made other important points: 'It is obvious that the present government is very weak, and especially with the loss of Victor Adler, the famous Social Democrat, it lacks a leader with impulse and energy.' Adler had been appointed Minister of Foreign Affairs in the new government, but he died a few days later. On the day of the proclamation of the Austrian Republic, shooting broke out in front of the Parliament building in which two people were killed and many more injured. It was said in Vienna that if 'there should only have been an organised force of one hundred men with any other government at hand, it would have succeeded in doing away with the young government just nominated.' As to the population of the city, it 'is forgetting all about war, thinks no more of government, politics, finances, in fact they are too much starved, as to be able to bring up the energy to occupy themselves with these'; they were only awaiting the moment when 'they get help from anywhere, until they get some food and coal'. The author even described the Austrians as 'a degenerated race ... unable to develop any energy at all. Consequently the Jews with their ambition are the leading people in the country and really have the government in their hands now. But they are hated everywhere.'[5]

It is true that among the members of the new coalition government two were of Jewish origin: Otto Bauer (who succeeded Victor Adler) and Julius Deutsch (the Under-Secretary in the Ministry of War); but this was a far cry from the claim that they 'have the government in their hands' or 'dominate the country'. As we shall see, the events of the war and its aftermath gave a strong impetus to anti-Semitism which had developed in pre-war Austria and was supported by the two important bourgeois parties, the Social Christians and the German Nationalists, who, together with the Social Democrats, formed the government. In stressing these points, the report accurately mirrored the prevailing tendencies among the middle and lower middle classes of Vienna with whom the author was in contact. He also mentioned 'people of the old political and social system', keen to 'safeguard their superior positions not by liberality, but by authocratic [sic] means ... thus still ignoring every democratic idea of the present time.' There can be little doubt that many of them remained bitterly hostile to the Republic, which they would conveniently blame for all the ills that had befallen the country.

The proclamation of the German Republic and the formation of a provisional government dominated by the Social Democrats (which was not the case in Austria) caused a growing agitation in Austria for the Anschluss (union) with Germany. This was strongly supported by the Social Democrats, who were aware of their weakness and isolation in a very conservative and Catholic country and hoped to gain succour from their German allies. As early as November 1918, the historian and civil servant Lewis Namier minuted in the Foreign Office: 'It seems probable that the German Austrians will finish by joining Germany', and he suggested the issue of an official communiqué:

> Rumours seem to be spread in German Austria by German agents alleging that Great Britain proposes to force the Austrian Germans into a Danubian Federation and to prevent them from joining Germany, should they wish to do so. No such intentions are entertained by the British Government which will respect the right of German Austria to settle her own fate, just as it respects the right of other nationalities to do so.

It was then arranged for a question on these lines to be asked in the House of Commons by Colonel Josiah Wedgwood. The answer, by Bonar Law, the Chancellor of the Exchequer, was that 'these rumours have no foundation whatever.' At the same time Arthur Balfour, the Foreign Secretary, wrote to George V's Private Secretary that to 'oppose the union of the Germans of Austria with the rest of the Germanic peoples ... would violate one of the cardinal principles for which the Allies have been fighting – the right of self-determination'. Such a union would not be 'politically disadvantageous', for 'it would greatly increase the strength of South Germany as opposed to the North and the leadership might pass from the hands of Prussia.'[6] A few weeks later a memorandum on 'German Austria' by the Political Intelligence Department stated even more unequivocally, and using very similar expressions:

> We cannot exterminate the Austrian Germans; we cannot make them cease to feel Germans. They are bound to be somewhere. Nothing would be gained by compelling them to lead an existence separate from that of Germany. Such enforced separation would merely stimulate German nationalism, but could not prevent co-operation between the two branches nor their final reunion. Lastly, the inclusion of German Austria in Germany is not altogether disadvantageous from our point of view; it would restore the balance between the Catholic south and the Protestant north, and help to check Prussianism in Germany.
>
> The idea of preventing the Austrian Germans from joining Germany, even if both parties concerned wish it, has therefore to be dismissed both on grounds of principle and of expediency.

This memorandum was approved by several senior officials, among them Sir William Tyrrell, the Assistant Under-Secretary of State.[7] It showed how clearly the problem was recognised in 1918, and how little opposition to the Anschluss there was at that time. The French, however, were determined to oppose it, and eventually a provision was included in the Treaty of St Germain, which declared the independence of Austria 'inalienable', unless the Council of the League of Nations approved a change in its status. The French also wanted to bind the Allies to oppose by force any future union of Germany and Austria, but this was not conceded.[8]

While more rational considerations were swept aside in the

political atmosphere of 1919, with passions aroused by the bitter warfare of the past years and the terrible devastations, the issue of the Anschluss would not go away. The Austrian socialists in particular were pressing for it as a means of alleviating the country's financial and economic problems. From Bern, Sir Horace Rumbold accused them, on the basis of confidential information received by the British Legation, of being 'imbued with what may be called pan-German ideas.... It is the expectation of the Vienna Socialists that they may succeed in avoiding state bankruptcy by means of the incorporation of German–Austria in the German Republic.' In spite of the fact that in the elections of February 1919 the pro-Anschluss parties (the socialists and German Nationalists) received a clear majority of almost 60 per cent of the vote, Rumbold still believed 'that the majority of the population of German–Austria are opposed to union with Germany.'[9] In April a British diplomatic representative reported:

> The agitation in favour of the Anschluss has continued to grow during the last few months and has now become so strong that no political leader opposes it openly. It has from the outset been quite clear that the Anschluss would sooner or later become inevitable unless the Succession States could be persuaded to drop their Chauvinistic tendencies and to open their frontiers to traffic with Austria.

He suggested a conference of the Succession States to discuss the issue; but Lord Hardinge minuted that 'all the jealousies and bitterness of the war are still rampant in these States.... A Conference at the present time would be far more likely to aggravate rather than to alleviate them, since it would demonstrate more clearly to the various States where their interests diverge.'[10] In June 1919 Otto Bauer wrote to the Austrian State Chancellor Renner, who was negotiating with the Allies at St Germain: 'Everybody says that no other way exists now but the Anschluss. Even in bourgeois circles which hitherto were extremely cool the Anschluss idea is now stronger than ever.' Any retreat on this issue 'would be the biggest mistake'.[11] Yet retreat there had to be, and this was one of the reasons why Bauer resigned some weeks later as Foreign Secretary. Lewis Namier commented rather surprisingly:

The change was clearly made with a view to pleasing the French & obtaining more favourable peace-terms.... But ultimately the policy of German Austria will from the logic of fact, have to go the way indicated by Bauer, i.e. towards closer union with Germany.... Bauer out of office may become an even greater power than in office, & anyhow the cooperation between him & Renner is likely to continue - which is not a bad thing. Austria in the days of her greatness has never had such a decent government & such able statesmen as she has got now.[12]

In November the British Foreign Secretary, Lord Curzon, was still convinced 'that a large number of Austrians consider that they could find salvation in such a union [with Germany], and in view of the fact that the Allied and Associated Powers have by Treaty prevented Austria from joining Germany, Lord Curzon feels that those powers are under a strong moral obligation to see that Austria is not reduced to ruin and starvation by being thus prevented from joining Germany.'[13]

A memorandum drawn up in the Foreign Office, on the other hand, pointed to the dangers implicit in the Anschluss: 'Once Germany is in Vienna she is again on the high road to the Balkans and Constantinople, and will resume her "Drang nach Osten" policy, one of the causes of this war. The problem of the German minority in Bohemia at once becomes acute; and the continuance of the Czecho-Slovak Republic is definitely threatened.'[14] Shades of 1938, but by then of course the whole situation in Central Europe had completely changed.

The large German minority in Bohemia who wished to join Austria presented another insoluble problem. In a conversation with a British military representative, Otto Bauer declared early in 1919 that the Czech claim to the German-speaking districts was

> the greatest political problem at present confronting the German-Austrian government.... The whole future of German-Austria depends on the solution of this problem.... If the Peace Conference supports the Czech claim there will be no peace for many years, as German-Bohemia under Czech rule will be a source of weakness to Bohemia and a constant source of nationalist agitation in German-Austria. The loss of the German-Bohemian coalfields would spell ruin to German-Austria.[15]

But it was in vain that the socialists quoted 'the right of self-determination, as laid down in the 14 points of President Wilson'; and equally in vain that 114 communes of South Moravia (which had a common frontier with Austria) out of a total of 195 expressed their wish to be united with Austria.[16] The decision of the Peace Conference went in favour of the Czecho-Slovak Republic and its claim to the 'historical' frontiers of Bohemia and Moravia. No concession was made to Austria in Southern Moravia, where it would have been possible to cede the German-speaking districts bordering on Upper and Lower Austria without inflicting any serious damage on Czecho-slovakia.

In the north the Austrian government was entirely unsuccessful in obtaining any adjustment of the frontier; nor did it gain any concession from Italy which insisted on the letter of the secret Treaty of London (1915) and on the Brenner Pass frontier. In July 1919, the French Prime Minister, Clemenceau and the British Foreign Secretary, Lord Balfour, wrote to the Italian Foreign Minister, Tittoni, and pointed out that this demand 'has caused a painful surprise among many admirers of Italy. ... If language, race and the voice of the population had determined the decision of the Conference, the South Tyrol would never have become Italian.'[17] But the principles of nationality and of self-determination were sacrificed to strategic considerations and Italy obtained what she desired. In North Tyrol too, the Italians in 1919 were 'carrying on a strong agitation for union with Italy', which 'would seem the only means of provincial reunion', as the British High Commissioner, Lindley, reported from Vienna.[18] Yet the strong 'provincial patriotism' of the Tyroleans and their opposition to Vienna did not tip the balance in favour of Italy, and the two parts of the Tyrol were to remain separate.

In the south, the Austrians were faced with the territorial claims of yet another state, the new Kingdom of Yugoslavia, which occupied the Slovene-speaking districts of Southern Carinthia and Styria, and demanded their cession. Early in 1919 Colonel Cuninghame, the British military representative, forwarded from Vienna resolutions voted by the town councils of Bleiburg and Tarvis in Carinthia, which were occupied by the Yugoslavs and the Italians respectively, but demanded 'to belong to an undivided province of Carinthia forming part of the

German-Austrian Republic', and thus refuted 'the Slovene assertions concerning the wish of the occupied territory of being incorporated to [sic] the Jugoslav Kingdom'.[19] To resolve the problem, the Allies decided to hold a plebiscite in Southern Carinthia, and a Commission headed by a British colonel arrived at Klagenfurt to supervise it, backed by an inter-Allied force of British, French and Italian troops. From Klagenfurt Colonel Peck reported in August 1920: 'many of the inhabitants of the Klagenfurt area have no strong feelings either towards the Austrians or the Jugo-Slavs, but ardently desire that the area itself should on no account be split up, and would be prepared to welcome either solution in order to gain this end.' He also complained strongly about the Yugoslav authorities which 'have openly defied ... the instructions of this Commission', encouraged by the French Commissioner, 'who either openly opposes any measure which he thinks to be contrary to the hopes and wishes of the Jugo-Slavs, or gives them only a very half-hearted support.... It is thus doubtful whether it will be possible to carry out a free and fair plebiscite.'[20]

The plebiscite took place, as planned, on 10 October 1920, without a serious incident, even though, as Colonel Peck reported, 'alarming rumours ... that an awe-inspiring reign of terror would be inaugurated three days before the plebiscite and would reach a maximum on the day itself'. Nevertheless, hundreds of outsiders had managed to enter the area in spite of all precautions;

> many of them were armed with revolvers, life preservers of horrible design, bludgeons or thick sticks. The Jugo-Slav Sokol bands numbered several thousands.... On the other side, were organised battalions of workmen and students similarly armed from Vienna and other parts of Austria, who had been smuggled ... into the area of the plebiscite.

At least 95 per cent of those entitled to do so voted. 'It also shows very conclusively that no one was prevented from voting by terrorism of any kind. This has been a matter of great surprise to the Austrians and a great disappointment to Prince Borghese [the Italian Commissioner]'[21]-22,000, many of them Slovenes, voted for Austria, and 15,000 for Yugoslavia. In Colonel Peck's opinion, the misgovernment and the harsh bullying methods of General Meister [Majster] who has been largely responsible for the administration for the previous sixteen months had done much to undermine the desires of those Slovenes who had no strong racial tendency to come under Jugo-Slavia. The Austrian representative a few days ago speaking on this point said he thought the Austrian nation should raise a monument to General Meister in the market square of Klagenfurt to commemorate what he had done for the interests of Austria by his methods.

Peck also thought that fear of military conscription in Yugoslavia 'caused many people to throw in their lot with Austria who has no military ambition'; and that people had voted 'without fear of anyone ever finding out which way they voted' – as the French Commissioner remarked after the announcement of the result: 'we have lost the plebiscite through the secrecy of the vote.'[22] In the conditions prevailing in Central Europe in 1919–20 it was quite a remarkable story, and Southern Carinthia remained Austrian, in contrast with Southern Styria which became Yugoslav.

Quite apart from all territorial claims, the dissolution of the Habsburg Monarchy which by and large had been an economic entity, led to a closing of frontiers and to endless economic conflicts. In November 1919 Lindley wrote from Vienna: 'At present Czecho-Slovakia and the Yugo-Slavs are following the suicidal policy of devoting their principal attention to mutual destruction. The difficulties of the various frontiers are inconceivable and it is almost impossible to get anything through them.' He had only heard one side of the story and did 'not doubt that the Austrians are also greatly to blame', for the Austrian government

> has no real authority over the Provinces, which actually constitute what amount [sic] to frontiers against the Capital. In short, everyone in Central Europe is bent on erecting a zareeba of the stoutest thorns round his particular plot of ground with the fond idea that he will prosper inside.

Four weeks later he added:

> For hundreds of years trade has followed certain channels in Central and South-Eastern Europe and lines of communication have been developed accordingly. These channels and lines have been suddenly

blocked without any time being allowed for readjustment. The result is economic chaos and the starvation of certain districts quite close geographically to other districts having a superfluity of foodstuffs.

Lindley suggested that the Allies should exercise 'effective pressure' on the new governments to adopt 'a friendly commercial policy towards Austria', but this was easier said than done. Early in 1920, writing specifically on the railways of the former monarchy Lindley noted that formerly they 'were managed as one concern and well managed. Now they are managed by seven different States ... all more or less at loggerheads.' He even approached President Masaryk to impress upon him 'the danger of the present situation', but he found 'that Masaryk's hatred of Vienna has in no way abated owing to the change of circumstances; it is unstatesmanlike and dangerous to the future of his own country which will break up if Austria goes to Germany.' He urged that the problem be 'taken in hand seriously', otherwise 'anarchy is, in my opinion, bound to lay waste the whole of Central Europe.'[23]

Similar difficulties arose with the governments of the other Succession States. In June 1919 the Austrians informed the Allied Trade Commission in Vienna that the Polish government was refusing to permit exports of coal, petrol, oil, etc., in spite of an agreement signed two weeks previously; if the prohibition were not lifted 'everything including lighting of Vienna must shut down'. All the Foreign Office could do was to forward the report to Paris for the attention of the Supreme Economic Council.[24] In October it was reported from Vienna that the Yugoslavs, while not actually repudiating the food contracts signed by them, 'are making all sorts of obstruction and have delivered nothing.... The City is without coal, with only 5½ days of grain, and without prospect of any sugar, meat or fat.' Coal trains sent from German Silesia to Austria through Czecho-slovakia failed to reach their destination. During the first week of December as many as 527 trucks went missing: 'coal must be somewhere in Czecho-Slovak..,' Lindley laconically recorded.[25] In the same month the Poles sent potatoes in 50 open trucks, 'with the result that all the potatoes were spoiled by the frost, etc., and could not be used', even though the Austrians had sent closed waggons for the purpose. When the British Minister in Warsaw delivered a strong protest, the Polish Minister of

Railways replied that 250 trucks with potatoes had been despatched to Austria, but he was unable to say whether closed waggons had been used. Commenting on his reply, the British Minister wrote to Vienna: 'these people are profoundly cynical and light-hearted in their habits. They take refuge behind their inexperience, and they do things which seem strange to our conception of fair dealing.'[26] Actions such as these prevented any improvement of the situation in Austria, and especially in Vienna.

Throughout 1919 and beyond the situation remained desperate. In January Colonel Cuninghame reported: 'Outwardly it is calm, inwardly there is a good deal of seething. Not related to theoretic Bolshevism, but to conditions approximating to destitution and despair.' 100,000 men were registered as unemployed. A few weeks later another British officer wrote: 'When I left Vienna on Feb. 16th there was sufficient flour to last for one week. British doctors visiting the hospitals report the mortality there is very high on account of the scarcity of meat and milk. . . . Bolshevism and Food are running a great race at present and the former is gaining ground.' In the large towns the poor were suffering badly 'from lack of food, clothes and coal'. Nevertheless,

> A great deal of food seems to be smuggled in from Hungary, Czecho-Slovakia and from rich peasants living in German Austria. . . . By means of the *Schleichhandel* [black market] almost everything is obtainable. The restaurants, for example, seem to be having no difficulty in supplying eggs and omelettes, whilst the hospitals find it almost impossible on account of the prohibitive prices to obtain them.

The food in the restaurants was 'equal in quality and quantity to that obtained in London', but outside poor people were 'waiting for small scraps of bread'.[27]

In March, a Dutch doctor wrote to the Regius Professor of Medicine at Oxford that the well-to-do, 'by paying incredible prices', were able to obtain a wide range of goods: 'all the people connected with this trade under the surface are gaining such a lot of money that they can afford to buy whatever they want'; but 'the poor and the low functionary and the enormous number of discharged soldiers and officers are starving.' In the hospitals things were even worse: 'the food we get for our patients is

"Hundefrass" [dog food] and this ugly stuff is given in such small quantities that half the patients run away on the second day. It breaks one's heart to assist these scenes and not being able to help.'[28] According to a British officer who visited Vienna in April, 'the poor people are in a pitiful condition', but the middle classes 'imagine themselves very much worse than they really are. The rich people can get what they want by paying exorbitant prices.' He found the Viennese 'extraordinarily docile and quiet', and a Bolshevist outbreak 'most unlikely'; at Innsbruck, on the other hand, food was not short and prices were reasonable.[29]

Meanwhile the first members of the relief mission sent by the Society of Friends had reached Austria and began to report on the conditions there. In Styria they found the most acute shortage was that of fats which were of 'an exceptional importance in that province'. Smuggling between the peasants and the towns was less openly practised than in Vienna, but the severe shortage of coal meant that only a few factories were operating; most of the blast furnaces of the 'Alpine Montangesellschaft', by far the most important Styrian industrial company, were closed down; however, recent shipments of food sent by the Allies made it possible to allocate small increases of the rations for Easter.[30]

In May, Dr Hilda Clark made her first journey to Vienna at the request of General Smuts to look into the medical conditions. She found the streets 'filled with a hopeless, and ill-looking people'; the children received a diet of only 800 calories (they needed 1500–2000). On 16 May, she recorded in her diary: '...went to one of the two places where the American feeding scheme starts today. The children are supposed to be selected as the most underfed, but the ones we saw in the schools who were not going [to participate] looked just as bad, and what we saw at the Kinder clinic there are many clearly worse.' The head of the British Food Commission told her that one of the main difficulties was that of transport: 'We had a thousand tons of condensed milk ready to come out – held up at Boulogne by the French – and by the time they had agreed to its transport only 400 tons were left.' Another urgent need, 'not met by anyone at present', was for soap and clothing, especially for babies. A few months later she reported that the Americans were feeding 100,000 school children betweer the ages of 6 and 14, but were not helping those under that age, who 'are in a very serious condition of rickets and stunted growth and all need help, especially fats.'[31]

In October 1919 another member of the Friends' relief mission wrote:

> What can we do? We feel quite powerless sometimes in face of the catastrophe which is bound to come. Surely any people but the Viennese would have risen up in revolt long ago and demanded some drastic action. Their friendliness and patience and free and easy ways are delightful, but often one longs that they had a little more go and grit and righteous discontent.

A few weeks later she mentioned just such an action witnessed by one of her Austrian friends, when coal was delivered to the house of a bank manager: 'People came with baskets, bags and rucksacks and simply took away what they could, the unloader helping and four or five policemen standing by looking on!' Her friend considered this 'the most hopeful sign he has seen for a long time' – a sentiment she shared.[32] Another Friend noted: 'it is dreadful to see the starved faces of the people in the streets – the ration for last week was 1¼lbs bread, ¼lb flour, ¼lb peas, and 2oz fat. But the trouble is that there is no fuel to cook the things with or very little.' In Graz in December the bread ration was larger than in Vienna, one big loaf per person per week, 'but the bread is made largely of maize and is distinctly worse than in Vienna.' There was the same lack of sugar, fats, milk and meat, the same shortage of coal and wood, and no petroleum or candles. Only the sick and babies under one year received fresh milk. As coal was unobtainable, it was reported, in the same month, that people chopped up their doors and stripped the bark off trees in the parks. In the woods the trees were cut down under police supervision: 'I have seen little emaciated boys, with spindle legs and worn, thin faces, crushed almost to the ground under a load weighing at least 100lb....The whole life of Vienna is haunted by this lack of fuel.'[33]

A letter written in December described the conditions in the shops and markets. Cabbages, swedes, carrots, turnips, small apples and potatoes could all be found, and delicatessen shops sold some foreign food but at enormous prices: 'the profiteering business has almost swamped the legal trade, and while the rations can frequently not be given in full, similar food may be obtained from the profiteers at exorbitant prices.' With the growing inflation wages had risen by 600–1000 per cent, but salaries had only doubled. Pedlars with their rucksacks dominated the blackmarket food trade, and 'the wood trade seems to be in their hands too'. Even the wooden crosses had been taken from the cemeteries.[34]

A month earlier, Lindley, the British High Commissioner, had written:

> Snow has been falling intermittently for a week, but not only is there no coal to heat the houses, but few persons have sufficient to light the kitchen fire. Nor is there either sufficient wood or peat to take its place. At the Hotel Bristol, where I am staying, the rooms are altogether unheated, and a small jug of water is all that each guest is allowed morning and evening. To-day's newspapers are full of a number of deaths of newly-born children owing to the low temperature of the hospitals.

As to food, 'the rations supplied by the Allies is [sic] sufficient to support life when eked out by supplies bought surreptitiously from local sources; the prices fixed by the Government for local produce having driven it totally from the open market.' On reading this despatch King George V was so shocked that he asked Curzon to send it to the Allied Conference in Paris, so that something could be done for the stricken city.[35]

In Vienna, Colonel Cuninghame found the authorities 'unable to cope with the accumulated difficulties . . . and the result is that the City of Vienna is now face to face with the rigours of winter without having at disposition any reserves of food or fuel.' The situation of the children, 'who are left by their parents – when absent – in ice-cold houses', rendered any provision charity could make for them quite useless. To try to alleviate the situation, Cuninghame called together representatives of all parties and social groups and urged them 'to save the children of the City from death and misery' and to support the efforts of the Quakers.

The response was immediate; almost 2 million kronen were subscribed on the spot and gifts in kind were made, sufficient to provide fuel for designated schools and crêches, and for the homes of mothers attending the Infant Welfare Centres: 'the scheme is in its infancy, and already remarkable results have been achieved.' From the meeting emerged a society called British Help for the Children of Vienna, with Cuninghame as President, and the British High Commissioner as Honorary President. Care was taken to co-operate with the government and the local socialist organisations. State Chancellor Renner expressed his gratitude and promised his support. As Lindley wrote, 'the population has become so apathetic and is so divided by mistrust of each other that I felt they would never succeed in helping themselves.'[36]

An Entente Food Mission was etablished in Vienna at the beginning of 1919, under another British officer, Major E.V. Bethell. When food trains arrived, (usually from Trieste) the consignments were handed over to the Austrian Food Controller, who 'distributes it, amongst the inhabitants and amongst the poor practically free of cost. Richer persons have to pay a graduated price according to their income.'[37] When the Friends' relief mission arrived later that year, they coordinated its work with the local socialist organisations. Two of its members attended a meeting of the Workers' Council ('an excellent set of people') and offered help – which was of course readily accepted. Cases of condensed milk, dried vegetables, egg powder and washing soap, as well as 50kg each of cocoa and sugar were promised for the central district of Vienna. Soon the Mission was able to dispense mugs of cocoa to infants between the ages of one (who no longer qualified for the milk ration) and school age (age 6, when their welfare was taken over by the Americans): 'this warm drink is the only nourishing food which these babies get.' Cod-liver oil, milk, linen and butter at much reduced prices were also supplied.[38] By November the Mission was able to report that its clothing scheme 'has really got going now. We hand over material ... to Tailors' Trade Unions, and they hand us back so many dozen garments weekly', which were given to hospitals and infant welfare centres to be sold at low prices; the money was then used to buy milk.[39] These efforts were to be continued on a much larger scale during the following two or three years.

Britain was able to help the Austrians in another matter – the serious shortage of rolling stock which hampered all relief shipments. But when it was proposed that 1500 British waggons from War Office stocks which were still in France should be diverted to Austria, the Ministry of Transport strongly objected and suggested that instead former German rolling stock, surrendered under the armistice conditions, should be lent by the French. In December 1919 Curzon wired to Paris to bring pressure to bear on the French authorities for the release of these waggons for Austria and Germany, where the shortage of rolling stock was causing anxiety in the occupied Rhineland; if need be the issue was to be raised at the Supreme Allied Council. Curzon emphasised that 'we are anxious to do something for Austria even at sacrifice to ourselves.'[40]

In the same month all passenger traffic in Austria came to a standstill for ten days, and Lindley expressed his fear that the provision of trucks by the Allies would only 'afford temporary relief, but would not really solve the problem'. The British government proposed the establishment of an authority, composed of railway experts, to control the distribution of rolling stock in all the countries concerned. It took another three months, however, before arrangements were made to lend to Austria the 1500 British waggons which were still in France. The Netherlands government had applied for trucks to transport relief goods from Holland to Austria, and it was agreed that the British waggons would be moved from France to Holland for the purpose.[41] (Nothing seems to have come of the other proposal.)

It is perhaps not all that surprising that comparatively little was done for Austria, at least during the first 15 months after the end of the fighting, and that the French were more reluctant to do anything than the British, for all the countries which had been involved in the Great War were experiencing enormous political and economic difficulties, especially France and Belgium which had been so badly devastated. On 31 December 1919, Lindley wrote:

> The greatest sufferers are undoubtedly the surviving members of the old Middle Class who are now financially worse off than the so-called proletariat and accustomed to a more comfortable mode of life.... The consumption of electricity is so restricted that very wealthy people are unable to live in more than two rooms of their large houses and these are almost in darkness after nightfall, one or at most two electric lights being allowed per household.[42]

The distress and suffering in the country were enhanced by

the strong antagonism which developed between the central authorities and the provinces and the growing hostility of the latter towards Vienna and its socialists. In September 1919 the head of the British Relief Mission wrote: 'The provinces utterly ignore the government who are quite unable to carry on for any great length of time. It seems pretty clear that the reactionary movement will gain increasing force with the distress which is ahead of the country owing to the lack of coal and approaching winter.' In November the British High Commissioner blamed not only the new political frontiers dividing Central Europe, but equally the frontiers erected by the Austrian provinces against Vienna:

> the reasons for the hostility of the Provinces to Vienna are various, but the principal seems to be the Socialist character of the Vienna authorities which does not correspond with provincial feeling. Then there has always been a good deal of jealousy felt towards Vienna in all the old parts of the Empire, and now they feel that the moment has come to humiliate her.

He was convinced that, as the government was powerless to enforce maximum prices, they should be abolished: 'there would be an outcry but the majority would be glad to acquiesce in a measure imposed upon them from outside.'⁴³ Yet such a step would not have abated the hostile attitude of the provinces towards 'red' Vienna.

One element of stability and continuity did exist, and that was the police under its efficient Director, Johann Schober. Lindley described him as 'perhaps the most capable official in Austria and absolutely reliable. He was habitually entrusted with care of King Edward when his late Majesty visited Marienbad and has kept both police and gendarmerie in a remarkable state of efficiency.'⁴⁴ Lindley made a similar point when the British military attaché in The Hague sent his opinion on the Workers' Councils, which he claimed 'are in a position to thwart the decisions of the authorities on every occasion' and tried 'to prepare the way for the "unlimited dictatorship of the Proletariat"'. The attaché further claimed that whoever was 'capable of comprehending the situation in Austria will agree that the present conditions in that country are identical *in essentials* with those in Hungary at the time of Béla Kun [the leader of the short-lived Hungarian Soviet Republic of 1919]'.

Lindley immediately countered that 'the institution of Workmen's Councils does not play the prominent part in the life of the country which the Memorandum describes.... No-one I have met thinks that the present conditions in Austria are identical "in essentials" with those in Hungary at the time of Béla Kun.' These were: 'absence of Parliamentary Government, trials and executions for political opinions, wholesale pillaging and a general state of terror amongst the upper and middle classes. None of these exist in Austria and I presume the writer of the Memorandum does not consider them "essentials".' Even more remarkable was the fact that its author did not mention at all 'the efficiency of the Police and the Gendarmerie under the direction of the Police President Mr Schober. This efficiency is perhaps the most surprising feature of the whole situation and it is due to the character of the Police President who has told me himself that he has the full support of Doctor Renner.'[45] Schober was to enjoy the full confidence and trust of British diplomats in the following years.

As to the Workers' Councils, which for some years played an important part in the life of Vienna and some other industrial towns, in July 1919 Colonel Cuninghame described the Central Council as 'a patriotic and level-headed body of men', but admitted that it 'has aroused considerable misgivings among the Bourgeoisie, who see in the concession the beginning of a Soviet institution'. There was a danger that 'junior members of the Socialist Party', who were 'discontented with the slow progress of Socialist legislation', might use the Workers' Council to overcome opposition and 'demand privileges which the Socialist leaders are not prepared to grant'. But as long as the Council followed the socialist leaders, 'so long we are safe from change'. Early in 1920 the Colonel reported that the Central Workers' Council (i.e. for the whole of Austria) 'remains in overwhelming majority in accord with the leaders of the Socialist Party'.[46]

In contrast with Germany, where the working-class movement was deeply divided and split among three major parties, the Austrian socialist leaders never lost control of the Council Movement. A memorandum by the Second Secretary of the British Legation, drawn up in December 1920, even described the Workers' Councils as 'little else but a Social-Democratic Party organisation'. This political control was consolidated at a conference held in June 1919. According to the memorandum, the development of the Councils at the local level was 'very uneven'. They were widespread and influential in Vienna and Lower Austria, and even more so in Salzburg, 'where they obtained a dominant position on the Provincial Boards of Food Control, Disposal of War Stores, Conversion of War Industry and Housing'. In Linz, the Workers' Councils had succeeded in stopping a riot; and in Carinthia they were 'chiefly occupied in opposing a Pan-German reaction'. But in the Tyrol they had failed to establish themselves. In the spring of 1919 certain Councils had assumed 'direct administrative authority', but later this changed: 'in fact they ceased to be potential Soviets.' Like all Austrian institutions, the memorandum continued, 'the Councils have a somewhat academic air. Nothing they can do or say can touch or alter the essential fact that Austria is starving and bankrupt and only existing by permission of her late enemies.' To the firmness with which they insisted on this fact, the Social Democrats owed their triumph at the conference of June 1919, when the communists demanded the immediate proclamation of a Soviet Republic. The Chairman, Friedrich Adler, replied 'in unanswerable fashion ... that in the first place Austria was economically dependent on the Western Powers, and in the second place that Communism could offer the peasants ... nothing that they had not already got. There were no large estates to be expropriated and divided.'47

A more radical Council existed in Wiener Neustadt to the south of Vienna. According to a report of April 1919, Social Democrats and communists cooperated there, in spite of their differences. The Workers' and Soldiers' Councils 'exercise an intermittent control, and in general determine policy'; food control was exercised by a committee of eight – four from the Town Council and two each from the Workers' and the Soldiers' Councils; their representatives participated in searches carried out by the Town Council. To enable the poor to buy meat, which was very expensive, the town had fixed special prices for about 5000 inhabitants with an income of less than 3000 kronen, the difference to be borne by the town. In each firm, the distribution of food was organised by a nominee of the employers who was controlled by workers' representatives. When the food shortage became acute in March, radical workers seized the food shops and sold the contents to the people 'at what they considered fair prices', but the price reductions were 'not very drastic'. As far as the writer knew, 'these semi-Soviet conditions ... are peculiar to this district'.[48] Indeed, Wiener Neustadt, a small town dominated by its industries, was a very exceptional case; even in 1919, nothing similar was reported from any other Austrian town.

In Villach in Carinthia, the Workers' and Soldiers' Councils similarly cooperated closely, trying, as a hostile memorandum put it, 'to get as much power as possible into their own hands'. They were represented in several administrative departments, such as the Food and Housing Offices. A Carinthian Soldiers' Council was formed for the whole province in December 1918, under Social Democratic influence. The local units were to be organised 'on the lines of election of commanders, abolition of ranks and the subordination of everything to the Soldiers' Councils'; these subordinated themselves willingly to efficient officers, but overruled others 'who were weak or lacking in energy'. Later, a central representative body of the Soldiers' Councils was founded in Vienna, on which the provinces were represented according to the strength of the local units. As most units were concentrated in the capital, the Vienna Soldiers' Councils dominated the central body. But the memorandum admitted that during the fighting against the Yugoslavs the Soldiers' Councils 'did their duty completely and well', although at first some of them hesitated on grounds of international working-class solidarity; but so as not to lose all their influence, the Councils had supported the national fight in Carinthia.[49] According to the Brigadier who headed the British Military Mission in Carinthia, the local population was 'strongly opposed to the system of the Government of Soldiers' Councils or any other "Councils"'. He also described the local *Volkswehr* units as 'quite unreliable for any serious purpose', 'a danger to the country', and 'nothing more than a partisan gang', organised by the socialists for political purposes.[50] As the Volkswehr fought reasonably well against the Yugoslavs, the Brigadier was only showing his own political bias, or that of the Austrian officers who advised him.

The large majority of the men in the new Volkswehr were undoubtedly socialists – especially in Vienna and some other towns – who had joined up at the prompting of their party.[51] The British government received several reports that they were dangerous and unreliable. In March 1919 the Swiss Minister in Vienna informed Sir Horace Rumbold in Bern 'that Volkswehr was unreliable and that there were 20,000 armed men in [the Vienna] Arsenal which was a regular fortress'. He urgently advised that Allied troops be sent to Vienna to restore order. In April Lord Acton wired from Bern, on information supplied by the Vice-President of the International Red Cross, 'that Dr Renner was unable to control troops which had practically become Red Guards. Scission between Government and Red Guard at Vienna appeared to be complete.'[52] A report from Vienna of the same month described the Volkswehr in Styria as 'the focus of Bolshevism in Styria, in so far as it exists' – which seemed to indicate that not much of it could be found there. Its ranks were swollen by sailors of the former Austro–Hungarian navy who 'are said to be imbued with revolutionary ideas'. But the same report stated that Styrian Volkswehr units had been employed to enforce government requisitions; that a unit at Leoben was 'on excellent terms with the Government officials, and with the (anti-Bolshevist) Social Democrats'; and that their main activity was the organisation of a weekly dance, which made them 'deservedly popular with the Leoben population'.[53]

All this was rather contradictory, but it may have reflected different tendencies among the local military units. In Vienna, as Colonel Cuninghame reported, Volkswehr men, in cooperation with members of the Workers' Councils, caused some alarm 'by carrying out requisitions on their own account into the houses of food hoarders'. This caused all the restaurants to close, and made it 'very awkward for us all, as food is absolutely impossible to buy.' He therefore complained to Julius Deutsch, the War Minister, and was given an assurance that these confiscations would be stopped.[54] By the spring of 1920 Cuninghame was convinced

> that the new Austrian army will in no sense be communistic.... At no time in the recent history of Austria has the danger of 'Communism', 'Bolshevism' or the 'institution of Soviet Government' been less, nor is the danger likely to increase, provided that there is not a general collapse in Central Europe.

His opinion of the Volkswehr was by no means purely negative, for he added: 'Of the old Volkswehr 11,000 men will be retained, and these will not be the worst element, but certainly the best element.'[55]

In its turn the British Legation stated: 'the Volkswehr and Workmen's Councils frequently interfered in the administration of the law, and arrogated to themselves duties which should have been left to the police. The middle classes complained frequently of a "terror", but there was no destruction of property beyond the looting of a few provision shops.'[56] And at the end of 1919 Curzon declared quite unequivocally, referring to the alleged intention of the Austrian government to recruit the new army 'exclusively from members of the Social-Democratic Party', that 'this is entirely a question of Austrian internal politics, and I do not consider that His Majesty's Government are called on, or have any right, to intervene therein.'[57]

During 1919 the so-called 'Red Guards', and the communist danger in general, received the constant attention of British officers and diplomats, especially after the proclamation of the Hungarian Soviet Republic in March of that year. A few weeks before that event a junior British officer had reported from Vienna:

> A new plan of the Bolshevists is to undermine the public services such as the railways, telegraphs, post and government appointment [sic] by secret confidential agents who are slowly to make themselves indispensable in these services. . . . As a large number of working men from various districts are supporters of the Bolshevist policy, this does not appear to be extremely difficult. . . . They receive great assistance at the present time from the high cost of living, scarcity of houses and accommodation, lack of employment, and shortage of food and clothing and coal.[58]

In April, the Swiss Minister in London called at the Foreign Office with urgent instructions from his government: the only way of preventing the proclamation of a Soviet Republic in Vienna was 'the despatch of a division of Allied troops'. Professor Lammasch, the last Imperial Prime Minister, even informed the British Legation in Bern that over 60 per cent of the Vienna Volkswehr 'might be considered as Red Guards' and that a Communist Republic would be proclaimed there on 14 April.

Even further removed from the truth was a message in June from the Legation in Prague that a Bolshevist *coup* was to be expected: 'Dr Bauer will probably be in the directorium, Dr Deutsch doubtful. Co-operation with the Magyars (Béla Kun) unquestionable.'[59]

On 21 April *The Times* carried a lurid description of the riots in Vienna around the Parliament House which resulted in 5 deaths and 40 wounded, and was quelled by a 'particularly stable' Volkswehr battalion: 'Yesterday's events,' the paper added, 'apparently were the work of a small band of agitators working in conjunction with the Bolshevists of Budapest and elsewhere. In addition to the native Communists, many Hungarian and Russian agitators undoubtedly took part in the demonstration.' And on the following day: 'In spite of various arrests, numerous undesirables are still in Vienna. This afternoon, for example, a man speaking in Russian declared that if the Government did not accede to the demands of the unemployed and the war invalids, before Tuesday, the Government would be swept away, in spite of the threats of the Entente to cut off food supplies.' If the man really spoke in Russian, his audience cannot have been very large.

On 17 June *The Times* published a more sober account of an abortive communist *coup* in Vienna, when the police had fired on a hostile demonstration attacking a police cordon, killing seven people. Volkswehr units supported the police and 'apart from the immediate scene of the excesses complete quiet prevails in the city.'[60] As the British Legation reported later, the communists had tried 'to take advantage of the unemployment existing in Vienna to provoke a "Putsch" and ... the attempt completely failed.'[61]

In the autumn of 1919 there were new reports of growing communist activity and preparations 'to take advantage of the unrest which will accompany any duration of the present misery'. When elections to the local Workers' Councils took place in Vienna in November, only 10–15 per cent of the electors voted and thus 'a large number of Communists have been elected'.[62] Early in 1920, however, Colonel Cuninghame could report that, in spite of the concentration of the Red Army on the frontier of Galicia, there was no 'recrudescence of Communist activity in Vienna'; 'the recognised Communist leaders are without serious following and do not seem to be equipped with money for any special proximate effort.' The Central Workers' Council was still firmly 'in accord with the leaders of the Socialist Party.'[63]

The Austrian Communist Party thus quickly became a minor political force on the fringe of the working-class movement, with hardly any influence in Vienna and even less outside the capital, unlike the German Communists who became a mass party. If it ever had any chance of seizing power – and this was slim enough even in 1919 – the collapse of the Hungarian Soviet Republic in August 1919 destroyed any such hope – a fact soon recognised by the British. In the same month, Colonel Cuninghame mentioned 'the collapse of the Communist movement in Austria. ... They are now quite innocuous.'[64] Within the Volkswehr too, communist influence rapidly declined and the one 'Red' battalion – no. 41 – was quietly disbanded, even though it had not participated in the attempted *coup*.

The dominant party in the coalition government formed in November 1918 were the Social Democrats, not by virtue of the number of ministerial posts they held, but on account of the strong personalities of the State Chancellor, Dr Renner, and the Foreign Minister, Dr Bauer. To both men the British representatives paid considerable attention, as they did to their Party. In November 1919 Lindley reported on the Party Conference which had proved 'that the Party as a whole realize that it is impossible for the State at present to carry out the Party's policy of the socialization of industries on any large scale' – a point stressed by Bauer, who declared that Austria was dependent on foreign capital.

> Members were depressed by the terrible food and fuel conditions in the Capital and the financial condition of the country and evidently felt that the moment was not propitious for any proposals of action of a startling nature. As Your Lordship is aware, the Social Democratic Party in this country has retained its unity, and most of the speakers laid stress on the need of continuing to show a united front to their enemies.

The socialist leaders did not fear that Bolshevism was 'a serious menace in the near future', but they did fear 'a state of general anarchy' on account of the prevailing misery. Two weeks later Lindley described the conditions of life in Vienna as 'intolerable'

and was afraid of 'a terrible upheaval'; 'it is not strange that the
Social Democrats call aloud for union with Germany and that
the cry is finding from day to day a deeper echo amongst the mass
of the population.'[65] In Colonel Cuninghame's opinion, the
socialists, by preserving their unity, 'have managed to avoid
Communism on the one side and reaction on the other'.[66] While
the German labour movement was critically weakened by the
split into rival and mutually hostile parties, the Austrian
Socialists remained united and comparatively strong. After the
break-up of the coalition government in 1920 however they were
permanently in opposition, and their strength was very unevenly
distributed throughout the country: apart from Vienna, it was
limited to a few industrial areas, such as parts of Lower Austria
and Styria.

The Christian Social Party, which rivalled the socialists in
strength, was mainly supported by the middle classes and the
peasants of the strongly Catholic villages of Austria. As early as
July 1919 Colonel Cuninghame drew attention to their efforts 'to
perfect a political organization which will give effect to the
wishes of the Provinces as apart from those of Vienna itself' and
'to arm and organize the peasants', in particular in Salzburg,
Styria and the Tyrol. 'Special precautions,' he added, 'have
already been taken to defend the harvests from all attempts at
forcible requisition by any local or central Soviet' (apparently
meaning the Workers' Councils which were not soviets). An
organised resistance movement to any attempt at establishing a
proletarian dictatorship now existed in the provinces: 'on the
whole the armed peasants can be taken as a loyal and law-abiding
group, not likely to give trouble', provided that the disarmament
prescribed by the Peace Treaty proceeded simultaneously for
peasants and workers. He believed that the organisation of the
peasant leagues was 'a great factor for stability at the present
critical moment'. In August he returned to the subject, reporting
a 'considerable recovery' from the feeling of hopelessness which
had prevailed in Austria in the spring: this recovery 'we have
principally to attribute to the success of the organisation of the
Peasant League – today a powerful conservative institution –
which has so directed its influence that the leaders of the Trades
Unions of Vienna have been obliged to be content with a
moderate policy.'[67] And in October, in Styria 'the relations

between the peasants and workmen are very strained. Both sides are armed and a conflict may arise any day.' But, according to a different source, at least in Upper Styria the Peasant Councils were working 'hand in hand with the Workmen's Councils in important questions, of distribution of food etc.', and were 'gaining more and more power and influence'.[68]

In Salzburg, Styria and the Tyrol the first *Heimwehren* were formed by the peasant leagues in opposition to 'Red' Vienna. They were to become one of the most important political movements in Austria in the 1920s and 1930s. As early as August 1919, Renner expressed his apprehension to Cuninghame about 'the increased strength of the Christian Socialist parties', which seemed to indicate a 'return to reactionary political influences'.[69] His apprehension was more than justified, for soon the Heimwehren were to menace the very existence of the democratic Republic, which seemed to have roused but little enthusiasm in the general population. On its first anniversary, in 1919, the Social Democratic meetings in its honour were 'fairly well attended'; but, as Lindley wrote, 'there was not the smallest sign of enthusiasm', and the general population 'took the opportunity of a fine day to spend some hours in the beautiful surrounding districts'.[70]

There was no desire for a return to the House of Habsburg, and the monarchist groups (mainly former officers) remained very small. As Cuninghame wrote in August 1919, 'the Monarchist groups have refrained from all attempts to influence Austrian politics, and from their own point of view, wisely so, as the tendency of both City and Province is against all return of the Habsburgs.' He added that this might change if the monarchists were successful in Hungary. In the spring of 1919 Butler, the head of the British Relief Mission, was approached by an emissary of the monarchists who informed him that 'the country was rife for a change of government', that 'at least 30 per cent of the population of Vienna' supported them 'and that the country districts would vote solidly for a change'.[71]

This was wishful thinking, and a memorandum drawn up in London for the War Cabinet stated succinctly that Austria 'has no desire for the return of the Habsburgs or the Habsburg régime'.[72] Commenting on the reactionary Kapp Putsch in Germany of March 1920, Lindley stated his belief that a similar attempt in Austria 'would be the wildest folly'; yet 'the miserable conditions of the Austrian officers and the irresponsible and adventurous temperament of the Hungarians made it not impossible that an attempt might be made.'[73] As anticipated, the former Emperor Charles' surprise landing in the Burgenland, in October 1921, to march from there to Budapest, aroused no echo whatever in Austria. It was only as a counter-move to the rise of National Socialism and to German interference in Austria that the monarchist movement acquired some credibility in Austria, and even then it did not become a mass movement.

Another reactionary movement did arouse great popular excitement in Vienna and elsewhere at a time of extreme shortages of food and other necessities; it was directed against the Jewish war refugees from Poland. In Vienna, mass meetings were organised at which violent anti-Semitic speeches were made and the expulsion of all refugees was demanded.[74] In September 1919 the *Manchester Guardian* reported the alarming news that, according to an announcement by the Austrian government, some 130,000 refugees must leave Austria within a few days, otherwise they would be 'forcibly expelled'. This order could not be carried out because of the shortage of rolling stock and coal, but there was grave danger of anti-Semitic riots. From Vienna a British officer wrote that the figure of 130,000 was exaggerated, and that about 60,000 refugees had already returned to Poland. None had been forcibly expelled, but 'there is no doubt that the anti-Jewish feeling is very strong in Austria and people would be very pleased to see the Government taking a stronger attitude'. The British member of the Inter-Allied Food Commission added that the number of Jewish refugees now in Vienna was only about 30,000, mainly from Galicia; 'the Poles are said to make great difficulties about re-admitting these refugees when they reach the frontier; but it appears that some 100,000 have succeeded in getting through.' Of the remaining 30,000 only 400 intended to go to Palestine 'by some means or other'; the large majority did not care 'where they go, so long as it is not Galicia'. Meanwhile, the Austrian government had prohibited further anti-Semitic meetings; the anti-Semites were planning demonstrations to be held every Sunday near the old Jewish district of Vienna, but their last one 'was broken up by the police'.[75]

In London, Lewis Namier (who was himself of Polish-Jewish origin) minuted that 'the Minority clauses of the Peace Treaty concede to all these refugees the power to claim citizenship, and the Austrian Government tries to forestall this possibility by expelling them *en masse*.' Citizenship had been granted only to those born in Galicia who had been resident within the new Republic prior to 1 August 1914, thus excluding the war refugees. Namier suggested that a demand should be put to the Austrian government to suspend the expulsion order so that further discussions could be held, 'and we ought to threaten them, should they proceed in such a drastic manner, in an equally drastic manner to cut off the supplies' on which Austria depended.[76] The file contains nothing more on this issue, and the matter seems to have been settled without an exchange of diplomatic notes. Certainly, the expulsion was not carried out in the envisaged form, but in Vienna anti-Semitism remained very strong, and could always be exploited for political purposes.

From its very inception the young Austrian Republic was beset by the most severe shortages of all necessities which were aggravated not only by the attitude of the Succession States, but also by the continuation of wartime controls. Time and again, the British representatives feared a complete collapse, 'anarchy' or 'chaos'. It was only with the aid of shipments of food and other commodities that the country was able to survive, however precariously, during the terrible winter of 1919–1920.

In the elections of February 1919 the Social Democrats polled just over 40 per cent of the vote – considerably more than their Christian Social rivals – but thereafter they declined, and never became a majority party. Thus the revolution of 1918 remained limited to the political and constitutional sphere, and Austria became a bourgeois Republic, dominated by the conservative and Catholic Christian Social Party, and not by the socialists. The relations between the two rival parties were marked by a growing antagonism which reflected the deep division between the few large towns on the one hand and the small towns and villages of the countryside.

Notes

1. 'Notes on the Situation in Austria-Hungary', August 1918: Public Record Office (PRO), FO 371, file 3136, fos. 559 f.
2. Lord Acton to FO, Bern, 31 October 1918: ibid., file 3134, fo. 26 f. For Korošec in 1918, see Hugh and Christopher Seton-Watson, *The Making of a New Europe – R.W. Seton-Watson and the last Years of Austria-Hungary* (London, 1981), pp. 303, 315, 319, 322, 326. Korošec visited Switzerland to contact the Allies on behalf of a newly-established Yugoslav National Council.
3. Memorandum by Acton, 19 December 1918: PRO, FO 371, file 3507, fo. 54.
4. Report by L.H. Faber, 8 January 1919: ibid., file 3514, fos. 298 ff. For a dramatic description of the disorderly retreat from Italy, see Ernst Fischer, *Erinnerungen und Reflexionen* (Hamburg, 1969), pp. 72 ff.
5. Report by Faber, loc.cit., fos. 303 f., 313. For details of the shooting affair of 12 November 1918, see F.L. Carsten, *Revolution in Central Europe, 1918-1919* (London, 1972), pp. 85 f.
6. Minutes by Namier, etc., 11 November 1918: FO 371, file 3139, fos. 123 ff.; Balfour to George V's Secretary, 11 November 1918: FO 800, file 200.
7. Unsigned P I D memorandum, 9 December 1918: FO 371, file 4355, fos. 192, 196.
8. M.L. Dockrill and J.D. Goold, *Peace without Promise – Britain and the Peace Conferences, 1919-23* (London, 1981), pp. 112 f.; Erich Zöllner, *Geschichte Österreichs* (Vienna, 1961), p. 499.
9. Rumbold to Curzon, Bern, 1 March 1919: FO 371, file 3529, fo. 447. In the elections of February 1919 the socialists gained 40.76 per cent of the vote and the German Nationalists, 18.36 per cent.
10. Memorandum by F.O. Lindley, 23 April 1919: *Documents on British Foreign Policy 1919-1939* (quoted as DBFP), 1st series, xii (London, 1962), no. 143, p. 177.
11. Bauer to Renner, 8 June 1919: Haus-, Hof- und Staatsarchiv Vienna, Nachlass Bauer, Box 261.
12. Minute by Namier, 2 August 1919: FO 371, file 3530, no. 110413.
13. FO to Treasury, 12 November 1919: DBFP, 1st series, vi, 1956, no.278, p.376.
14. Memorandum by C. Howard Smith, 13 August 1919: FO 371, file 3530, fo. 523 f.
15. Rumbold to FO, Bern, 4 January 1919: FO 371, file 3529, fo. 359.
16. Report by Lt.-Col. Sir Thomas Cuninghame, February 1919, and note sent to FO by Swedish Legation, 5 March 1919: FO 371,

file 3529, no. 27254, file 3541, with minute by Namier of 7 April.

17. Clemenceau and Balfour to Tittoni, Paris, 29 July 1919: FO 371, file 3509.

18. Lindley to Curzon, 9 December 1919: DBFP, 1st series, vi, no.363, p.498.

19. Resolutions of January 1919, sent by Lt.-Col. Cuninghame on 22 April: FO 371, file 3508. In spite of this, Tarvis was ceded to Italy, to become Tarvisio.

20. Col. S. Capel Peck to Curzon, Klagenfurt, 28 August 1920: FO 371, file 4628.

21. Ibid., 13 October 1920: DBFP, 1st series, vii, 1962, no. 248, pp. 292 ff.

22. Ibid., 20 October 1920: ibid., no. 257, pp. 309 ff. For the Klagenfurt plebiscite in general, see K.R. Stadler, *The Birth of the Austrian Republic, 1918–1921* (Leiden, 1966), pp. 121-7.

23. Lindley to Curzon, 7 November, 5 December 1919, 1 January 1920: DBFP, 1st series, vi, nos. 265, 356, 406, pp. 352, 494, 550. A 'zareeba' or 'zariba' means an enclosure of thorn-bushes, built for defence against enemies or beasts.

24. Cuninghame to War Office, 3 June 1919, minutes of 7-12 June: FO 371, file 3543.

25. Cuninghame to FO, 17 October 1919; Lindley to Curzon, 16 December 1919: DBFP, 1st series, vi, nos 219, 378, pp. 298 f., 514.

26. Rumbold to Lindley, Warsaw, 13 December 1919: PRO, FO 120, file 924.

27. Reports by Lt.-Col. Cuninghame, 26 January, and Lieutenant W.A. Reaves, 24 February 1919: FO 371, file 3529, fos. 399, 434 f.

28. Prof. K.F. Wenckebach to Sir William Osler, 2 March 1919: FO 371, file 3530, no. 56830.

29. Notes by Captain John de Vars Hazard, s.d.: FO 371, file 3508, no. 66064.

30. Report on Styria, 20 April 1919: Society of Friends Library, Papers relating to Friends' Relief Mission in Austria, box 5, parcel 3, folder 1.

31. Diary notes by Hilda Clark, May 1919: ibid., box 4, parcel 2, folder 4; *The Friend*, new series, lix, 28 November 1919, p. 724.

32. Helen Fox to Friends, 16 October and 7 November 1919: Papers relating to Friends' Relief Mission in Austria, box 4, parcel 3, folder 3a, and parcel 2, folder 4.

33. Letters by E.M. Pye, Francesca Wilson and M.A.L., 30 November, 9 and 23 December 1919: ibid., box 4, parcel 3, folder 3a, parcel 3, folder 1, and box 5, parcel 3, folder 1.

34.   Letters by B.B. Hoysted and Fritz Schwyzer, 20 November and December 1919: ibid., box 4, parcel 3, folder 3a.
35.   Lindley to Curzon, 4 November, and Lord Stamfordham, the King's Private Secretary, to Curzon, 14 November 1919: DBFP, 1st series, vi, no. 252, pp. 327 ff., p. 329 note 1.
36.   Cuninghame to Lindley, 25 November, and Lindley to Curzon, 22 November 1919: FO 120, file 925; DBFP, 1st series, vi, no. 297, pp. 399 f.
37.   Lt. Reaves to War Office, 24 February 1919: FO 371, file 3529, fo. 434.
38.   Reports of 3 September and 9 December 1919: *The Friend*, lix, p. 612; Papers relating to Friends' Relief Mission in Austria, box 4, parcel 3, folder 1.
39.   Helen Fox to Friends, 7 November 1919: ibid., box 4, parcel 2, folder 4.
40.   Curzon to Norman, 12 December 1919: DBFP, 1st series, vi, no. 368, p. 507.
41.   Earl of Derby to French Foreign Ministry, Paris, 9 January 1920, quoting Lindley's report of 1 January: ibid., xii, 1962, no. 69, p. 98 f.; FO to Sir Ronald Graham in The Hague, 13 March 1920: FO 371, file 3535.
42.   Lindley to Curzon, 31 December 1919: FO 371, file 3533.
43.   C.K. Butler to Sir William Goode, 4 September, and Lindley to Curzon, 7 November 1919: DBFP, 1st series, vi, nos. 171, 264–5, pp. 222, 351 f.
44.   Lindley to FO, 10 January 1920: FO 371, file 3548. In later years Schober twice became the Austrian Chancellor.
45.   Report by military attaché at The Hague, 16 December 1919, and comments by Lindley, 14 January 1920: FO 371, files 3532–3.
46.   Cuninghame to Col. Twiss, 1 July 1919, and his report, 21 January 1920: DBFP, 1st series, vi, no.3, p. 5; FO 371, file 3534 (fortnightly report, 21 January).
47.   Memorandum on *Arbeiterräte* by G.M. Young, 6 November 1920: FO 371, file 4655, fos. 198–204.
48.   Report by C.K. Butler, 25 April 1919: FO 371, file 3530, fos. 147–52.
49.   'The Carinthian Soldiers' Council', 3 August 1919: FO 371, file 3510.
50.   Brigadier-General Delme Radcliffe to Chief of Imperial General Staff, Klagenfurt, 18 September 1919: FO 371, file 3510, no. 135177.
51.   For the Volkswehr, see Carsten, *Revolution in Central Europe*, pp. 79–107.
52.   Rumbold to FO, 20 March, and Acton to FO, 27 April 1919: FO

371, file 3529, fo. 486, file 3530, no. 65363.

53. Report of 20 April 1919: Papers relating to Friends' Relief Mission in Austria, box 5, parcel 3, folder 1.

54. Letter by Cuninghame, 23 March 1919: FO 371, file 3525.

55. Lindley to Curzon, 19 June 1920, with Cuninghame's report of 5 June: FO 371, file 3524, fo. 534 f.

56. 'Austria. Annual Report, 1920', p. 10, 23 June 1921: FO 371, file 5786.

57. Curzon to Lindley, 15 December 1919: DBFP, 1st series, vi, no. 376, p. 514.

58. Report by Lt. Reaves, 24 February 1919: FO 371, file 3529, fo. 436.

59. Rumbold to FO, Bern, 5 April, with minute of 7 April, and Cecil Gosling to Curzon, Prague, 16 June 1919: FO 371, file 3530, fos. 36, 42, 242.

60. *The Times*, 21-22 April and 17 June 1919 (reports of 19 April and 16 June).

61. Memorandum by G.M. Young, sent to FO 6 December 1920: FO 371, file 4655, fo. 200.

62. Cuninghame to Oliphant, 17 October, and Lindley to Curzon, 25 November 1919: DBFP, 1st series, vi, nos. 219, 305, pp. 299, 408.

63. Report by Cuninghame, 21 January 1920: FO 371, file 3534, p. 7.

64. Cuninghame to Sir Ronald Graham, 28 August 1919: FO 371, file 3531, fo. 23.

65. Lindley to Curzon, 7 and 22 November 1919: FO 371, file 3531, fos. 244, 516.

66. Cuninghame to Graham, 28 August 1919: FO 371, file 3531, fo. 22.

67. Reports by Cuninghame, 8 July and 28 August 1919: DBFP, 1st series, vi, nos. 22, 147, pp. 37 f., 194.

68. Report by Cuninghame, 17 October, and report 'from a sure source', 29 July 1919: FO 371, file 3530, nos. 144566 and 115336.

69. Cuninghame to Balfour, 10 August 1919: DBFP, 1st series, vi, no. 101, p. 140.

70. Lindley to Curzon, 14 November 1919: FO 371, 3531, fo. 456.

71. Reports by Cuninghame, 28 August, and C.K. Butler, 4 September 1919: DBFP, 1st series, vi, nos. 147, 171, pp. 194, 221.

72. Memorandum by C. Howard Smith, 15 August 1919: ibid., no. 112, p. 156.

73. Lindley to Curzon, 19 March 1920: FO 371, file 3536.

74. For details of these meetings, based on Vienna police reports, see Carsten, *Revolution in Central Europe*, pp. 264 ff.

75. *Manchester Guardian*, 16 September 1919; Captain Marochetti to War Office, and R. Butler to Marochetti, both 28 October 1919:

all in FO 371, file 3544. Other sources give the figure of the remaining refugees as about 25,000.

76.　Minute by Namier, 16 September 1919: FO 371, file 3544.

2 Years of Crisis, 1920–22

The early 1920s brought Austria no relief from her economic and political difficulties, and the state remained substantially dependent on the Allies for the most essential supplies as well as for financial credits. Social distress was exacerbated by ever-rising prices causing accelerating inflation. Early in 1920 Colonel Cuninghame reported:

> The principal cause for anxiety in Vienna is due to the continued rise in the price of food. Only the most meagre ration of bread and flour is in any case available for ordinary distribution, and the price of the 2-lb loaf is to-day 3.80 Kronen and will shortly be raised to 5 Kronen. . . . The hardship involved falls principally upon persons of fixed income, of whom an increasing number are faced with sheer starvation, thus increasing the number of those in despair. . . . The working classes who benefit to a certain extent by the corresponding rise in wages, which is made possible by the continued inflation of the currency notes, are better off. But lately their position has also been aggravated by the complete stoppage in the coal supply, involving the cessation of the trams and the practical stoppage of the issues of fuel, whether of coal or wood, to households.

The issue of coal to households would shortly be resumed, but no coal whatever was available for factories.[1] The distress equally affected the British community in Vienna. Its members were allowed a 'totally insufficient' quantity of meat and fat, a small loaf of bread 'made of anything but flour' per week, per person; 'the principal food upon which they live is a soup made from cabbages and turnips' – a diet which the children could not digest and refused to eat. Before the war, the burial rate in Vienna had averaged 40–50 a day: now it was closer to 2000, and soldiers had to be detailed to assist the gravediggers.[2] In February 1920 Otto

Bauer told a member of the British Legation that in Vienna alone 60,000 war invalids were receiving relief; they, their dependants, and the widows and children of those killed in the war together with the dependants of POWs formed one-sixth of the total population, and another sixth were officials of the former Empire and their dependants: thus one-third of the population of Vienna depended on government support and did not produce anything. The employees of the Ministry of Justice complained bitterly that their income had fallen behind that of the workers who also received charitable gifts: the employees had 'silently starved till now', but sheer want compelled them to apply for foreign help.[3]

When a member of the Quakers' Relief Mission visited Linz in February 1920 he saw two large demonstrations. In the morning the war wounded, the widows of soldiers and their children 'gathered in hordes to attest their misery and starvation. Battered men and emaciated women stood there silently.... They remained there motionless for an hour, and then, as peacefully as they had come, they dispersed.' In the afternoon about 1000 shipwrights staged a demonstration in the same place. When a socialist speaker told them to maintain their discipline and to control their eagerness for action, the workers heckled him continuously: their wives and children were hungry and they knew where to find food. 'We are hungry,' they muttered, and some of them swore at the speaker and shook their fists in anger. Prelate Hauser, the head of the Upper Austrian government, told the visitor that there was an 'imminent peril of a hunger revolution'.[4]

In March, State Chancellor Renner called a meeting of the representatives of the Allies to inform them of the critical position; the general strike in Germany (which defeated the Kapp Putsch) was aggravating the situation, and he hoped that it would be possible to transport the stocks held at Rotterdam through the occupied Rhineland or by sea to Trieste, the 'only sure port of entry'; if the general strike in Germany continued for another two weeks, Austria would have no coal even for food trains, because the Czechs had stopped all deliveries. Renner stressed 'that Austria had for fourteen months remained true to the cause of order and civilization', even when Munich and Budapest were in the hands of the Bolshevists. If a sufficient supply of food were assured 'she would continue to be a moderating influence', but no government could keep order if people were starving: anarchy would prevail if the food situation did not improve.[5]

In May a British relief worker described the situation:

> It is impossible to pass from one province to another without being held up and searched for foodstuffs or any other articles which the provincial powers that be consider should not leave the particular province. Starving Vienna itself has such barriers. You cannot enter the city by any of the main roads without coming into contact with a 'control' of some sort, and if you happen to have with you a little more than the amount of food allowed to be imported it is taken from you.... Truly the Viennese are a patient people – too patient methinks. They put up with any amount of 'control' and allow the foreigner to feed them by charity.

He had just heard of a most absurd case: no one visiting Upper Austria was allowed to stay longer than three days; a Viennese lady who was in poor health went there to recuperate and was able to stay a fortnight in collusion with her landlord, but when her husband arrived he was seized by two gendarmes, marched through the village and detained; the couple were then given two hours to leave Upper Austria. 'The provinces take good care not to help one another, and the Central Government is powerless.'[6]

The same relief worker described the existing 'contingent' system by which the government bought in the peasants' produce at fixed prices below the cost of production; the peasant was not even allowed to dispose of any surplus (after contributing his 'contingent') on the open market, but had to sell it at the controlled price. He therefore produced as little as possible beyond his own needs, and if he had a surplus he fed it to his animals or sold it on the black market. Thus the government was 'directly discouraging any effort to increase production', a system which 'makes the peasant bitter against the Government and creates in him a hostile feeling towards the townspeople', for, if he needed to buy anything in town, he had to pay a high price corresponding to the fall of the krone. In Vienna prices were now 30–40 times what they had been before the war and as the peasants had to pay them for clothes, boots or any other immediate requirements, it was almost impossible for them to buy any manufactured goods. 'So long as this vicious system lasts there can be little progress in agriculture and the real basis of a revival of industrial life in Austria will be retarded.' In the writer's opinion, relief should be concerned less with importing food supplies and more with the development of Austria's own resources. The Inter-Allied Relief Commission had repeatedly applied for seeds, artificial fertilisers and other agricultural necessities, but its appeals had met with little response, yet 'there is room for a great development in the agricultural resources of Austria.' He also pleaded for the abolition of the 'contingent' system and for the payment of 'a fair market price for his produce' to the peasant.[7] Another relief worker found that in Graz the prices were 50–100 times above their pre-war level, but wages only 20–30 times higher; 'many families are selling their furniture and other belongings to get food', among them 'many highly educated people, whose learning now counts for nothing'.[8]

Among the worst sufferers were the small children. In the annual report of the British Legation for 1920, the total child population of Austria (up to 15 years) was given as 1,182,000, of whom 930,000 (nearly 80 per cent) were classified as undernourished. In Vienna alone, 327,000 children (96 per cent) were undernourished, just under half of whom received a school meal supplied by the Americans – often their only meal of the day, apart from black bread and *ersatz* coffee. When the Americans examined 206,000 children in August, nearly half of them were found to be 'extremely undernourished', only 6000 not undernourished, and the remainder 'undernourished in a lesser degree' – and that at a time when most of them were receiving some food from American or British relief agencies.[9] From Graz it was reported that the death rate was so much in excess of the birth rate 'that, if it were to continue as at present, there would be nobody alive in thirty years'. Many children and students possessed no underclothes and were 'almost in rags'; at the time of reporting neither meat nor flour was available.[10]

Throughout the summer of 1920 the Society of Friends distributed weekly rations of milk, cocoa, sugar, fat, flour and soap to 40,000 Vienna children under school age. By the end of the year the figure had risen to 55,000; at the same time, the most urgent demand from the Relief Mission was for warm clothes. In February the Mission reported that the weekly ration consisted of two tins of condensed milk, half a pound of oatmeal, 125 g each of fat and sugar, and 100g of cocoa; 'rice, soap and dried vegetables are added when in stock.' The many depots also sold clothes at low prices and got wood for the women attending the depots. This large enterprise relied on the 'support and co-operation not only of the doctors and nurses at the Welfare Centres, but also of groups of women of each District willing to staff the Depots and carry out the work involved.' In each district a committee of local women was formed under a responsible head to run the depots, conduct the sales, keep the index cards, etc. They had to live on insufficient rations but were willing to do the work voluntarily for the sake of the children. The doctors were working under great pressure and had to face 'immense difficulties', but they were full of enthusiasm for the scheme. The members of the Mission felt that least was done for the youngsters of 15 to 20 'who are most necessitous'.[11]

By December 1920 the Mission, run jointly by the British and Americans, was 'a vast organisation'. There were 25 'food depots' in the different districts of Vienna, where the weekly rations could be drawn; food and medicines were distributed to hospitals; holidays and homes were organised for children, and students were cared for. 'This necessitates a large organisation – offices, warehouses, packing rooms, motor transport, etc.', with a personnel of 70 English and American volunteer workers, 80–100 Austrian employees, and at least 500 Austrian voluntary workers.[12] In addition, children were sent to England – as well as Scandinavia and other countries – for successive periods of three months under the auspices of the Society of Friends. Their visas were granted at the request of the British Minister in Vienna; but in December the Home Office objected to the practice and demanded that no further visas should be issued, except 'under the scheme organised by the Famine Area Children's Hospitality Committee', because under this scheme the children had to undergo careful medical examination 'in interests of the health of this country': the use of any other channel created a risk and 'the precautions may be rendered nugatory'.[13]

In Salzburg, during the winter of 1920, the American Red Cross fed 2000 children and the Society of Friends ran a convalescent home for children suffering from malnutrition: 'with no food, no coal, no money and prices daily rising the distress is as great as in Vienna, with the added grievance against

Vienna thrown in'; food could be bought by those willing to pay the high prices, and the worst distress was among the middle class. 'Unless help comes at once the position is hopeless: and "at once" is no longer a matter of months but of days.'[14] From Innsbruck a visiting British journalist described the breakfast in his 'first-class' hotel:

the only real article of food it included was an egg apiece. The 'coffee' was a sticky brown liquid of unknown origin, beside which the Government war time 'acorn coffee' would be delicious – the slice of black bread and slice of cake seemed to be composed of bad potatoes and glucose. After two and a half years of peace, the Austrians are suffering privations unknown to us in the worst days of war.[15]

In October 1920 the Austrian Minister in London, Francken-stein, described to the Foreign Secretary, Lord Curzon, the plight of Vienna:

a great Capital, with more than two million of people, situated in a country the population of which has been reduced to six million . . . surrounded by a ring-fence of embittered enemies. . . . There were indeed two alternatives before this mutilated and impoverished Austrian State: either to throw in her lot with Germany, or to come to some reasonable arrangement as regards trade and supplies with her hostile neighbours.

He asked Curzon which of these two policies he favoured. He also made 'a final and urgent appeal' for coal. The Foreign Secretary replied that Britain undoubtedly favoured the second policy and had done everything to promote it. The other 'would be entirely contrary to the policy for which we had fought and won the war.' A week later the Foreign Office stated that the supply of coal from Czechoslovakia was improving, as was trade between the two countries; in addition, Austria was receiving a fair share of coal from German Upper Silesia – 'nearly as much as Poland got'.

In January 1921, Curzon wired to the British Minister in Prague:

Present critical state of Austria is a menace to her neighbours, and her collapse might constitute positive danger to them. Economic distress in Austria is partly due to the "blockade" policy of neighbouring States, and removal of obstruction to trade is one of the most practical remedies to be applied.[16]

As Curzon claimed, the British government attached the greatest importance to the improvement of the relations between the Succession States, but improvement was very slow.

In April 1921, Lord Parmoore addressed the House of Lords on the conditions prevailing in Vienna, where 200,000 meals were provided daily by the relief organizations 'at a very cheap rate indeed', less than one penny in English money; 'but there were large numbers of half-starved poor children', most of whom 'look three years younger in size and in general physique than they ought to look'. He also stated 'that tuberculosis is a perfect scourge among the children in Vienna'. The Lords were told that the lives of many children could be saved if they got adequate supplies of milk and food, 'but, unfortunately, there was neither the one nor the other'. The Quakers had imported 'a most admirably kept herd of cows' from Holland but the milk supply was still 'wholly inadequate'. Lord Parmoore paid particular tribute to the work of the military attaché, Sir Thomas Cuninghame, who had urged him to say that 'it would be a national calamity of the worst kind if the relief works were suddenly stopped'. In reply, Curzon declared that the Austrian government had to pay vast sums 'in its depreciated currency for goods which it buys abroad and sells to the consumer at an uneconomic price'; every such purchase, if not balanced by export, led to a further fall in the value of the krone. He thought that the Austrian government lacked initiative and courage; they always hoped for assistance from the Allies: 'at every stage ... this spirit of rather helpless, I will not say hopeless, dependence has manifested itself.' In 1920 a special grant was made available by the Treasury to supply Austria with English seed potatoes. Full of enthusiasm for the scheme Lindley reported that on arrival only 2½ per cent of the seed was found too damaged to plant; the Austrian authorities 'bestirred themselves vigorously to make the new seed acceptable'. He felt certain that 'the crop produced by it will far exceed what could have been expected from the degenerate native seed.' The whole enterprise was 'an excellent advertisement of British methods and agriculture'.[17]

The Vienna Emergency Relief Fund continued to feed the children under the age of six, either through the Society of Friends or through Austrian welfare organisations, and also donated large supplies of food to hospitals. The Friends made special efforts to help the professional and salaried classes by distributing food and clothes. As many were unable to afford the high prices of new clothes and had to sell or pawn their valuables for food and fuel, the Friends 'undertook to clothe 20,000 of the most needy families of the middle classes'. They also supported 'the very efficient system of welfare centres in Vienna', in cooperation with the American Red Cross. In April, Dr Hilda Clark was able to report that, thanks to the help given, 'the condition of the younger children has improved wonderfully'; those still showing strong signs of privation were young boys and girls under 20 years, who received little attention. In July, the vienna Emergency Relief Fund stopped its work, having raised more than £500,000, and four of its officers, including Colonel Cuninghame, received the 'Iron Salvator Medal' from the grateful municipality.[18]

But the Friends continued their work, indeed, at the beginning of 1922 they reported from Vienna that financially the situation was 'very bad again'; large-scale unemployment was expected, and there were no funds to pay benefits; in spite of the further depreciation of the krone, foreign trade was suffering too; the manufacturers had to pay such enormous sums for raw materials that their price level reached world prices. 'We have so often been told that a catastrophe was going to occur, and it has so often been tided over ... but, certainly, things do not look cheerful at the moment.'[19] During 1922, the Friends' Mission continued to assist children and the middle classes. Milk from its dairy herd was distributed to children and tubercular patients, and clothes were either distributed free or sold at a fraction of the wholesale price. Old people and needy families received special allocations of coal. Oil cake was imported from Hungary to increase the milk yield of the Mission's cows. By 1923, however, it was felt that it was unnecessary to continue the work of the Mission 'in view of the general improvement in the condition of Austria', and it was discontinued after Christmas.[20] It had been a very remarkable effort, entirely achieved by voluntary help.

Life in Vienna during these years was not miserable for everybody. As early as November 1919 Lindley wrote: 'The shops are thronged with foreigners who are buying up everything at prices which, though ruinous for Austrian purchasers, are cheaper than now obtain in any other place in the world.... The quality of the goods is often quite first-rate, but in another fortnight there will be nothing left.' Because of the lack of fuel and food, the skill and industry needed to produce the goods would be wasted. Early in 1921 he stated that 'Vienna forms no exception to the rule that a desire for feverish amusement springs up in communities on the brink of financial and social dissolution', and the members of the Reparation Commission (which was dissolved in April 1921), with their salaries 'on a scale unheard of in His Majesty's Diplomatic Service' and their ample funds, 'amused themselves in the same way as that part of the population who was in the same position. Their behaviour caused no outraged feelings in Vienna and 'no scandal': 'if it was desired that they should lead a life of retirement', they should be paid smaller salaries.[21]

For the unscrupulous there was ample opportunity to exploit the situation. In 1920 the Duke of Manchester bought some furs from a small Vienna shopkeeper, for which he paid 50,000 kronen in cash and promised a remittance of the balance, another 590,000 (then equivalent to £230) within a few days. But he left Vienna without paying, and in 1921 the Vienna police informed the London police who issued a warrant for the Duke's arrest. Lindley wrote twice to the Duke's uncle asking him to use his influence to obtain a settlement. Eventually, the Duke's solicitors replied, contesting the claim, and promising a cheque for the amount for which liability was admitted. The cheque was not sent and there was no reply to further letters. In 1923 (!) the Duke finally admitted that the sum of £18 was still outstanding and promised to pay it, but even this was not done. As the British Minister put it, 'the affair has made a very unpleasant impression here.'[22] There must have been many more of a similar kind.

The Viennese workers responded to the rising cost of living, caused by the fall in the value of the krone, with protest demonstrations. In December 1921 violence broke out during such a protest march, many windows in the city centre were broken, hotels were attacked, and shops and cafés looted; 400 people were arrested. The Legation reported: 'hand in hand with exasperation caused by the continual rise in prices goes a feeling of intense resentment and hate against all those who have made money out of Austria's misfortune, the "schiebers", speculators on the exchange market, and their like, who are mostly Jews.'

The Legation commented that it was not surprised at the outbreak, but rather by the fact 'that the class who have been hardest hit of all ... namely the middle class, have not yet taken any effective public action'; but 'few people have such a capacity for long-suffering as the Austrians.'[23] A deputation from the demonstrating workers was received by the Chancellor and the Finance Minister; they demanded, among others, a seizure of gold, including that in churches and monasteries, a progressive property tax, a system of child benefits, prohibition of the import of luxury goods, and control of foreign exchange markets. The Finance Minister promised to control the currency and securities markets, as well as the introduction of a property tax and child benefits. Quiet returned to Vienna, and no further outbreaks were reported.

However, if the workers could voice their protest through their trade unions and socialist organisations, any such organised protest was much more difficult for the middle classes. And all social classes suffered from the ever-accelerating rate of inflation. Early in 1920, when £1 equalled 820-50 kronen, a report pointed out that 'wages have not increased in anything like the same proportion'; a man who before the war earned 48 kronen (about £2) a week, now got about 400 kronen, but in real terms this was worth 'one quarter the wages he earned before the War'. In August 1920 Lindley mentioned that an official with an annual salary of 20,000 kronen would have to spend 18 per cent of it to buy one suit and one pair of boots. Three months later, he wrote that 'the rise in the exchange has produced such a rise in prices as to make purchases of the most necessary articles an impossibility for the majority of the population'. Nevertheless, there were only 14,000 unemployed in Vienna, and the shops 'have larger stocks on hand than they had six months ago and trade in the retail business is brisker.'[24]

In the same month the British representative on the Austrian Reparations Commission stated: 'It is evident that no Central Government can continue ... to purchase from abroad 75 per cent of the fundamental food supplies by pawning, as they are at present, State-owned objects of Art.' Opinions differed 'when the collapse of Central Government will occur', whether in three, or six months' time, but he thought 'the latter estimate the more probable'. In early December 1920 £1 was worth more than 2000 kronen, and the British Minister wired: 'The conviction seems suddenly to have seized many people that things cannot continue like this and that it does not matter how soon inevitable crash comes.' He considered that the government was 'incapable of governing [the] country and their advent to power a contributory cause of present situation'. The diplomatic representatives of Britain, France, Italy and the USA agreed 'that time has come when anything might happen'.[25]

In January 1921 Lindley saw Schober, the head of the Vienna police, who predicted 'chaos' within a few weeks if foreign credits were not forthcoming. The crisis might be precipitated by extensive strikes which would prevent food from reaching Vienna; every fall in the value of the krone caused a new price rise. Schober even claimed that 'the existence of Vienna is now depending upon myself and the banknote printing press.... The State has no money – new notes must be issued hourly – every new issue reduces the value of the krone'; but he was willing to 'guarantee order for 14 days longer'. In August 1921 the krone stood at 4000 to the pound, and the Chancellor requested the British Minister to urge that the Allied Supreme Council must discuss the question of Austria's finances; the delay in adopting the rescue scheme, which had been agreed in principle in March, had had 'a disastrous effect'. Meanwhile Schober had become Chancellor and was, Lindley wrote, 'in fact, regarded as the last horse in the stable, and it is difficult to see what Minister could replace him' if he failed to secure help from abroad: all who 'have studied the situation consider [this] necessary for the stability of the State.'[26]

The krone continued to fall, bringing about labour unrest and a general conviction of 'the necessity for some radical, even violent change'. In September an unauthorised strike occurred on the railways which lasted two days. The unions negotiated with the government over wage increases but were unable to control the movement. The Legation also reported that unemployment was increasing, that industry was feeling the strain, and that merchants were unable to restock the goods sold. Hitherto the low value of the krone had helped the export trade, but if the manufacturers could no longer replace their raw materials, an industrial crisis would be added to the financial crisis.[27] By mid-October a loaf of bread, which had cost 9 kronen on 1 August, had risen to 34 kronen, and 1 kg of potatoes had rised from 10 to 42 kronen, while an egg cost 35 compared to 11 kronen. By that time the pound stood at 11,450 kronen, and four weeks later it was worth 24,000 kronen.[28]

When two experts from the League of Nations drew up a memorandum on Austrian finances in November 1921, their picture was by no means all gloomy: 'Trade and industry are flourishing; unemployment does not exist. A progressive control of agriculture is already making Austria markedly more self-sufficing in foodstuffs.' As Austria exported to Hungary on a large scale, more food could be bought there because Hungary had a food surplus; there was no longer a coal problem, and industry was able to accumulate reserves which previously had not existed; the orders placed at the Vienna fair 'were gigantic, and the manufacturers preferred to fulfil these orders, rather than to sell for Austrian crowns to the shops.' Some shops asked for payment in foreign currency, but these were few, and the fair had caused the shortage of goods in the shops. Foreign credits should be given, but not, as the British and French governments had done hitherto, without conditions: 'credits are the only weapon by which the control of Government expenditure and taxation can be enforced.'

This rosy picture was to some extent modified by a report of the Commercial Secretary of the British Legation drawn up five weeks later. He too stated that exports were booming because Austria was able to undersell all competitors and that there was very little unemployment – only 21,000 in Vienna, mainly in the hotel and coffee house trades. But the prosperity of the export trade was 'based on a continuous consumption of the country's capital'; many manufacturers only realised that they had made a loss when they wanted to restock and found their capital insufficient to buy the required raw materials. The public were hoarding foreign currency on a large scale, and while threats were made to seize these hoards, this only had the effect 'to spur people to new purchases while they are still able to do so'; and in any case the foreign notes were kept in stockings and similar hiding places. Real wages were now between a quarter and a half of what they had once been, and that constituted 'an enormous advantage' to the industrialists.[29] These facts explain why labour unrest was mainly confined to the state and public employees whose wages lagged far behind.

In January 1922 the krone sunk to a level of 44,000 to the pound, but then it improved a little. The Austrian Minister in London made urgent appeals for an advance on the credit promised by Britain and France. A panic had broken out in Vienna, causing a 'terrifying drop of the krone' and 'a renewed immense increase in prices'; his government could 'no longer bear the responsibility for a situation caused by the non-fulfilment of the repeated promises of the Powers to grant credits to Austria. Only if the advances of £2½ million are forthcoming within the next few days, a catastrophe can be avoided.' Britain should not allow 'a people of such high civilisation, occupying an important place in the centre of Europe to be submerged'. A few weeks later a British credit of £2 million was indeed offered to Austria, with the effect that the krone rose to an equivalent of 27,000 to the pound. Schober expressed his deep gratitude and told the British Minister: 'it was a particular source of gratification to him that England should have thus shown her confidence and interest in Austria, and ... should have been the first to come to Austria's aid in her hour of need'; among all parties and classes 'there was undoubtedly the greatest feeling of trust' in Britain.[30] The credit, however, only brought temporary relief, as had all previous credits granted to Austria, for they were mainly used to buy essential supplies of food and other necessities.

In November 1920 Lindley had pointed out that, with the exhaustion of foreign credits and 'a staggering deficit in the budget', there would be 'starvation and the disruption of society' unless Austria received further assistance. Three courses were open to the British government in his opinion: to refuse to make any grant, 'to join with the other Powers in granting the same sort of doles as have been granted in the past', or to 'make a serious effort to put Austria on her legs': if put on her legs, 'Austria would exercise a civilising and steadying influence in a region which the war and its aftermath have thrown back a hundred years.' But this last, more sensible, course was not adopted. Twelve months later a joint advance of £500,000 was made by the British and French governments 'for the purchase of food supplies outside Austria', and a hope was held out of further credits to come.[31] But, according to the Austrian Minister in

London, the small amount offered created 'the worst impression'. Since the Armistice, the British government had granted credits to the value of £12,000,000, while the French and Italian governments 'have hitherto given practically nothing', the Foreign Office claimed; apart from their credit of £250,000 of 1921, the French had now 'voted' £1,000,000 and the Italians had done the same; but the krone continued to fall – 'the downward course has since been so headlong that it now stands at anything between 200,000 and 250,000 to the pound.' Trouble was avoided by the grant of higher wages which depressed the krone still further, but if supplies ran short, 'the mass of paper money which the worker earns will do him no good' and disturbances would break out; the government could not rely on the small army 'and the country may be left a prey to anarchy'. In summing up the memorandum stated pessimistically in August 1922: if the credits merely achieved a prolongation of the agony, 'it is obvious that no real good is being done, and it is possible that this policy may even be doing harm, as the longer the "collapse" is postponed, the worse it may be when it comes.'[32]

In the same month it was reported from Vienna that the new Austrian government, headed by Dr Seipel, was 'becoming extremely anxious as the financial situation grows worse owing to the further great fall of the krone, and their fear is that, if they have to give up hope of securing financial help, they would have to convoke the National Assembly and state their inability to carry on the administration'. The situation was made worse because the peasants were holding up supplies and refusing payment in local currency; the government was unable to meet the demands of the provinces for money; and their attitude was causing anxiety. Another urgent appeal for foreign help went out from Vienna: if none was forthcoming, 'Austrian finance is threatened by immediate collapse. Only foreign credit can restore confidence, both inside Austria and abroad, in the Austrian currency.'[33]

In September 1922, Dr Seipel and the Foreign Minister, Dr Grünberger, went to Geneva where they met Lord Balfour, the Lord President of the Council. They admitted that the provincial authorities often prevented the transport of food to Vienna, but argued that the provincial contribution to the needs of Vienna in any case was small because only Lower and Upper

Austria had a sizeable food surplus. Dr Seipel complained that the Austrian army was unreliable and 'an obstacle to the financial restoration of Austria'; the police and gendarmerie might be increased at the expense of the army, but Grünberger said that the French objected to this, though he did not know why.[34] In August the representatives of the Allied Powers discussed an Austrian request for the guarantee of a loan of £15,000,000, but they could not hold out hope of any further financial help and agreed to refer the question to the League of Nations on account of the 'discouraging results' of the previous efforts. The League, they hoped, would work out a 'programme of reconstruction containing a definite guarantee that further contributions would produce substantial improvement and not be thrown away as in the past.'

A special committee of the League Council was appointed to carry out the complicated negotiations and an agreement for 'The Restoration of Austria' was concluded and signed at Geneva on 4 October 1922. By this a loan of 650 million gold kronen (£26,000,000) was guaranteed by the governments of Britain, France, Italy, Czechoslovakia and other countries, and as security Austria pledged the receipts of the customs and the tobacco monopoly; the rates of the Austrian posts, telegraphs and railways were to be increased; and the budget was to be balanced within two years. A Commissioner General appointed by the League, and based in Vienna, was to supervise a programme of financial reforms, and a Committee of Control was to be formed by the governments guaranteeing the loan and its annuities. The Anschluss was prohibited for a period of 20 years. The states with reparation claims against Austria agreed to defer them, so that she would be able to offer the required security for the loan.[35]

At the signing of the agreement Lord Balfour warned that there was still much to do and that Austria would have to undergo more suffering before she would be able to overcome the crisis, but he felt certain 'that if the Austrian people and Government will throw themselves wholeheartedly into the work of reform, then Austria will become again a great factor in European civilisation.' From Vienna the new British Minister, Akers-Douglas, reported that all was quiet; a threatening strike of metalworkers had been settled by a compromise; the rate of exchange was improving 'slightly but steadily'; all classes, even the socialists, recognised the necessity of serious reforms, and the atmosphere was favourable for their introduction: 'The bad moment, however, will be when the period of real reform begins. Many classes will have to endure greater hardships than they have ever known before, and in spite of the meakness of the Austrian character the strain may be too great to be endured quietly.'[36]

Opposition to the agreement came from the Social Democrats, who protested strongly against the 'Geneva Bondage Treaty', with its system of international control, which was 'tantamount to a foreign government in the country', and was making Austria pay for help 'by the loss of its liberty and the right of a nation to self-government'. The party summoned a special conference at which Otto Bauer made the principal speech. He warned his listeners 'that they must fully realise the gravity of the moment, and that this was Austria's last chance of obtaining foreign help.' If they rejected the League's offer they must have an alternative plan 'which would save Austria from the humiliation of selling her freedom for a few hundred million gold crowns'; this would include levies on banks and industries, and higher taxes for the rich. But would such levies produce a sufficiently large sum? According to the British Legation, the Social Democrats claimed that they were fighting for their existence, for 'Control and the grant of full powers to the Government will destroy their power as a Party, at all events for the time being.' But the speeches at the special conference were 'for the most part couched in moderate language', and the party's history 'has always shown their leaders on the side of moderation', so that no violence or sabotage of the execution of the agreement was to be expected. This opinion was confirmed by Chancellor Seipel, who told the British Minister that 'the Socialists were as usual attacking him, trying to make out that he was sacrificing Austria's independence; but it was rather a personal and political vendetta': they would accept the control, provided that it did not mean foreign administration and police. In the opinion of the British Minister, 'their only avowed policy appears to be one of attack upon the Banks and upon private property, in the belief that there is sufficient money to be obtained within the country in the shape of holdings of foreign securities.'[37]

The delegates of the League who visited Vienna in November 1922 were anxious to establish the exact attitude of the opposition, and the Commercial Secretary of the Legation was sent to interview Dr Renner. Renner complained bitterly 'that Dr Seipel was making too much party capital out of the whole business' and was 'riding the party horse too hard'; he would use the scheme to reduce the influence and the economic strength of the working class; he would carry it out in a party spirit; the chief burden would fall on the working class by stepping up indirect taxation, and if the number of state employees were reduced, the socialists would be dismissed and the Christian Social officials retained. Seipel, Renner added, should have formed a coalition with the Social Democrats when they proposed this three months earlier. In the end, the party decided not to oppose the constitutional law by which the Austrian Parliament had to approve the Geneva agreement. They considered it a partial success that they 'have prevented the elimination of Parliament and the establishment of a financial dictatorship of the Government'; and they agreed to the formation of an Extraordinary Cabinet Council, composed of members of the government and 26 Deputies, chosen according to the parliamentary representation of the parties, to supervise the execution of the Geneva agreement.

When the Seipel government decreed an increase of certain taxes without consulting Parliament, the Social Democrats protested, but their motion of censure was defeated by 99 to 67 votes. The British Minister reported that 'the Socialist policy of obstruction' was likely to continue, at least until some progress had been made 'with the actual raising of the loan'.[38] The Socialist International also sent some prominent leaders to Vienna to concert measures with the Austrian socialists. Discussions took place with Otto Bauer, Friedrich Adler, Karl Seitz and others, and it was established that the Austrians 'did not count on the Socialists of Great Britain, France, etc. refusing the scheme of assistance for Austria, but on their opposing anything which gives the Commission of Control and the Commissioner General the power of constantly placing the Austrian Government ... between the refusal of credits and measures against the working class' in matters of wages, working hours and trade union rights. The French socialists therefore proposed to voice in the Chamber their 'protest against the suppression of the independence of a free nation' and to attack 'the alliance formed against the working class' by Austrian capitalism and the foreign powers – a policy which they expected would be approved by the Labour Party.[39]

At the beginning of 1923 Akers-Douglas wrote that Seipel and Grünberger were ready to start for Geneva to make the definitive arrangements for the floating of the loan and the provision of interim credits. If they failed to do so, there would be a new political crisis and a new fall in the rate of exchange, which had remained steady for the past four months. Although 'the coming weeks will be a critical period and probably decisive of [sic] the fate of the Republic', the daily papers devoted most of their columns 'to discussion of German affairs, almost to the exclusion of home political problems', and the National Assembly had sent a message of sympathy to the German Parliament. (The French had marched into the Ruhr and Germany had proclaimed a policy of passive resistance.) The February Budget estimated that the League of Nations scheme would reduce the deficit from 5.2 to 2.3 billion, an improvement of 56 per cent; altogether 75,000 state employees were to be pensioned off, and, in particular, railway personnel was to be reduced; but 'the Government has walked very warily as it is afraid of a general railway strike'. The draft budget was showing 'the beneficial influence of the League of Nations delegates', although it did not go quite as far as they wished. The largest share of taxation was to come from income tax, followed by an excise on beer, wine, sugar, etc., and a tax on shares and dividends.[40]

In June 1923 – with the accelerating rate of the German inflation – Akers-Douglas reported that the rate of exchange had been stable for six months but that prices had risen considerably so that the government had to grant slightly higher allowances to its employees. But the great success was the floating of the Austrian loan in London and elsewhere which 'has surpassed all expectations', while Germany was 'passing through a financial crisis worse than any which has afflicted this country'. If one remembered 'the chaotic state of affairs' of 1922 'and the imminence of a crash', the Seipel government 'have every reason to congratulate themselves on their success'; and the Social Democrats, who had prophesied the failure of the League scheme were 'reduced to silence or feeble gibes'.

In August Akers-Douglas repeated that the public and press were 'watching the course of events in Germany' with 'a comfortable feeling of satisfaction that, whereas a year ago the Austrian crown was setting the example which is now being followed by the mark, for the last ten months it has been as stable as the dollar or the pound'. When it was reported from Berlin that the mark stood at 40 million to the pound, 'there was some nervousness on the Stock Exchange ... but there was no sign of panic.' In Parliament, the Social Democrats continued to oppose the budget and other legislation, but Seipel was confident that 'by making a concession here and there' and by negotiating with the parties, it would be possible to pass 'the remaining measures of economy and reform ... more rapidly'.[41] There was a marked improvement in the economic and financial situation: Austria had overcome a crisis which shook the very foundations of society – but only with the help given by the League of Nations and the great powers, rather than by the efforts of the government. This also showed that the institutions of the League could be used for constructive purposes, to benefit a former enemy country.

That the bureaucracy was far too large was admitted by the Austrians themselves. When the Federal President, Dr Hainisch, invited the British Minister on a shooting trip, he made this point very strongly – a 'prodigious growth' in the number of officials had occurred during the war, so that notices appeared with the slogan 'May God punish England with the Austrian bureaucracy'; after the war thousands of officials were expelled by the Succession States and were granted Austrian pensions. Some years later, the Minister of Finance calculated that the small Austria still had about 200,000 state employees and about 130,000 state pensioners. With their families, the government probably had to support no less that 800,000 people; and if the officials of the provinces and the municipalities were included, the figure would reach about 1,500,000 – and that in a country of only 6,000,000 inhabitants. Far too many men were employed on the railways, but a reduction of their number would be highly unpopular, and 'such a measure could [only] with difficulty be faced either by the Railway Board or the Federal Government.'[42] Therefore the reduction demanded by the League proceeded more slowly than the experts desired.

Another difficulty caused by the stabilisation of the currency was that the export boom, due to the low value of the krone, came to an end. In November 1922 the Legation reported a 'great stagnation in exports in nearly all branches'. In many enterprises the plant was inefficient or antiquated but could not be replaced owing to lack of funds; there was a 'serious shortage of working capital', brought about by selling at a loss during the years of inflation and a failure to calculate the real cost in stable currency. Quite apart from that, before 1914 the Austrian industries had found their chief markets among the 50 million inhabitants of the Habsburg Monarchy, and now they had 'to compete with the whole world on equal terms in selling their goods in the other Succession States'. There was therefore a problem of a permanent stagnation of exports, and the prospects for the industries depending on them were 'distinctly gloomy'. Indeed, one of the results was a quick growth of industrial unemployment (which had hardly existed during the crisis years), which, by the end of 1924, had reached 120,000, or 2 per cent of the population.[43]

The weakness of the central government and its helplessness *vis-à-vis* the provinces were recurrent themes in the despatches from Vienna. In 1920 Lindley wrote rather optimistically: 'both sides have recognised that Vienna cannot live without the Provinces and that the Provinces cannot rule the industrial population of Vienna, that the present combination [the coalition government] has been able to survive so long the constant quarrels between the two Parties' (the Social Christians and the Social Democrats); in the conditions of Austria, only a government 'in close touch with the industrial population ... could possibly maintain a semblance of order'; and he had 'never given the smallest encouragement to the many people' who hinted that the socialism of Bauer and the other leaders prevented Austria from receiving more Allied help. But the Christian Social leaders, Kunschak and Seipel, believed that, if they withdrew from the government, they could 'form a solid "bourgeois" block ... and secure the downfall of the Social Democrats'. Only three weeks later, the coalition disintegrated when Deutsch, the War Minister, was sharply attacked in Parliament for issuing new regulations for the Soldiers' Councils without government approval and the Christian Social leaders declared his action illegal. Such heat was engendered 'that latent hostility between two groups broke out openly and led to mutual insults and threats'; the socialist members of the government 'have applied to their party leader for permission to resign', and this would be granted. As Lindley commented:

> Parliamentary Government is not possible unless a certain regard is shown for the susceptibilities and interests of minorities and unless the vast majority of the population are ready to abide by the decisions of their elected representatives. But the signs of the times all point to a growing disregard of all but purely selfish considerations.[44]

When the new Austrian Constitution was adopted at the end of 1920, it was also submitted to the provincial Diets and became 'the occasion for significant expression of feeling,' Lindley reported. The Diet of Upper Austria qualified its adherence by adding the words 'so long as Austria remains a state organism capable of life'. Vorarlberg openly expressed its preference for union with Switzerland, and the Diet emphasised this. The Tyrolese Diet protested formally that its demand for a debate of the draft Constitution before it was introduced in Parliament was completely ignored and saw in this 'a violation of the rights belonging to the Province in virtue of the right of self-determination ... and of the rights enjoyed by the Diet'. A British memorandum on the federal problem of the same year stated unequivocally:

> The struggle between the Provinces and the State is therefore part of the class struggle between the propertied classes and the working classes.... The Provinces insist upon their economic independence, they close their frontiers against Vienna, and they formally constitute independent economic districts, solely for the purpose of not giving their agricultural produce to starving Vienna.... The Provinces do what they like, and the Provincial Governments do not trouble about the laws and ordinances of the State.

In truth, Austria was 'a Federation of Provinces', and the new Constitution would not be able to change this.[45] In the summer of 1921 the Tyrolese Diet even voted a law introducing a new currency based on the German mark and independent of the krone. But the central government submitted a complaint to the Supreme Court which declared the step illegal. Even in the Tyrol itself it aroused the opposition of hotel managers and tradesmen who feared that their trade would suffer.[46] Especially in the Tyrol, feeling remained strong against Vienna. In 1922 it 'manifested itself in appeals from the Provincial Authorities to the summer visitors to cut short their holidays', pleading an alleged shortage of food. Agitation was carried on 'in favour of the confiscation of foreign money', not from the tourists, but from the hotels and shopkeepers who allegedly hoarded their profits from the tourists, while the poorer classes suffered from the rising prices.[47] As we shall see, this strong local 'anti-foreign' feeling was to find expression in the *Heimwehr* movement, and continued for many years, even after the return of greater stability.

The Federal President, Dr Hainisch, was described by Lindsey from good personal knowledge as 'probably not a great man, but he well represents the best type of citizen to be found in this country'. He was 'on terms of life-long intimacy with the Social-Democratic leaders', whose views he did not share, and he personally knew all the leading German Nationalists, 'with whom he has, probably, closer affinities than with any other party'. He was 'not free from the mild form of reasoned anti-Semitism' which was 'almost universal' in Austria. For example, he considered the well-known historian, Professor Redlich, 'a man of first rate ability but not altogether reliable politically', a man who 'could not get away from the fact he was of Jewish origin'.[48]

Elections were due to take place in October 1920. In September the First Secretary of the British Legation reported that the election campaign was conducted with a large amount of personal abuse:

> The principal topic is the responsibility of the Christian Socialists and the Social Democrats for the shortage of white bread. The facts appear to be that the maize ordered by the Government in the spring did not arrive till the greater part of the American wheaten flour had been eaten, and the brusque change over from a fairly appetizing to a distinctly unsavoury loaf is being exploited by the leading parties at the expense of each other and by the Communists at the expense of both.

The Christian Social Party emerged considerably stronger than the Social Democrats after the election, with almost 42 per cent of the vote as against 36 per cent. They remained the leading party for many years, with the bulk of their strength in the conservative countryside. After the elections the Social Democrats went into permanent opposition: but the Christian Social Party never gained an absolute majority, and usually formed a coalition with the smaller bourgeois parties.

The French Legation in Vienna took sides more or less openly in party politics; it 'consistently supported the Christian Socialist Party', partly because the Social Democrats and the German Nationalists favoured the Anschluss, partly because of 'the supposed interests of their foreign bondholders'. The Italians, on the other hand, according to the British Legation, in those days 'supported the Social Democrats, presumably because the latter are hostile to Hungary and prefer the "Anschluss" to any form of Danube Confederation'. Lindley himself favoured a 'neutral' Cabinet as offering 'the best chance of getting through the winter without a collapse' and 'the most desirable for the Allies to deal with in the event of a programme of reconstruction and control being adopted'. A 'neutral' government would also be supported by the French, 'provided it has no "Anschluss" leanings'.[49] Under 'neutral' Lindley understood a government of experts and officials, headed by the Vienna Director of Police Schober, who did not belong to any party.

Support for Schober was the guiding-line of British policy in Austria. In December 1920 Curzon instructed the Minister

> that all possible support should be given to the particular Government that gives most hope of being able to guide Austria through the critical times which lie ahead.... You are therefore authorized, if and when Herr Schober is called upon to form a Ministry, to inform him that in the opinion of His Majesty's Government a "neutral" Government ... is the surest means of maintaining internal order and restoring Austria's credit and prosperity.[50]

Schober had maintained law and order in Vienna during the critical months of 1919, and continued to enjoy the confidence of British diplomats and ministers for many years. He was a civil servant rather than a politician and had no strong party leanings – clearly an asset in British eyes on account of the bitter party conflicts in Austria. In February 1921 Colonel Cuninghame reported that the Social Democrats had sent men they trusted to

Schober 'to see whether the latter is still willing to head a Government of Officials', which was later confirmed by Schober himself. Twelve months later Akers-Douglas wrote that, although the Schober government 'can hardly be said to have a working majority, it is hoped that they will be able to carry on the administration of the country during the present critical time.' Later, he added that the government's position was 'shaky', but it was hoped that the negotiations between the party leaders 'will result in securing a bare majority in Parliament but sufficient to enable the Government, with perhaps a change of one or two Ministers, to carry on.' Eyre Crowe, the Permanent Under-Secretary of State in the Foreign Office, added the comment: 'gratifying'. Before he became Chancellor, Schober informed the British Minister that 'the first thing he would do ... would be to refuse supplies to any recalcitrant province', for he considered provincial plebiscites on the Anschluss issue 'politically idiotic' and was opposed to them; 'he would let the Parties go to the devil and have nothing but non-party men in his Cabinet.'[51] Schober was a strong man after the British heart, one of the very few who in their opinion might be able to cope with the mounting crisis. But his government barely lasted twelve months.

The alternative to a 'neutral' government was a coalition of the Christian Social and German Nationalist Parties, the latter being by far the weaker. But on account of its right-wing pro-German politics it received a good deal of attention from the British diplomats. In 1920 Lindley reported:

> The Pan-German Party ... is confined to the towns and in its essence resembles the old National Liberal Party of Germany. It numbers 25 in the present National Assembly and is the only Party left which represents educated middle-class opinion. The University Professors and professional classes belong to it almost to a man, and it keeps in a certain touch with the working population through the clerical staff of the railways and the more educated of the workmen.

It had refused to support either of the big parties, but more recently had moved closer and closer to the Christian Social Party. Indeed, after the October elections, the two parties formed a coalition; but Lindley's scepticism was justified when he wrote: 'I do not believe that such a combination could last more than a few months, unless the Social Democrats give it their tacit support.'

In June 1921 he reported that more than 100 Austrian students, mainly from Graz and Innsbruck, had left the country to fight with the German Free Corps against the Poles in Upper Silesia; the responsibility rested with the professors who 'belong almost to a man to the German Nationalist Party', whose 'pernicious proceedings' he had mentioned several times. On informing the Chancellor of the students' departure, Schober replied that he had drawn 'the attention of the Provincial Authorities in Styria and Tyrol to the inadmissability of such an enterprise'; none had gone from Vienna, and 'he was determined to put a stop to students being organised for party political purposes.'[52] Among the Austrian intelligentsia, German nationalism was an old tradition, especially among the students, going back to the days of Georg Ritter von Schönerer in the late nineteenth century, and it went hand-in-hand with a virulent, racialist anti-Semitism.

The German Nationalists were not anti-British, and in an interview in 1922 their parliamentary leader, Dr Franz Dinghofer, stressed his friends' 'most friendly feelings towards England'; 'the only Entente Power against which we feel any hostility is France and we regard her as the disturber of the peace in Europe.' Their propaganda for the Anschluss was 'not in any degree incompatible with feelings of cordial friendship for England. We are fully aware that we can only achieve union with Germany by way of London, with the full approval of England'; and he wished to establish 'the most cordial relations between England and Austria'. In the same year, the Party brought about the fall of the Schober government, and then formed a new coalition with the Christian Social Party under its leader Dr Seipel. The new Chancellor told Akers-Douglas that a change of government at such a critical time might perhaps be considered a mistake abroad, but 'things in Austria could not go on unless there was a Government with a Parliamentary majority'; the presence of the German Nationalists in the government might be misunderstood too, but 'he could assure me most emphatically that there was absolutely no ground for misgiving'; he would not remain Chancellor if the government programme included the Anschluss. Akers-Douglas was very favourably impressed by Seipel:

He is a man of intelligence, tact and moderation, and he possesses one great advantage over Mr Schober in that he is an expert parliamentarian and has a much firmer hold on his Party ... than his predecessor who was not a professional politician. ... I must confess that it is very refreshing to find an Austrian Statesman who is both confident and determined, and does not sit with crossed hands waiting for something to happen.

As to his German Nationalist partners, 'their political stupidity is so great that it is to be feared that they will always be ready to overthrow the government, however much they may harm their own position thereby.'[53]

At the end of 1922 the Legation's annual report endorsed the favourable assessment of Seipel. He was 'a man of subtle intelligence and considerable courage', who 'gave to Austrian foreign policy an importance hitherto unrecognised'. While Schober was 'generally able to count upon the support of the Social Democrats', Seipel 'was anathema' to them and they 'made every effort to break his power'. The Christian Social Deputies had deserted Schober because they felt that he 'was not strong enough to deal with the party wranglings' and preferred a Chancellor from their own ranks 'who might be accepted by the German Nationalists and thus form a new *bloc* against the Social Democrats.' The conflicts between the political parties, the report added, 'are the curse of Austria'.[54] In 1923 – after the French occupation of the Ruhr – the worst suspicions of the British diplomats seemed confirmed when the German Nationalists sent their 'brotherly greetings to the people from whom we feel ourselves more inseparable than ever'.[55]

It seems that this strongly pro-German policy was not supported by the electorate, for in the general election of the same year the party lost heavily; their fraction of the vote dropped from 17 to less than 13 per cent, with its parliamentary representation reduced from 28 to 10 seats.[56] Yet this defeat did not bring about a change of policy, nor any more inspiring programme. The German Nationalists remained a small but vociferous Party agitating against the Jews and in favour of the Anschluss, and there can be little doubt that they prepared the way for the National Socialists. And however much Seipel and his Party might disapprove, no parliamentary majority could be formed without them.

In the early 1920s, however, the longing for union with Germany was by no means confined to the German Nationalists and extreme right-wing circles. As Lindley put it early in 1920, the feeling 'has now extended to a great part of the population, who are ready to welcome any solution which offers them a chance of escaping from their present misery.' The only staunch opponents of union were the avowed monarchists 'who realise that it would signify the final end of their hopes of a restoration'. If Austria joined Germany, Vienna would soon regain her 'preponderant position in South-Eastern Europe which she enjoyed in the past thanks to her geographical position on the Danube, her highly civilised population and her scientific and cultural institutions. She remains the real outpost of civilisation towards the Near East.' The next step after union would be 'an irredentist movement amongst the Germans under alien rule', which neither the Italians nor the Czechs would be able to contain. A few weeks later Lindley added that, if Germany should 'settle down under a really Socialistic and orderly regime', the Austrian socialists, 'who regard Berlin as their spiritual home', would 'redouble their clamour for Union'; but outside Vienna the result would be the opposite, and the Christian Social Party would hesitate to join a state that was more socialist than the Vienna which they disliked so much.

This was written soon after the defeat of the Kapp Putsch by the German workers when it seemed that Germany might be moving to the left, but in reality the opposite tendency prevailed. According to 'a well-informed observer', the enthusiasm of the Austrian socialists for the Anschluss could 'very simply' be explained by the personal ambition of Otto Bauer 'who is supposed to consider that his exceptional talents require ... a larger stage than Austria can provide' and Lindley thought there might be some truth in this.[57] But Renner, the other prominent leader, declared in answer to nationalist critics that he had supported union with Germany from the first and throughout the peace negotiations; he attributed the responsibility for the failure to the Christian Social Party, and he still preferred union with Germany to a Danube Federation. His first duty was to see to it that Austria was fed: as long as French imperialism 'plays first violin in politics', union was out of the question. Colonel Cuninghame thought that 'the efforts of the Clerical Party' favoured the Habsburgs against 'Pan-Germanism'; and that in the Tyrol the opponents of union were predominant. Sir William Goode of the Reparations Commission, on the other hand, believed that Upper Austria, Salzburg and Tyrol desired to join Bavaria.[58]

Certainly, for the strongly Catholic Tyrol, a combination with their equally staunchly Catholic neighbour to the north must have seemed preferable to union with 'Red' Vienna. It may well have been this feeling which produced overwhelming majorities in favour of the Anschluss when local plebiscites were held in Salzburg and Tyrol in the spring of 1921, and there can be little doubt that the mood of the time favoured union with Germany. The French government suggested a sharp protest by the Allied governments against the plebiscites, but Curzon considered such a step 'unnecessary and injudicious'. The Austrian Minister in London explained that his government, in authorising the plebiscites, 'intended rather to control and direct such a movement into the right channel than to give it an impetus, which unfortunately it did not require.' The intention was to decide 'whether or not the Austrian Government should apply to the League of Nations to obtain their sanction' for union with Germany, so that his government had done nothing contrary to the Treaty of St Germain.[59] As such a sanction was clearly unobtainable at the time, no further plebiscites were held. It would in any case have been extremely unwise to provoke the Allies, as Austria depended so much on their good will. This, however, did not mean that the idea of the Anschluss was no longer alive. Many Austrians continued to 'regard the artificial severance of Austria from Germany, as laid down in the peace treaties, as the chief source of all the miseries, both material and spiritual' of their country: a feeling which was still strongly expressed by a well-known Austrian exile *after* the Germans had marched into Vienna in 1938.[60]

In yet another plebiscite in the small province of Vorarlberg, 70 per cent of those entitled to vote opted in favour of joining Switzerland as a new canton. But strong opposition arose in Switzerland, partly by the French and Italian-speaking cantons, who feared a stronger German preponderance, partly by the textile manufacturers who feared competition, and partly by the Protestants who did not desire an increase in the Catholic minority in their country; the attempt was abortive.[61] There was no secession from Austria and, much as they disliked being ruled from Vienna, the provinces had no option but to acquiesce.

Although the Social Democrats in 1920 moved into permanent opposition, the reports from Vienna paid considerable attention to the party's activities and the opinions of its leaders, perhaps because of the radical stance of some of them, perhaps because of its attitude to the communists and its success in containing them, which compared so favourably with Germany or France. Early in 1921 Lindley wrote:

> There can be few countries in Europe so well provided with organs for concentrating and expressing the ideas and wishes of the working classes. The Social Democrats have, in fact, succeeded in constitutionalising what they would call the proletarian movement to a degree which, if one considers the catastrophe with which the war ended for Austria and the desperate situation in which she is left ever since, is remarkable.... So far as I can see, the numerical insignificance of the Communists fairly represents their political and moral importance in the country. Allowance must of course be made for the orderly, good-natured and cheerful disposition of the Austrians themselves, and even more for the instinctive conservatism of the large agricultural population. But none the less, I think a full share of credit ought to be given to the Social Democratic leaders who have shown a statesmanlike capacity for enforcing unpleasant truths and imposing unacceptable restraints on their followers.

A few weeks earlier Lindley had stated: 'The Social Democratic leaders are not Muscovites and probably saved the country from a Bolshevik régime in 1919', but now they seemed 'to be veering to the Left' and were 'determined to make it impossible for the Christian Socialists to govern the country.' He saw evidence of the 'semi-Bolshevik' attitude of the party in its appeal for the foundation of a new Socialist International which 'openly reviled' the government and its institutions.[62] An intelligence report written by a British Colonel claimed that when in office the Social Democrats had confined their conflicts with the other parties to Parliament, but 'since their defeat they desire to remove the battlefield from the Parliament to the Country, knowing that the Government has no effective weapon with which to put down any open outbreak.' Colonel Cuninghame found this conclusion 'wholly unfounded and unjustified'. In his opinion, the party wanted 'to return to power when conditions – if ever – are such as to make their policy feasible'; a breakdown of the government would therefore oblige them to do what they did not want to do, or would bring to power 'the forces of disorder with whom the Socialist Party, as such, are not associated': they had nothing to gain by a breakdown of the government.[63]

This assessment was confirmed by Bauer's speech at the Party Conference held in November 1920. He declared that the need for a coalition government had, fortunately, come to an end; the bourgeois parties had recovered from 'their first fright' and regained 'confidence to resume the direction of affairs'; the Social Democrats 'could now devote themselves whole-heartedly to opposition, until such time as public opinion was ready to welcome a purely Socialist government.'[64]

Reports on the conferences of the Workers' Councils emphasised the clashes between the socialists and communists. In February 1920 the communist delegates left the hall when the chairman ruled 'that they had not the right to interrupt the debate'. When several speakers urged an immediate mass demonstration in the streets, Bauer succeeded in postponing a decision by pointing out 'that the moment was not well chosen for such a demonstration'. The conference also objected to the proposal of the Minister of Finance for a capital levy because payments in War Loan were permitted and this favoured the wealthy: 'the War Loan should be left to take care of itself.'

Another conference of the Workers' Councils in June 1920 brought a widening of the gulf between socialists and com-munists, and 'the proceedings ... were marked by constant scenes of regrettable disorder'. The communists were accused of engaging 'in an underhand agitation against the Councils and their authority' and of preventing a 'united front against reaction'. Bauer spoke seriously about the crisis which resulted in the end of the coalition government: if the bourgeois parties 'tried to get together an armed force ... as they seemed to be trying to do, it would be the business of the Workmen's Councils, who knew that they could rely on the new Army, to show that they were the stronger.' In May the Social Democrats organised a mass demonstration to hasten the imposition of the capital levy, and the communists a separate and much smaller one of their own. In Linz the communists used the occasion to force their way into the government offices and were dispersed by the police; ten people were killed and thirty wounded.

In a conversation with the British Minister, Dr Renner said that the Social Democrats aimed at the isolation of the communists 'who, in Austria, consisted mainly of adventurers and criminals'; recent events had proved 'the extreme numerical weakness of the avowed Communists'. On a different occasion Renner observed that 'all his information went to show that the Soviet Government would quickly disappear with the return of the Red Army to a life of peace. It was inconceivable that a nation, of whom 95 per cent were peasants, could long remain Bolshevik if left to themselves.'[65] Renner's 'usual optimism' was more justified with regard to his native Austria than with regard to Russia.

In general, Lindley found that 'Austrian Social Democracy is not badly equipped for the leadership' of the moderate wing of the Central European labour movement;

> it has a good intellectual tradition, it has shown remarkable discipline and solidity in two very trying years of power and it is not, like the corresponding parties in some other countries, encumbered with the bourgeois instincts and conservative methods of old-fashioned labour. Its efforts to tread the narrow path between the second and the third International deserve to be watched with attention and I think with sympathy.

Six months later he again praised the 'very good' discipline of the party: 'it cannot be easy to hold a party together on a policy of moderation and expectancy with nothing but disappointed hopes behind them and little likelihood of office in front.' A comparison with their Christian Social rivals and the quality of their leadership 'leaves little doubt as to where the political intelligence of Austria is to be looked for these days'[66] – rather surprising assessments for a conservative British diplomat who had just accused the socialists of a 'semi-Bolshevik attitude'.

Early in 1921 Lindley reported in great detail on 'a remarkable profession of policy by Dr Bauer' at the annual conference of the factory councils of the Metalworkers' Union. In Bauer's opinion, they were 'the educational organ by which the working class would become fitted, in due course, to take the place of the capitalist in the direction of industry'; they were to ensure that the growing profits 'were not engrossed by the capitalist but were made available for the benefit of the workers'. While in Britain and America millions were unemployed, in Austria there were practically none because of the low cost of production; this would attract foreign capital provided it was safe from expropriation and political instability; if any violent interference with private industry were attempted, they would be 'blockaded by a ring of non-socialist powers'; it was better to work in a capitalist factory than to starve 'on the pavement outside'. Lindley commented: 'There is no doubt that Dr Bauer has for some time past been working hard for moderation and I have little doubt that the eclipse of Communism in Austria is in a large measure due to his influence.... And he must be very sure of his standing in his Party to be able to administer as many unpalatable truths in one dose.'

Lindley's opinion of Bauer had changed a good deal. At about the same time the Commercial Secretary of the Legation talked to Bauer about the vexed question of the denationalisation of the Austrian Länderbank and the proposal to transfer its seat from Vienna to Paris so as to facilitate the settlement of the bank's pre-war debts. Bauer believed that such a transfer 'might involve serious dangers': the French had large interests in certain Czech industries, particularly in iron and steel, while the Czechs prohibited the import of some Austrian industrial products. If the French through the Länderbank were to control certain Austrian factories 'they could manage them in such a way as to favour the interests of the Czech competitors' of Austria; it was therefore preferable for the bank to remain in Austria, but much would depend on the safeguards to be introduced. Bauer stressed that his attitude was not influenced by political motives, but would be guided by the economic welfare of Austria: 'as usual he gave the impression of frankness and sincerity as well as being very competent in economic affairs.'[67]

In 1921 Colonel Cuninghame wrote that the socialists 'remain determined to stand outside all responsibility for Government'. They feared to destroy the solidarity of the party and to lose their left wing, but so far they had kept their following intact. The Legation's annual report for 1922 repeated that the party showed no sign of wishing to enter the government; and, in any case, the resolutions of the 'Vienna International' – formed the previous year on the initiative of the Austrian Socialists – forbade any cooperation with bourgeois parties.[68] An agent's report of the same year gave the strength of the party's membership as almost 1 million and 'constantly increasing'; its leaders 'never go to the extremes for the sake of a theory and practically protect the interests of the working class.' The workers, organised in trade unions, 'have an enormous sense of their power'. 'The only illegal activity of the party', according to the report, consisted of the *Ordnerwehr*, a well-organised force of about 120,000 men, with 'purely passive functions', to oppose any attempt at a restoration or a possible attack from Hungary. Since the elections of March 1919, the Legation reported, the municipality of Vienna was in the hands of the Social Democrats, after 25 years of Christian Social rule. Among the party leaders, there was 'a very large sprinkling of Jews', and this had led to the slogan 'Los von Wien' (Let's separate from Vienna), which appealed 'to everyone who was interested in preserving his own food supply or who disliked Socialists or Jews'.[69] The refusal to enter a new coalition government distinguished the Austrian Socialists from other Social Democratic parties and gave them a more radical air: 'It puts them in the comfortable position of being continually in opposition' and helped them to gain electoral successes – about 40 per cent of the total vote.[70] But their hope of winning a majority by democratic means was never fufilled. This was the case only in Vienna which was only one among eight provinces.*

After the stormy events of 1919, the communist danger was not considered very serious, and alarmist reports received little credence. When the Brigadier of the Inter-Allied Military Mission in Budapest early in 1920 sent a memorandum to Admiral Horthy claiming 'that the Bolshevist organisation in Austria constituted a very serious danger to the whole of Europe, and that the Austrian Government ... takes no serious steps to combat it', the historian Harold Temperley minuted: 'This does not seem very convincing in detail.' In June 1920 the head of the Styrian gendarmerie supplied 'secret information' to Colonel Cuninghame on 'the riotous and extreme left wing led by notorious Communists acting on international and non-local impulses', which was equally exaggerated. In September Dr

---

*The others are from West to East: Vorarlberg, Tyrol, Carinthia, Styria, Upper Austria, Lower Austria and Burgenland.

Rintelen, the head of the Styrian provincial government, claimed 'that Communists and Social Democrats were now working together' and that 'Communism had made considerable progress in the last few weeks'; but he combined this information with a request for 7000 rifles for the local *Heimwehr*.[71] After the general election of October 1920 the British Legation reported more soberly that the communists had failed to win a single seat and even to poll more than a fraction of their own membership; in three of the poorest Vienna districts, they won 740, 1175 and 1400 votes respectively, out of a total of 185,000 votes cast (1.8 per cent), and in the whole of Austria only 20,000 votes.[72]

In May 1921 violence for which the communists were held responsible occurred in the Styrian village of St Lorenzen, where Dr Rintelen was prevented from speaking by left-wing miners. Rintelen and one of his friends were thrown out of a window, knocked down and stoned until Rintelen lost consciousness. The gendarmes arrested four suspects and intended to take them to Graz by rail. But when they heard that armed workers were searching all the trains to release their comrades, the gendarmes with their prisoners set out on foot. They found the passes too occupied by armed men and so decided to release those arrested. There was a great outcry and an interpellation by a Christian Social deputy in Parliament. In July twelve men were tried in Graz for participation in the attack, but only three were found guilty and sentenced to two months of imprisonment; the others were acquitted. The violence was condemned by the local Social Democrats, and some of their leaders paid a visit of condolence to the maltreated Rintelen.[73] They were fully aware that violence of this kind would play into the hands of the reactionaries and serve to strengthen the Heimwehr movement.

After the failure of the 'March Action' of 1921 in Germany (a disastrous communist Putsch instigated by the Comintern), heated discussions broke out, not only in the German but also in the Austrian party. One section, led by Joseph Strasser and the leaders of the communist soldiers' group, 'violently condemned those responsible for the German Putsch and those holding similar views among the Austrian Communists' and sided with the German communist leader, Paul Levi, who was expelled from the German party. But then a meeting was convoked on orders from Moscow, which dutifully condemned Levi. Strasser was removed from his post as editor of the Vienna *Rote Fahne*, and he and two others were expelled temporarily from the party. At a later meeting they were reinstated as members of the steering committee when they renounced their earlier attitude, but the meeting ended in such an uproar that even the minutes 'went west' and no copy could be obtained by the agent reporting the meeting.

At a meeting of the enlarged steering committee in July the differences reappeared. One of those who had been suspended earlier proposed 'the adoption of a more moderate course towards the Social Democrats', especially by the party paper, *Rote Fahne*. This indicated that a 'right' faction was in the process of being constituted to oppose the extremists among the leaders; preliminary discussions had taken place in a café to determine the general line of action and the members – ten names were given – would continue to meet secretly once a week and would defend their views whenever possible at party meetings. At the enlarged steering committee the number of paying party members was given as 16,824, and that of the soldiers' group as 3460, giving a total of just over 20,000. The 'considerable shortage of funds' which had existed during the past six weeks was overcome 'thanks to fresh reinforcements from Moscow', and normal pay was resumed at party headquarters.[74] No source was given in these Intelligence reports, but they probably came from the police. Whoever made them seemed very well informed.

In August 1922 the British Minister reported on demonstrations of the unemployed in Vienna which were 'poorly attended'; but a group of the demonstrators tried to break into the Parliament building in the centre of the city where a Social Democratic conference was held. In the resulting clashes ten policemen and eight demonstrators were injured. 'In spite of many rumours of possible disturbances', the week had otherwise passed quietly. An agent's report of the same month stated 'that it looks as if we could reckon with a sharp split between the country districts swinging to the Right and the industrial districts towards the Left.' As the workers were 'much more radical than the Social Democratic leaders, Communist influence will play a large part, and will certainly prove extremely dangerous'; but in spite of all promptings from Moscow, the party did not intend 'to undertake any action on its own responsibility'.

A report of September 1922 gave the party's income for August as 7 million kronen, but its expenditure as 80 millions, more than half of which was spent on salaries and office expenses. An 'axe' would have to be wielded to reduce the number of paid officials, and this was likely 'to lead to serious internal discussions' as no one wished to be the victim; 'any attempt at violence would be a flash in the pan' because the masses were against any such action.[75] The Legation's annual report gave the membership for the earlier months of 1922 as 'about 15,000 active Communists and from 10,000 to 30,000 sympathisers'; shortage of funds was greatly hampering all activities, and by October the number of active members had fallen to 11,000, and by December to about 7000, but the number of sympathisers had increased. It was estimated that in Vienna 30 per cent of the unemployed followed the party. An 'illegal apparatus' had been built up by Franz Koritschoner, consisting of 'a secret army with some 300 rifles and some 250 rounds of ammunition to each, together with a number of hand grenades and revolvers', and of a 'sudden alarm group' of young party members; they were to create disturbances and to stir up the workers to deeds of violence, and 'in the summer they succeeded in aggravating the situation and in spreading a great deal of discontent'.[76] This may have been so, but the report also made it clear that, with the improvement in the financial and general situation in the autumn of 1922, the party's membership steeply declined. In municipal elections in Vienna in October 1923 the party polled a mere 13,559 votes, compared with 569,226 for the Social Democrats, or hardly more than 2 per cent of the socialist vote.[77]

A number of strikes reported to London mainly affected the public sector. In April 1920 there was a serious railway strike on the southern and western lines which was due to a cut in the flour ration. It lasted four days. The union leaders were willing to accept a settlement suggested by the government, but their advice was disregarded by a mass meeting; more radical younger men took the lead, and no trains reached Vienna for a few days. 'Long continued distress seems at last to have exhausted the patience of the population,' Lindley wired. According to Dr Renner, the direction of the movement passed to 'Communists and Pan-Germans', but on 20 April 'work was resumed on all lines'. The month before an ugly incident had occurred in a cotton mill at Neunkirchen when a worker was discharged after a clash with a manager, a Swiss citizen. The workers of the district demonstrated against him a few days later, and some invaded his office, dragged him out and beat him up so badly that he was taken unconscious to hospital. A British diplomat discussed this and other incidents with Otto Bauer as he feared that it might develop into a movement 'against the employers with a view of setting up Workmen's Councils to run the factories if the employers decided to close them.' Bauer however, assured him 'that the better-class workers in the district had not approved . . . and felt ashamed of what had taken place', and that the trade unions had no part in it: the courts must deal with any criminal proceedings arising out of the incident, and official regrets were expressed to the Swiss Minister.[78]

At the end of 1920 the civil servants struck for higher salaries, but the government did not intend to raise them 'and had no means of doing so except by means of [the] printing press'. Early in 1921 there was a strike of railwaymen on the southern line with its centre at Graz; and a strike of postal workers and telephone operators in the course of which the main post office of Vienna was occupied by strikers. They were ejected by the police. After a few days the strike was 'settled by so-called compromise which really amounts to victory for strikers', Lindley wired; if it had not been settled the outbreak of a general strike was feared. An unauthorised and short railway strike which affected all the Vienna stations occurred in September 1921, while the government was still negotiating with the unions over wage increases, and caused a complete cessation of all rail traffic with Hungary. Twelve months later the printers came out. The Legation attributed the unrest to 'the growing desperation over the delay in the Credits'.[79] More serious was a 'general strike' declared in June 1922 which cut off Vienna from the outside world, except by car or air. After three days the strike was ended by a concession made by the government, according to which its employees would receive the same automatic increases as workers in the private sector, in line with rises in the cost of living index.

These were virtually all the strikes reported by the Legation, and they were all short. But it also attempted to answer the hypothetical question whether the army could be used in the case of a strike on the railways or in the public utilities. The answer given by Colonel Cuninghame in 1922 was that the army could not prevent any such strike and that in certain circumstances soldiers might be willing to act as strike-breakers; but they could 'hardly be required to support and protect civilian strike-breakers, because of the natural cowardice of Austrians and their reluctance to act as individuals'.[80] This assessment, of course, came from a professional soldier, but his remark about the Austrians was rather nasty, and completely disregarded the military valour shown by Austrian soldiers during the war. Many years of residence in Vienna clearly had not endeared the Austrians to him.

The British diplomats often mentioned the easy-going, law-abiding, long-suffering and non-violent character of the Austrians, but this was only part of the picture. Apart from the incidents already mentioned, others occurred. In April 1920 anti-Semitic excesses took place at Vienna University, instigated by Christian Social and nationalist students 'who realised that the number of posts open to them in this country will in the future be very restricted'. They aimed at excluding Jewish students from the university, but socialist and communist students took the side of their Jewish colleagues and the Rector had to close the university for a time. Three years later several hundred National Socialists who had gone to drill in the Vienna woods clashed there with Social Democrats, hundreds of shots were fired, and a few people were wounded. After further anti-Semitic demonstrations at the university a memorandum was drawn up in the Legation which stated:

> The impoverishment of the landowners has left the Jews the only wealthy class in the Republic. To-day they practically monopolise finance, industry and commerce; they dominate in art, music, letters, science and medicine. The principal newspapers are owned and managed by Jews, and even the Catholic *Reichspost* acknowledges their superior talents by employing them on its staff. The traveller who finds the theatres, restaurants, and shops in Vienna almost exclusively filled with Jewish profiteers of extremely unprepossessing appearance, is easily inclined to exaggerate their numbers. In fact

they constitute but 7 per cent of the whole population of Austria, and in Vienna where they are most numerous, not more than 22 per cent.... Some few with political ideals or ambitions become leaders of the Social Democrats or the Communists because the other parties will not have them, but generally the Jews take but little part directly in politics. Their international sympathies and lack of patriotism lead them to prefer business.... The wealth and abilities of the Jews has [sic] naturally accentuated the jealousy and natural antipathy of their less successful and less gifted fellow citizens, and there have in the last few months been several anti-Semite demonstrations at the University, where their intelligence and wealth threatens [sic] to give the Jews the monopoly both of teaching and learning.

This memorandum not only very much exaggerated the role and importance of the Jews in the economic, artistic and academic life of Austria, but it was also based on incorrect figures. It is true that the Jewish population of Vienna had grown on account of the war and its aftermath, but it was less than half the figure quoted. In 1910 Jews formed 8.6 per cent of the population of Vienna, and in 1923 10.8 per cent.[81] The sources used by the writer, and the writer himself, must have been strongly anti-Semitic.

Political violence emanated above all from the para-military associations which remained the bane of Austrian political life. In the early 1920s the principal ones were the *Arbeiterwehren* of the socialists and the *Heimwehren*, which were supported by the bourgeois parties and received considerable help in money and weapons from Bavaria. This was well known to the Allied officers in Austria. In October 1920 the Intelligence Section of the Military Control Commission (which was to supervise Austrian disarmament according to the provisions of the Peace Treaty) reported that the Heimatwehren of Salzburg and Tyrol had close connections with the Bavarian para-military formation, the *Orgesch* (Organisation Escherich) and had even accepted directives from it at a meeting in Munich held in July. Thereafter the *Orgesch* penetrated the whole Austrian movement to Styria in the south. In September three Bavarians met representatives of the Christian Social and German Nationalist Parties in Vienna and tried to obtain the military leadership of the *Orka* (Organisation Kanzler) for General Krauss; but in fact General Metzger was appointed military leader for Austria. The Orka

aimed at a centralisation of the Austrian Heimwehren, but this
was impeded by the particularist tendencies of the provinces: a
remark which proved how well informed the author, a French
officer, was, for this aim was never achieved. In his accompany-
ing note Colonel Gosset agreed that the Heimwehr movement
had made 'considerable progress in organisation' and 'that it will
be difficult to bring it under a central authority', but the
Germans 'are using every means to extend their influence over
the Heimwehr'. He also informed London that at Innsbruck the
Heimwehr had about 1000 members, former officers, students
and young men of the upper classes, all armed; in the Tyrol
outside Innsbruck, it had about 9000–10,000 peasant members;
it possessed no guns but 'about 300 machine-guns and several
armoured motor machine-guns'. Many of the weapons had
recently come from Bavaria 'with the support of the Tyrolese
authorities and the connivance of the Customs Officials'. The
strength of the Styrian Heimwehr was given by Dr Rintelen to
the Colonel as 50,000 men, but without sufficient arms, so that
he asked for more rifles[82] – surely a strange request to address to
the officer of an authority sent to supervise Austrian
disarmament! Rintelen also admitted his good connections with
the Orgesch.

In November 1920, Lindley reported that the Heimwehren
were organised against 'Bolshevism and the town population'
and were not connected with the monarchist movement; they
were 'in close touch with the Orgesch', and General Ludendorff
was active in Austria, trying to organise former officers and
soldiers. He was supposed to have won over 1200 officers of an
ex-servicemen's league under General Krauss. When Lindley
expressed his apprehension to Police Director Schober, the latter
replied that Rintelen 'was by no means the hot-head he
represented himself to be'; even if he intended to use the
Heimwehr 'for some adventure, the peasants would not follow
him.'[83] In the same month the President of the Inter-Allied
Control Commission for Austria, General Zuccari, protested to
the Austrian government that the planned Heimwehr shooting
contest at Innsbruck would be attended by people 'armed with
weapons of war', which according to the Peace Treaty should
have been handed over to the Commission. He urged the
government that 'the festival should ... not bear the character of

a public demonstration with arms which are prohibited by the Treaty'.

In spite of the protest and against the wishes of the government, the contest took place. The railwaymen came out on strike in protest and prevented several thousand Bavarians from crossing the frontier: only about 100 managed to get through and they were not armed. An Allied officer who attended the meeting was convinced that, if the Bavarians had come, everything was ready for the announcement of the union of the Tyrol with Bavaria, and that the Heimwehren were only waiting for a more propitious moment. Colonel Cuninghame, on the other hand, believed that, in spite of their Bavarian links, they were 'instruments of the Christian Socialist Party and are as such potentially pro-Habsburg and anti-Gross Deutsch'; their principal purpose was 'the combat of the growing power of the Socialists and the armed associations of workmen'.[84]

At the beginning of 1921 an intelligence report of the Military Control Commission gave the strength of the Tyrolese Heimwehren as over 22,000 (compared to 2500 of the Arbeiterwehr); membership in the much smaller Salzburg was estimated at 15,000, commanded by Colonel Kerner with the Bavarian Major Hörl as his Chief of Staff, and ample stores of weapons sent from Bavaria. Little information was available on Upper Austria where the Heimwehren were 'scattered throughout the province'. In Styria, they were tolerated by the provincial government 'as an efficient protection against Socialist plots', and 'attempts to thwart them met with no success'. Lindley felt certain that the movement was kept together by 'the fear of Bolshevism and the resolve not to allow Austria to submit to the experience of Bavaria and Hungary' in 1919, but did not aim at the overthrow of the Constitution and the restoration of the Habsburgs.

In June 1921 it was reported that the Tyrolese Heimwehren had celebrated the first anniversary of their foundation in military fashion at the Isel mountain. They were addressed by their leader Dr Steidle and the Orgesch leader Escherich, who distinguished between 'the lovers of order and those who wished to stir up trouble': 'all who stood up for order and the reconstruction of their much-tried country' were welcome to join their ranks to promote 'national recovery'. It was added that

Heimwehr members had apparently been busy raiding army depots to add to their stores of weapons.[85]

The information available on the Arbeiterwehr was less precise. Early in 1920 Colonel Cuninghame noted that 'drilling groups' existed in four Lower Austrian towns and the Vienna Arsenal, as well as in Graz, Bruck, Leoben 'and other Styrian mining centres'; thus the declaration by Deutsch, the War Minister, that there were no workers' battalions, 'is only nominally true'. Lindley wrote at the same time that the workers of Wiener Neustadt had intercepted 122 machine-guns on their way to Vienna and that four lorry loads of arms were removed from a depot in Graz. When disturbances broke out there in June 1920 armed workmen occupied a section of the town and one of the main bridges, and demanded that those arrested by the police be freed; when this was done the workers disbanded.

Colonel Cuninghame estimated that the Styrian Arbeiter-wehren were several thousand strong and armed with rifles. But in his opinion it was 'certain that the arms in the hands of the peasants are much larger in number' and that the workers were 'interested in giving the impression that they have more than is really the case'.[86] The Tyrolese government claimed that the Arbeiterwehren of Innsbruck and surrounding districts consisted of eleven companies with one or two machine-guns each, and detachments in all industrial centres and at important railway stations. The annual report of the Legation for 1920 even claimed 'that the Arbeiterwehr is the best organised and . . . in a much stronger tactical position than its rival'; but it was 'not a Bolshevik organisation as it is so often accused of being, but a force animated by the resolve to prevent the return of the monarchy and to intimidate the employers of labour and the Government sufficiently to prevent any attempt' at reducing the power of the socialist organisations; it was therefore not 'organised for subversive purposes',[87] which was quite correct.

By the early 1920s both sides had their para-military formations – very roughly representing the sharp conflict between town and country – and a clash between them seemed possible or even likely. As early as October 1919 Colonel Cuninghame commented on the 'very strained' relations between peasants and workers in Styria: 'both sides are armed and a conflict may arise any day. The workmen are secretly forming armed associations, and it is entirely desirable that no time should be lost in carrying out the work of general disarmament.' Six months later, after the German Kapp Putsch was defeated by a general strike, he reported that the Austrian workers too were excited, 'and advantage has been taken of these events to preach to them the necessity of retaining their arms in order to counteract the influence of the newly formed army'. The movement was spreading rapidly, the workers relied on their weapons, defying the managers of the factories, and were in favour of direct action; forcible resistance was rendered to any efforts to prevent the formation of armed groups and to collect information about them. When another British officer saw Deutsch, the Minister of War, in June 1920, Deutsch claimed that 'there was a serious danger of civil war' and told his interlocutor that the 'Entente should tell us to do away with Burgherwehr, Heimwehr and Arbeiterwehr, and threaten not to give us any more credit unless this is done at once.' As the interview took place at the time of the government crisis which led to the resignation of the socialist ministers, Colonel Gosset feared the outbreak of disturbances in certain industrial areas 'to show necessity of continuance of Social Democrat preponderance in the Cabinet', especially in Graz.[88]

Lindley reported at the same time: 'There is no doubt that peasants who have all along had arms are now being organised into regular formations both in the Tyrol and Styria to resist any attack from armed workmen or perhaps to attack them. In short, scene seems to be set rather for a civil war between town and country than for a new Coalition Government'. Previously, he had often urged the necessity to disarm both sides so that a repetition was not necessary, but 'it is now difficult of accomplishment'. A few days later he wrote that, as both sides were organised, they might 'shrink from an armed conflict and become more inclined for compromise'; but the best hope of avoiding civil war rested on the fact that Austria depended 'on the good will of foreign countries for food'.[89]

Disarmament was repeatedly urged by British officers, but in vain. Early in 1920 Colonel Cuninghame informed the War Office that he had always been in favour of the removal of the arms depots of the workers' associations, not because he feared any revival of Bolshevist activities, 'but because it seems to me that chance events of an untoward type, such as sudden increase in the number of unemployed, complete breakdown of railway transportation owing to snow or strikes, etc., might lead to street fighting'. The situation in Styria was 'delicate', with workers opposing peasants and possible threats to the border areas from Hungary or Yugoslavia. The first task was the confiscation of arms in the arsenals and depots, and 'any risk there may be of resistance should be taken'. As Vienna depended on food imports, the workers knew that their arms would have to be surrendered; it should be explained to them at the same time 'that there is no intention of leaving the industrial classes in an inferior position from the point of view of effective influence', and they should be assured 'as to the attitude of the Entente towards the reactionary tendency in Hungary'. This applied in particular to Styria, where Dr Rintelen had openly supported the White forces in Hungary in the summer of 1919. When the First Secretary of the Legation saw Rintelen in April 1920 and mentioned the difficulty of simultaneous disarmament of peasants and workers, and especially the mutual suspicion that the other side would keep their weapons, Rintelen found these apprehensions exaggerated. 'He spoke with a good deal of bitterness of the Communists and of the influence which they exercised over the Social Democratic members of the Government', and he gave the impression 'that, provided the townsfolk were disarmed, he would not much mind if the peasants remained in possession of their arms.' When Lindley discussed the same issue with Schober, he told the Minister 'that disarmament could not be carried out until [the] Austrian Government possessed a reliable force'; if he were given a free hand, he could create in a few months 'a small but reliable' force from the present army; 'then he could disarm both workmen and peasants':[90] but this was a pious hope.

In December 1920 Colonel Gosset lunched with Deutsch (the latter no longer Minister of War), and stressed that it was the responsibility of the Austrian government to bring about disarmament, but that no measures had been taken five months after the Peace Treaty had come into force. Deutsch replied that he was all in favour: the Arbeiterwehr would give up their weapons freely, 'provided the Heimwehr were disarmed first'; a law should be introduced offering rewards for arms surrendered and the Allies should exercise pressure on the government. In Gosset's opinion, it was immaterial whether they began with the one or the other force, but the government had to do it. The War Office, on the other hand, sided with Schober, who believed that the existence of a reliable army was a precondition of disarmament: 'in view of the weakness of the present Austrian Government they are doubtful as to the feasibility of carrying out the disarmament simultaneously with the re-organisation and reformation of the Wehrmacht, which they regard as a matter of urgent and paramount importance'; immediate steps must be taken 'to re-organise the Wehrmacht and to turn it into a disciplined force, capable of carrying out its duties'; disarmament would have to wait.[91]

In retrospect it seems strange that no more was done to achieve the disarmament of the para-military organisations or to stop at least the arms traffic across the Bavarian frontier, which the Allies were well informed about, partly by the British Consul in Munich.[92] But in the much more important issue of German disarmament, greater efforts were made by the Allied Military Control Commission and they equally failed. It may well be that only direct military intervention could have achieved more, and that certainly was a course Britain would not have contemplated, either then or later. A threat to cut off food supplies to Vienna unless disarmament was carried out by the Austrians would have caused a public outcry in Britain. And effecting the disarmament of the peasants in the mountainous areas of Styria and the Tyrol where they had always possessed their own rifles was highly problematic. A disarmament of the workers in the towns was easier to carry out, but it would have remained a one-sided affair.

When the Austrian Chancellor, Dr Mayr, visited London in 1921 to seek further assistance, Lord Curzon expressly warned him that Austria 'must give a definite guarantee as to the execution of the Military Clauses of the Treaty of Saint Germain, which his Government had hitherto shown a marked reluctance to fulfil'; this failure was most conspicuous with regard to the reduction of the army to its stipulated size, the surrender and the sale of war material, for example to Poland. In the spring of 1920 an Army Bill had been passed which permitted a strength larger than laid down in the treaty (30,000 men); since then there had been an amending Bill, but there was no serious effort to pass it. Dr Mayr raised no objections to these strictures and defended himself by airing the difficulties of his parliamentary position: the opposition was nearly as strong as the government and forced him to adopt measures which he would have shunned if he were stronger. Early in 1922 the War Office stated that some of the conditions had since been fulfilled: the army was reduced to a figure below its stipulated size; the strength of the gendarmerie and police did not exceed the limit fixed by the Conference of Ambassadors; the destruction or export of the surrendered war material should be completed by April, as should the establishment of the single state factory for the manufacture of arms and material for the Austrian army. But, owing to the weakness of the Austrian government and the unsettled state of Central Europe, 'no appreciable progress has been made in the surrender of arms by the civil population nor in the disbandment of unauthorized organizations', such as the Heimwehr and Arbeiterwehr. In spite of this, the Army Council did not suggest the continuation of military control and recommended its termination 'as soon as the destruction or export of the remaining war material ... and the Control of the single State Factory for the manufacture of war material has been completed.' The British military attaché in Vienna should in any case 'not be concerned in any way with the work of control'.[93] The view that some of the outstanding matters could be settled within a few months proved over-optimistic, however. Especially the concentration of the manufacture of arms in one single factory was difficult to achieve, so that the so-called 'Organ of Liquidation' continued to function for several more years. As we shall see, no progress whatever was made in the disarmament of the para-military organisations.

During the six months from October 1922 to March 1923 the 'Organ of Liquidation' succeeded in finding at different depots sizeable quantities of illicit war material, including 44 mine-throwers with mountings and platforms, 66 artillery tractors, 14 guns of an older model, 40 trench mortars, 475 Stokes mortars, as well as very large quantities of mountings and spare parts for them, and of ammunition. The comment of the British section of the 'Organ of Liquidation' was a simple admission that arms and ammunition were probably hidden in quantity, but 'most of these will come to light in time; these possible stocks are held by dishonest Government Officials and Jew traders [sic] for disposal to whoever can pay the highest sum and undertake the risk of getting them out of the Country.' A danger was seen in 'the eagerness with which German firms gain a footing and controlling interest in Austrian factories', but the para-military associations and their stores of weapons were not mentioned. When a Vienna newspaper reported that the Hirtenberg arms factory had sold 35 million rifle cartridges to Yugoslavia, the factory was inspected, but nothing was discovered to prove 'any illegal manufacture of ammunition', and it was assumed that the cartridges came from the branch of the factory at Warsaw to which much of the machinery had been transferred.[94] But in 1924 an incident occurred which indicated that this assumption was incorrect (see below pp. 113–14). It would seem that the 'Organ of Liquidation' was kept busy with fairly minor issues and tended to neglect the more important tasks.

The British officers and diplomats were not so much concerned about the size of the Austrian army, but more so about its composition and political persuasion. A special issue was that of the Soldiers' Councils, which had fulfilled important functions in the *Volkswehr* and which the Social Democrats tried to retain in the permanent army. This was a question of great importance which caused the break-up of the coalition government in June 1920. In February Colonel Cuninghame wrote: 'The persisting evil of Soldiers' Councils and Men of Confidence remains, as before, an object of criticism and attack.' This applied in particular to the inclusion of their representatives in the selection committees for the new army; the provincial authorities of Salzburg and the Tyrol were determined to expel from these committees any members of a Soldiers' Council, and to prevent any private soldier from sitting on the committees for the selection of NCOs and any NCO from sitting on the committees for the selection of officers. In June 1920 a mass meeting of about 10,000 soldiers was held in front of the Vienna Town Hall to pass a resolution in favour of the retention of Soldiers' Councils in the new army. Deutsch claimed that it was the Councils' task to defend 'the Austrian body politic against extremists of both sides'; but privately he declared that 'the object of this demonstration was to take the wind out of the sails of the extreme and communist element' as represented by the old Soldiers' Councils. His opponents pointed out that the demonstration was instigated by the Social Democrats and openly associated the new army with the party's political aims.[95] Colonel Gosset of the Military Control Commission went much further and claimed that the new army 'is universally recognised as the tool of a political party: the Social Democrats, with a strong element of communism'; the people feared and distrusted the army, and this had induced the peasants to arm themselves and to form the Heimwehren; the large majority of the soldiers were men of the old army 'who have no trade or other means of earning their livelihood' and the remainder were 'unemployable, work-shy men and communists'; the army was practically in the hands of the Soldiers' Councils and the soldiers' trade union, the *Militärverband*. It was thus hopeless to expect the army to become a force of law and order as intended by the Peace Treaty. On the contrary, it was a danger to the peace of the Republic, and the majority of Austrians preferred to do without an army for the time being and to rely on the police to maintain order. This was the view not only of Colonel Gosset but also of Dr Rintelen when he was seen by a British diplomat. As planned, the army would be 'a purely Social Democratic Army, of little military value, and extremely obnoxious to Christian Socialist opinion', which would prefer to have no army at all.

In June 1920 Colonel Gosset stated that the Military Union, the Militärverband, supported by the Soldiers' Councils, would have 'complete control' over the army; the officers 'will only be tolerated as long as they are sufficiently malleable in the hands of the red Trades Unions'. When Deutsch was questioned by an officer about how the soldiers would behave in case of strikes or disorders, he had replied that they would no doubt join the strikers; if an army was established on these lines 'with apparent legality', the example would be followed by other countries and the outcome would be 'the complete collapse of all middle-class and peasant elements, and confusion and chaos in the whole of Europe.'[96] These apocalyptic statements by a British professional officer had little to do with the reality of Austria in 1920.

The assessment of Colonel Cuninghame was more realistic. He wrote in the same month: 'I am fully persuaded that the new Austrian Army will in no sense be communistic.... The proposal of General Soos that the Entente should "hinder the formation

of an Army on the basis of the dictature [sic] of a single class"
amounts in fact to a proposal that the Entente should alter the
terms of the Peace Treaty' on the conditions of military service;
only 11,000 men of the old Volkswehr would join the new army,
and they would be 'the best element'. When rioting in Linz was
quelled in May by a battalion of the new army, Lindley found it
satisfying 'to have this practical proof that the New Army is, at
any rate in part, ready and able to intervene effectively in the
cause of law and order'. The Military Control Commission for
Austria even raised the question of the Soldiers' Councils with
the Interallied Military Committee at Versailles, arguing that
they were 'destructive of all discipline and . . . incompatible with
the organisation of an army . . . for the maintenance of order.'
The question was then referred to the Conference of
Ambassadors in Paris, where the British representative, Lord
Derby, expressed his doubts whether it came within the
competence of the Conference. It was decided to refer the issue
to the Allied governments, and the Foreign Office considered it
'inexpedient to interfere', at least for the moment; only
unofficially the President of the Conference of Ambassadors,
Jules Cambon, should speak to the Austrian Minister in Paris,
but there was no official intervention.

In Vienna, Schober suggested that the army should be made a
proper army of order by compelling the soldiers to live in
barracks and forbidding them to do any outside work; the army's
size should be reduced, and the gendarmerie be transferred to
the army (clearly as a more trustworthy element). Over dinner
Colonel Gosset discussed the reduction of the army with a
prominent Christian Social leader. When another guest
suggested that Deutsch was the only man to carry it out
gradually, Gosset and the Christian Social leader expressed their
doubts whether Deutsch 'would agree to kill his own child' and
rejected any cooperation with him.[97]

In October 1920 Gosset reported on the composition of the
new army in Styria. The establishment for the province was 4000
men, but only 1800 applied to join, of whom 1200 were accepted,
including 700 transfers from the Volkswehr. Only about ten
officers were Social Democrats, and the rest belonged to one of
the bourgeois parties. The political affiliation of the NCOs was
similar, but about 80 per cent of the men were Social Democrats;

the Soldiers' Council of Graz had even decided to bar communists from enlistment. In December, Cadogan minuted at the Foreign Office that all reports showed

> that the Wehrmacht is a tool of the Social Democrats, especially fashioned ... for political purposes. Whatever its immediate tendencies may be it is obviously wrong, and dangerous, that the only organized force should be loyal to a party rather than to the State. The first step to be taken by any strong Govt. in Austria must be to rid the army of this party spirit.

In February 1921, Lindley reported that thousands of soldiers had paraded in uniform to greet the International Socialist Conference held in Vienna; it was true that the present government was trying hard to reduce the army 'without attracting attention'. The gendarmerie and police, on the other hand, 'remain in a high state of efficiency to which is largely due the great security of life and property in this country.' Lindley hoped the Conference of Ambassadors for the time being would drop the question of a reduction of either force. When Colonel Cuninghame inspected the battalions guarding the eastern frontier against Hungarian incursions in the autumn of 1921, he found the units from Styria, Tyrol and Upper Austria 'reliable', but those from Vienna and Lower Austria 'poor', 'surly and discontented', and 'not in a martial frame of mind'. There was 'an intense feeling of animosity amongst the men against the Hungarians, due to the behaviour of the bands towards the Austrian population, and to the murder of prisoners captured in action.' While the Ministry of Defence considered 'the troops as a whole capable of the tasks asked of them', the opinion among the Allied observers was that they would not be able to stand up to the Hungarians if it came to a serious conflict.[98]

By March 1922 Colonel Cuninghame was convinced 'that progress has been made, and no doubt as the old tradition fades, the relations between Officers and men will improve'; but many of them 'are serving semi-reluctantly, being compelled to do so by stress of circumstances'. Officers and men did not share the same 'attitude of mind'; the Soldiers' Councils remained opposed to the 'old Imperialist mode of discipline', and the attempts to dispense with it were neither happy nor successful.

Cuninghame suggested a change in the structure of the army as it was 'not fit for its task': a change to a militia system 'might get rid of its undesirable partisan character'. This, as he pointed out in June, would reduce the cost of the army from 40 to 7 milliards of kronen.

The British Army Council, however, rejected the scheme of a militia proposed by the Austrian government, although it admitted that it 'would probably be superior to the existing Wehrmacht, in discipline, morale and efficiency'; the long service prescribed by the Treaty of St Germain had to remain in force, 'in view of the fact that any concessions to the Austrian Government would have an immediate repercussion in the other ex-enemy States'. As the French government was equally opposed to a militia, the Austrian request was rejected.[99] In other words, a very sensible request which would have saved the Austrian government a large sum of money (one of the Allied aims) was turned down not on its merits, but because Germany and Hungary might follow suit. Yet in the case of Germany such a change would have been equally desirable: it would have made the highly-trained, long-service Reichswehr far less dangerous from the Allied point of view, and it would have done away with the political threat it constituted as 'a state within the state' and hostile to the democratic Republic. Thus political as well as financial considerations spoke for granting the Austrian request, but unfortunately such rational counsels did not prevail.

Summing up the debate, Colonel Cuninghame still suspected that 'the Bourgeois Parties desire to alter the organisation of the Austrian Army in such a way that it can no longer be looked upon, as it is now, as an instrument to safeguard the Republican Constitution of the country'; they wanted to use the need for economies to get rid of the existing force; but the Social Democrats were 'bound to support the continuation of the Professional Army in its character as a Republican Force', and any suggestions to change its character were unacceptable to them, unless they were entirely free from any attempt to restore the old regime. He had watched the men 'at work and at play, in barracks and in the field': 'they are really much better than is generally supposed, and have to a very great extent freed themselves from the subversive elements which once justified the bad opinion formed of them.' He attributed 'the strong bias against the Federal Army' shown by the representatives of the League of Nations to the fact that their principal advisers were men of the old regime, such as Prince Liechtenstein and Count Mensdorf with their 'natural political bias'.[100] On the extreme right this bias took scurrilous forms. A journal published in Graz, the organ of the 'Anti-Semitic Proletarian Union', referred to the new army as the 'Jews' Defence Force', the 'Pillar of the Jews' Republic' and 'a choice collection of specimens from the criminal albums of Central Europe', and devoted an entire issue to the subject of 'Our Army' on these lines.[101] In any case, whatever socialist influence there was in the early 1920s was fairly rapidly eliminated by the new Minister of War, Carl Vaugoin, a Christian Social deputy: under him, the political leanings of the army were to change completely.

Another political issue which involved the army was that of 'Western Hungary', or, as the Austrians came to call it, the 'Burgenland', which historically belonged to Hungary but was inhabited by a German-speaking population as well as Hungarians and other national groups. By a decision of the Allied Powers, this territory was allocated to the Austrian Republic in September 1919, but the Hungarians disputed the decision and refused to evacuate the Burgenland, the fate of which could in their opinion only be decided by a peace treaty. The result was a severe conflict and fierce fighting between irregular forces, similar to that taking place in Carinthia at the same time. When Colonel Cuninghame visited the territory early in 1920 his impression from conversations with prominent citizens and personal observations was that the people 'desire attachment to Austria, but that the Officials, including particularly the priests, are vehemently opposed to it'. When the Bolshevists were in power in Budapest in 1919, the Hungarian officials were less averse to union with Austria, but things had changed with the advent of the Horthy regime in Hungary. In Austria, 'the reactionary element', including a large section of the Christian Social Party, were 'anxious to keep on good terms with the present regime in Hungary, and would sacrifice the chances of securing territorial extension'; but the Social Democrats were hostile to the Hungarian regime and did not share this view.

Another British officer sent to study the local situation reported that 'villages which during the Bolshevism were clamouring to become Austrian are now totally opposed to the annexation. ... Many villages have changed their views as they fear that the Austrians will immediately make a clean sweep of every available grain of food in order to meet the present need.' Or as Lindley put it: 'The majority of the inhabitants are now in favour of remaining Hungarian, since they have no wish to join a State which is starving and bankrupt.'

Another report also found that economic considerations strongly influenced national feelings: 'This is especially shown from the fact that there is far greater pro-Austrian feeling in the Comitat of Sopron than in either Moson or Vas, the first mentioned Comitat having traded a fair amount with Vienna'. In the villages and country districts feelings were more or less evenly divided for and against Austria, but in the bigger towns they were 'decidedly against' Austria and especially in Sopron and Wieselburg (Moson); even some German-speaking people who had no Hungarian opposed separation from Hungary.[102]

Early in 1920 Chancellor Renner informed Lindley that he 'had full confidence that Powers would see [to it] that Austria secured Western Hungary', but that he had no intention of using force; Austrian units should replace the Hungarians as soon as Hungary had signed the Peace Treaty. In May a mass meeting in the Vienna Town Hall called by the Social Democrats protested against the imprisonment of hundreds of people 'under appalling conditions' by the Hungarians and their 'unbearable vexations'. In the Foreign Office Cadogan minuted: 'We cannot intervene usefully in this discussion.'[103] As the Military Control Commission reported in 1921, Austrian opinion was 'unanimous that no Austrian lives should be sacrificed to gain possession of the territory'; the Allies alone were responsible for the execution of the Peace Treaty, and they were 'generally and rather bitterly reproached' for their failure to do so; the Austrian units deployed along the frontier 'are showing a patriotic and war-like spirit for which they were not given credit', and the relations between officers and men were 'excellent'. From Vienna a British diplomat wrote that the Social Democrats were violently opposed to the Horthy regime in Hungary, and those of Wiener Neustadt were spoiling for a fight; while the Christian Social Party 'would have preferred an accommodation' they had to 'proceed cautiously in order to avoid the charge of royalism or sympathy with the supposed White terror' (which in reality was quite formidable). In August 1921 the Allied officers in Sopron informed the Austrian Chancellor 'that as Hungary had failed to deliver the territory to them, they could not deliver it to Austria.'[104]

In the end the fate of the Burgenland was decided by a plebiscite, which was held under Allied auspices in December 1921 in the district of Sopron. The result was a substantial majority for Hungary – 15,334 votes against only 8227 for Austria. In Sopron itself the majority was even more decisive: 12,327 against 4620 votes, but in the surrounding villages there was a slight majority for Austria: 3607 compared to 3007 for Hungary. As the administration and police were left in Hungarian hands, it was hardly a free plebiscite; but in the Foreign Office Harold Nicolson minuted that he hoped 'that the overwhelming Hungarian majority will induce the Austrian Government to see reason.'[105] Thus Sopron remained Hungarian, but part of the surrounding district became Austrian, and the 'Burgenland' became a new Austrian province within the federal structure. It was a compromise, even if it resulted in a partition and did not fulfil Austrian aspirations.

Indeed, joining Austria, with its rampant inflation, chronic food shortages and bitter internal conflicts, could not have seemed a very attractive proposition to the inhabitants of the small towns and villages of the Burgenland. Whatever their national leanings the majority decided to play safe. In comparison the 'White' regime of Admiral Horthy in Hungary appeared stable and reassuring: had he not coped successfully with the 'Red' terror, while in Austria the 'Reds' were still powerful? Economic and political considerations, rather than national ones, won the day, with the result that Sopron was separated from its natural hinterland and the Burgenland had to find a new capital, Eisenstadt, which was hardly more than an overgrown village.

In Austria, as in the Germany of the Weimar Republic, the early 1920s were plagued by the constant fall in the value of the currency, ever-rising prices, and the terrible shortages of food, coal and all other basic commodities. If anything, political antagonisms between town and country, between 'red' Vienna and the Catholic and conservative countryside, were even sharper than they were in Germany. To be able to survive at all, Austria remained heavily dependent on foreign help and foreign credits. Economic weakness and the growth of large, hostile, para-military forces did not augur well for the future.

Notes

1. Cuninghame's fortnightly report, 21 January 1920: FO 371, file 3534.
2. E.E. Massey to S.P. Waterlow, London, 14 January 1920: FO 371, file 3550. Apparently, the British only received the standard rations.
3. Report by E. Bridgeman, 9 February, and letter by Dr E. Krautmann, 31 March 1920: FO 120, files 929 and 936.
4. Report by Fritz Kuh, 6 February 1920: Society of Friends' Library, Papers relating to Friends' Relief Mission in Austria, box 5, parcel 3, folder 1.
5. Lindley to Curzon, 15 March 1920: DBFP, 1st series, xii, no.125, p. 156 f.
6. J. Lockhart Dougan to Lindley, 17 May 1920: FO 120, file 957.
7. The same, 8 and 27 May 1920, ibid.
8. Report by Jenny Willison, 8 May 1920: Papers relating to Friends' Relief Mission in Austria, box 5, parcel 3, folder 1.
9. 'Austria. Annual Report, 1920', p. 65 f., and Lindley to Vienna Emergency Relief Fund, 2 August 1920: FO 371, file 5786, file 4651, fo. 73 f.
10. Report by Jenny Willison, 8 May 1920: Papers relating to Friends' Relief Mission in Austria, box 5, parcel 3, folder 1.
11. Report by Ruth Fry, *The Friend*, xx, 16 July 1920, p. 442; Minutes of the Austria & Hungary Sub-Committee of the Friends' Relief Council, 23 December 1920; report of the Friends' Relief Mission, 11 February 1920: FO 120, file 935.
12. Report of the Friends' Relief Mission, 1 December 1920: Papers relating to Friends' Relief Mission in Austria, box 4, parcel 3, folder 1.
13. Home Office to FO, 17 December 1920: FO 120, file 974.
14. Report by Olive Haseltine, January 1921: Papers relating to Friends' Relief Mission in Austria, box 5, parcel 3, folder 1.
15. G.E.R. Gedye, 'Is Austria Starving?', Imperial War Museum, GERG 10.
16. Curzon to Bridgeman, 7 and 15 October 1920, and to Clerk, 18 January 1921: DBFP, 1st series, xii, nos 241, 250, pp. 281 f., 296;

Harry Hanak, 'The Problem of the Nationalities in Czechoslovakia as seen from London, 1918-1926', Conference paper 1984, p. 12.

17. Speeches of Lords Parmoor and Curzon in House of Lords, 13 April 1921: FO 120, file 977; Lindley to Curzon, 14 July 1921: FO 371, file 5786, fo. 46.

18. 'Austria. Annual Report, 1921', p. 46 f.; H. B. Johnson to Curzon, 1 July 1921; and Hilda Clark's report: FO 371, file 7359, file 5742, fo. 68 ff.; *The Friend*, xxi, 8 April 1921, p. 212.

19. Kathleen D. Courtney to Alice Clark, 24 January 1922: Papers relating to Friends' Relief Mission in Austria, box 4, parcel 2, folder 2.

20. 'Austria. Annual Report, 1922', p. 41 f.: FO 371, file 8551; Minutes of the Austria & Hungary Sub-Committee of the Friends' Relief Council, meetings of 16 March 1922 and 4 October 1923.

21. Lindley to Curzon, 7 November 1919, 30 June 1920 and 3 May 1921: DBFP, 1st series, vi, no. 265, p. 353; FO 371, file 5783, fo. 152, file 4645, fo. 168.

22. Akers-Douglas to Crowe, 5 January 1923: FO 371, file 8548, fo. 120 ff.

23. Keeling to Curzon, 2 and 7 December 1921: FO 371, file 5788, fos. 114, 117-20.

24. E. E. Massey to S. P. Waterlow, 14 January, Lindley to Vienna Emergency Relief Fund, 2 August, and to Curzon, 14 November 1920: FO 371, file 3550, file 4651, fo. 74 f.; DBFP, 1st series, xii, no. 277, p. 333.

25. William Goode to Chancellor of the Exchequer, 22 November; Lindley to Curzon, 9 December 1920: FO 371, file 4647, fo. 262; DBFP, xii, no. 288, pp. 343 ff.

26. Lindley to FO, 7 January, 4 and 8 August 1921: FO 371, file 5738, fo. 20 ff., file 5743, fos. 221, 226.

27. Intelligence Report for period ending 29 September 1921, and Keeling to Curzon, 23 and 30 September 1921: FO 120, file 991, FO 371, file 5744, fos. 141, 150 f.

28. Price details from letter by Alice Clark: Minutes of the Austria & Hungary Sub-Committee of the Friends' Relief Council, 17 October 1921.

29. Memorandum by M. Aaenol and F. H. Nixon, 1 November, and report by O.S. Phillpotts, 6 December 1921: FO 371, file 5745, fos. 12-15, 103-6.

30. Franckenstein to Lloyd George and to Curzon, 24-25 January 1922, and Akers-Douglas to Curzon, 16 February 1922: FO 371, file 7335, fo. 262 f., file 7336, fo. 112.

31. Lindley to Curzon, 3 November 1920, minute by Cadogan, 7 October, and statement by the Earl of Crawford in House of Lords, 3 November 1921: FO 371, file 4646, fo. 202 ff., file 5744, fo. 163, file 5744, fo. 94.
32. Franckenstein to Waterlow, 5 October 1921, and FO memorandum, 9 August 1922: FO 371, file 5744, fo. 164, file 7339, fos. 103-6.
33. Akers-Douglas to Curzon, 4 August, and Legation Vienna to FO, 11 August 1922: FO 371, file 7338, fo. 20 f., FO 120, file 995.
34. Phillpotts to Akers-Douglas, Geneva, 7 September 1922: FO 120, file 998.
35. FO to Akers-Douglas, 18 August 1922: FO 371, file 7339, fo. 128; *The Times*, 5 October 1922: file 7342, fo. 14.
36. *The Times*, 5 October 1922; Akers-Douglas to Curzon, 6 and 20 October 1922: FO 371, file 7342, fos. 8 f., 197. The full text of the Geneva Agreement in file 7343, fos. 41-69.
37. Akers-Douglas to Curzon, 21 September and 20 October 1922: FO 371, file 7341, fo. 280 f., file 7342, fo. 196 ff. The French Socialist Bracke to Arthur Gillies, 27 November 1922: Labour Party archives, Labour Party International Advisory Committee, memo no. 263.
38. Akers-Douglas to Curzon, 3 and 24 November 1922 and 5 January 1923: FO 371, file 7343, fos. 73, 232, 234, file 8537, fo. 223.
39. Bracke to Gillies, 27 November 1922: Labour Party International Advisory Committee, memo no. 263.
40. Akers-Douglas to Curzon, 19 January and 22 February 1923: FO 371, file 8538, fo. 45, file 8539, fos. 187-91.
41. The same, 15 June and August 1923: FO 371, file 8542, fo 18 f., file 8545, fo. 137; Keeling to Curzon, 13 April 1923: file 8540, fo. 228.
42. Lindley to Curzon, 16 May 1921, and Chilston to Chamberlain, 3 November 1926: FO 371, file 5785, fo. 241, file 11211, fo. 45.
43. Report by Phillpotts, 30 November 1922, and memorandum by Dr Tugendhat, London correspondent of *Neue Freie Presse*, January 1925: FO 371, file 7344, fo. 153 ff., FO 120, file 1009.
44. Lindley to Curzon, 22 May, 11 and 14 June 1920: FO 371, file 3538.
45. The same, 1 December 1920, and unsigned memorandum of 1920: FO 371, file 4654, fo. 140 f., FO 120, file 954.
46. Lindley to Curzon, 1 July 1921: FO 371, file 5776, fo. 103.
47. Akers-Douglas to Curzon, 8 September 1922: FO 371, file 7360, fo. 126 f.
48. Lindley to Curzon, 16 May 1921: FO 371, file 5785, fo. 242 f.
49. Bridgeman to Curzon, 21 September, and Lindley to Curzon, 17

December 1920: DBFP, 1st series, xii, nos. 225, 296, pp. 270, 356.

50. Curzon to Lindley, 31 December 1920: ibid., no. 301, p. 361.
51. Report by Cuninghame, 17 February; Lindley to Curzon, 16 June 1921; Akers-Douglas to Curzon, 3 and 16 February 1922: FO 371, file 5747, fo. 117, file 5776, fo. 62 f., file 7335, fo. 297, file 7336, fo. 113.
52. Lindley to Curzon, 14 June and 6 November 1920, 6 June 1921: FO 371, file 3538, file 4644, fo. 223, file 5776, fo. 95 f. The party called itself 'Grossdeutsche Volkspartei', which is not quite the same as 'Pan-German'.
53. Dinghofer interviewed by H. A. White, 4 April 1922, and Akers-Douglas to Curzon, 1 June 1922: FO 120, file 994, FO 371, file 7349, fo. 110 f.
54. 'Austria. Annual Report, 1922': FO 371, file 8351, p. 3 f.
55. Akers-Douglas to Curzon, 19 January 1923: FO 371, file 8538, fo. 45 f.
56. C. A. Gulick, *Austria from Habsburg to Hitler* (Berkeley, 1948), i, p. 690.
57. Lindley to Curzon, 28 February, 21 March and 1 April 1920: FO 371, file 3535, file 3536.
58. Bridgeman to FO, 15 September; Cuninghame to Bridgeman, 20 October, and Goode to Chancellor of the Exchequer, 22 November 1920: FO 371, file 4643, fos. 138 and 209, file 4647, fo. 262.
59. Curzon to Lindley, 12 May 1921: FO 371, file 5775, fo. 150.
60. Franz Borkenau, *Austria and After* (London, 1938), p. 10.
61. FO minute signed A.W.G.R., 31 March 1919: FO 371, file 3541.
62. Lindley to Curzon, 5 January 1921, 17 and 22 December 1920: FO 371, file 5770, fo. 93 f., file 4642, fo. 375 f.; DBFP, 1st series, xii, no. 296, p. 355 f.
63. Intelligence report by Col. Wethered, 11 December, and Cuninghame's reply, 20 December 1920: FO 371, file 4642, fos. 386, 391 f.
64. Lindley to Curzon, 6 November 1920, quoting Bauer's speech: FO 371, file 4644, fo. 251.
65. The same, 4 February, 13 May, 3 June and 13 August 1920: FO 371, file 3534, file 3538, file 3546, file 4649, fo. 249.
66. The same, 10 October 1920 and 30 May 1921: FO 371, file 4644, fo. 256 f., file 5756, fo. 117.
67. The same, 22 February, and report by Phillpotts, 14 April 1921: FO 371, file 5756, fos. 71–4, file 5784, fo. 63 f. No other Austrian politician received so much attention in the British reports.
68. Report by Cuninghame, 17 February 1921, and 'Austria. Annual

Report, 1922', p. 4: FO 371, file 5747, fo. 117, file 8551, fo. 102.
69. Agent's report, 19 June 1922, and 'Austria. Annual Report, 1920', p. 11: FO 371, file 7350, fo. 136 f., file 5786, fo. 2.
70. Borkenau, *Austria and After*, pp. 216 ff.
71. Brig.-General R. I. G. Gorton to War Office, 8 January, with minute of 26 February 1920; Cuninghame to Lindley, 22 June, and Col. Gosset to same, 6 September 1920: FO 371, file 3553, file 4637, fos. 259 f., 421.
72. Bridgeman to Curzon, 20 October 1920: FO 371, file 4643, fo. 201.
73. Reports by Cuninghame, 26 May and 16 July, and by Lindley, 11 May 1921: FO 371, file 5747, fo. 168 f., file 5752, fo. 103 f., file 5777, fo. 74 f.
74. Intelligence reports for periods ending 5 May and 21 July 1921: FO 120, files 960 and 961.
75. Akers-Douglas to Curzon, 25 August, agent's report, 11 August, and monthly communist report, 28 September 1922: FO 371, file 7350, fos. 196, 209, FO 120, file 985.
76. 'Austria. Annual Report, 1922', p. 12 f.: FO 371, file 8551, fo. 102.
77. Keeling to Curzon, 26 October 1923: FO 371, file 8553, fo. 145 f.
78. Lindley to Curzon, 16-20 April and 5 January 1921; reports by Bridgeman, 6 and 10 March 1920: FO 371, file 3559, FO 120, files 964 and 951.
79. Lindley to FO, 7 December 1920 and 16 January 1921; Keeling to Curzon, 23 September 1921; and Akers-Douglas to Curzon, 8 September 1922: FO 371, file 4654, fo. 162, file 5770, fo. 115, file 5744, fo. 141, file 7360, fo. 127.
80. 'Austria. Annual Report, 1922', p. 11; Cuninghame to Keeling, 3 November 1922: FO 371, file 8551, fo. 102, file 7356, fo. 263.
81. Bridgeman to Curzon, 1 May 1920, and memorandum by Keeling, sent to London 10 April 1923: FO 371, file 3537, and file 8552, fo. 14 ff., with minute by Cadogan 'quite interesting': ibid., fo. 12. For the correct figures see: P. G. J. Pulzer, *The Rise of Political Anti-Semitism in Germany and Austria* (New York, 1964), pp. 10, 347.
82. Reports by Col. Gosset, 6 and 28 September and 23 October 1920 (enclosing a French memorandum of 22 October): FO 371, file 4637, fo. 421, file 4639, fo. 317, file 4625.
83. Lindley to Curzon, 3 and 17 November 1920: DBFP, 1st series, xii, no. 264, p. 317; FO 371, file 4644, fo. 282.
84. General Zuccari to Dr Mayr, 8 November, and report for period ending 4 December 1920 by Inter-Allied Military Control Commission for Austria: FO 120, file 978, FO 371, file 4642, fo.

292 f.; Cuninghame's report, 13 December 1920: FO 371, file 5747, fo. 58.

85. Intelligence reports for periods ending 9 and 16 January and 9 June 1921; Lindley to Curzon, 11 January 1921: FO 120, file 960, FO 371, file 5750, fo. 297 f., file 5750, fos. 69–75 (summarising a French military report).

86. Cuninghame's report, 3 February; Lindley to Curzon, 12 February and 11 June; Cuninghame to Lindley, 5 and 22 June 1920: FO 371, files 3534, 3546, 3538, file 4637, fo. 261 ff., file 3524, fo 535.

87. Government of Tyrol to Innsbruck Sub-Commission (Armaments), 2 December 1920; 'Austria. Annual Report, 1920', p. 27: FO 371, file 4654, fo. 31, file 5786, fo. 2 (more or less identical with Lindley to Curzon, 11 January 1921, FO 120, file 980, with a very detailed report by Col. de Ligny).

88. Cuninghame to Oliphant, 17 October 1919, and to Lindley, 1 April 1920; Col. F. W. Gosset to Director of Military Intelligence, 11 June 1920: FO 371, file 3530, no. 144566, file 3536, file 3538.

89. Lindley to Curzon, 11 and 14 June 1920: FO 371, file 3538.

90. Cuninghame to Director of Military Intelligence, 4 January; Bridgeman to Curzon, 30 April; Lindley to FO, 15 November 1920: FO 371, file 3546, file 3537, file 4640, fo. 242 f.

91. Col. Gosset to General Zuccari, 6 December, and War Office to FO, 11 December 1920: FO 371, file 4642, fos. 247, 257 f., marked 'secret'.

92. In July 1920 Consul Smallbones reported that 40 railway trucks with small arms had passed the frontier into Tyrol: F. L. Carsten, *Britain and the Weimar Republic* (London, 1984), p. 102.

93. Curzon to Young, 17 March 1921; War Office to FO, 28 January 1922: FO 371, file 5739, fo. 245 ff., file 7352, fo. 98. Art. 132 of the Treaty of St Germain stipulated: 'The manufacture of arms … shall only be carried on in one single factory, which shall be controlled by and belong to the State.'

94. War Office to FO, 10 April; Lt.-Col. E. T. Hynes to War Office, 30 March 1923 and 3 November 1922: FO 120, file 957, WO 155, file 21.

95. Cuninghame's reports, 3 February and 18 June 1920: FO 371, file 3534, file 4643, fo. 43 f.

96. Col. Gosset to General Zuccari, 7 September, and to War Office, 1 June 1920; Bridgeman to Curzon, 30 April 1920: FO 120, file 938, FO 371, file 3562, file 3537.

97. Cuninghame to Lindley, 5 June; Lindley to Curzon, 13 May; Lord Derby to FO, 20 October (with minute by Cadogan);

Gosset to Zuccari, 26 November, and to War Office, 21 October 1920: FO 371, file 3524, fo. 534 f., file 3546, file 4639, fo. 41, file 4642, fo. 171 f., FO 120, file 938.

98. Gosset to War Office, 3 November; minute by Cadogan, 30 December 1920; Lindley to Curzon, 28 February, and report by Cuninghame, 30 September 1921: FO 120, file 959, FO 371, file 4642, fo. 373, file 5753, fo. 220, file 5764, fos. 227, 232.

99. Cuninghame's memorandum, 10 March; Cuninghame to Akers-Douglas, 23 June; War Office to FO, 15 June, with minute by M. Lampson, 17 June; wire from Paris Embassy to FO, 30 June 1922: FO 371, file 7355, fos. 151–5, file 7356, fos. 227 f., 237, 240 f.

100. Cuninghame to Keeling, 3 November 1922: FO 371, file 7356, fo. 258 ff.

101. Intelligence report, Military Control Commission for Austria, for period ending 27 March 1921: FO 371, file 5750, fo. 20.

102. Reports by Lindley, 27 November 1919, Cuninghame, 9 February 1920, and Capt. D. B. Aitken, 1 March 1920: FO 371, file 3517, no. 157588, file 3519, no. 178589, file 3520, fo. 297 f.

103. Lindley to Curzon, 30 January and 15 May 1920, with minute of 26 May: FO 371, file 3518, fo. 461, file 3523, fo. 5 ff.

104. Intelligence report for period ending 29 September 1921; Keeling to Curzon, 2 September 1921: FO 120, file 991, FO 371, file 5759, fos. 26–31.

105. Hohler to Curzon, Budapest, 18 and 23 December 1921, with minute of 19 December: FO 371, file 5768, fo. 127 f., file 5769, fo. 93 ff. For the Burgenland issue in general, see Stadler, *The Birth of the Austrian Republic*, pp. 136–41.

3 Years of Progress, 1923–27

The mid-1920s for Austria were not only years of a new and stable currency, but also years of a partial and hesitant economic recovery and greater political stability. The Social Democrats remained in opposition, and the government was dominated by the Christian Social Party under the leadership of Dr Seipel who became the leading Austrian statesman. In the summer of 1925 a newly-arrived British journalist wrote: 'Though all the world has heard of the tragedy of Vienna, few have heard of her recovery. ... Vienna the metropolis ... presents a smiling, nonchalant face to the world again.... To those who saw her in the days of her worst trials, the change is striking.' But, he added, the future was still dark and beneath the surface all was not well. Another British visitor, after four years' absence, found an 'air of general prosperity': 'the buildings have been redecorated, railways electrified, there are more taxis about, and wonderful new houses and flats have been built with extremely low rents.' But he too uttered a warning; in the autumn of 1926, there were 200,000 unemployed in the country, and in Vienna alone 70,000, and wages were very low compared with the high cost of living. A member of the Society of Friends believed that, in view of the unemployment and the serious financial situation, the only solution for Austria was 'back to the land' and the promotion of land settlements.[1]

Severe unemployment, after the end of the export boom during the inflation period, was recorded by British diplomatic observers. In January 1925 Akers-Douglas reported that the unemployment figure had risen to 145,000, about half of whom were in Vienna. In May the figure was given as 170,000 and still rising, and the state of the industry as 'almost paralysed'. By the end of the year the British Legation considered the situation was getting worse; more than 200,000 people were receiving relief (more than 3 per cent of the total population) and the number was likely to grow.[2]

In 1924 the Dutch Commissioner General, Dr Zimmerman, installed by the League to supervise Austrian finances, was 'rather pessimistic as to the Government's ability to effect any real economies'; he complained about 'the lack of energy and courage of Austrian politicians, as well as the indifference and slackness of the Austrian people in general'. The government ought to show more courage and have less recourse to parliamentary compromises. Akers-Douglas agreed, and regretted that the constituencies did not demand greater economy, while 'in England there has often been a call by the people and by the Press for the use of the axe'; the Austrian Parliament and public opinion 'do little more than complain of the "sacrifices" imposed upon the country by the acceptance of the foreign control for its salvation!' Recently a political crisis had arisen over the salaries of civil servants who demanded higher pay and pensions. As no authority could be obtained from Geneva for such a large permanent charge on the budget, they even presented an 'ultimatum' to the government, and pressure in the same direction was exercised not only by the socialist opposition, but by many deputies of the government parties. Giving way would make it 'quite impossible to fulfil the obligations to the League of Nations' and would bring the budget far over the figure of 520 million gold kronen which had been submitted to the League. 'Fortunately' the government was standing firm, and leading Ministers declared that, while they recognised that the officials' claim was justified, 'they will not take the responsibility of thus wrecking the whole of the Reform Scheme'. On the other hand, the Minister thought 'neither Dr Seipel nor any of his Cabinet are fighting men', and political manoeuvring was 'so deeply ingrained in the life of this country' that 'more energy is devoted to the working of the Party machines than to collaboration for the real interests of the State.' As to the outlook, he believed that economic difficulties had 'slightly shaken Austria's credit and affected public confidence', but he saw no reason to despair: 'it must be admitted that much has been done in a short time, and Austria stands in a far better

position than would have been thought possible two years ago.'
At the end of 1924 the government applied to Dr Zimmerman for
another instalment of the balance of the international loan 'in
order to meet the State expenses and reduce the current deficit'.
Zimmerman agreed, on condition that further stringent
economies were made and the number of civil servants was
further reduced.[3]

Early in 1925 the new Chancellor, Dr Ramek, informed the
British Minister that the industrial situation was far from good;
industry badly needed new capital, and he feared that London
'had lost confidence in Austria's progress'; he was doing all he
could to combat 'one of the most serious features, which was the
growing cost of living'. A week later Akers-Douglas added:

> A foolish and harmful wave of pessimism is passing over this
> country. The irresponsible cries of despondency to which a part of
> the Austrian press is giving vent do not excuse the alarmist articles
> appearing in certain American and English journals, as, for example,
> in the 'New York Times', which is reported here as declaring Austria
> to be 'on the brink of the abyss', or the article in the 'Morning Post',
> entitled 'Austria *infelix*'.

Although trade and industry were languishing and
unemployment figures growing, 'some bright features' could
also be found: the stability of the currency, the return to the gold
standard, and the growth in state revenues, such as the tobacco
monopoly. Dr Zimmerman's report for January 1925 was more
favourable than the December one had been. Although the
budget deficit was still considerable, it was due partly to the
financing of public works, and partly to measures adopted in
1924 which had caused higher public expenditure. It was
encouraging that the public was attracted to investments at a
fixed rate of interest and showed a marked tendency towards
thrift. In April the Austrian government decided to ask the
League to institute an inquiry into the state of the economy in
Central Europe, 'the difficulties encountered by Austrian
industry, and the question of how existing restrictions on trade
and communications can best be removed'.[4] The barriers to
trade erected by the Succession States to the Habsburg
monarchy made economic progress impossible.

This was fully recognised in London. A Foreign Office official
stated in May 1925 that, thanks to the League, Austria 'has

passed the critical stage of her financial troubles', but 'she can find no outlet for her produce and she is surrounded by hostile countries who maintain against her high tariffs, import prohibitions and transit difficulties.' Three possible solutions existed. The first was the Anschluss. This was 'the rational, and, I believe, in the end the inevitable solution, both on ethical and economic grounds', but Czechoslovakia, Italy and France would fight to prevent it, and 'Germany would not at the moment adopt a ruined Austria'; nor would the democratic Austrians favour union with a Germany which 'they believe will be under Prussian reactionary domination' after the election of Hindenburg as President of the Weimar Republic: 'for the moment the idea of the Anschluss is not practical politics.' The second possibility was a Danube Federation, or 'the reconstruction under another name of the old Austro-Hungarian monarchy with Vienna as the centre', which neither Italy nor the Succession States would accept. The third possibility was a customs union among the latter, but 'each state is now busy endeavouring to promote and consolidate its own national industries. They would never consent to alter this policy', and within such a union 'Vienna would return to her own again', which would be opposed by the Succession States.

What was to be done? The only possible solution consisted in 'breaking down the tariff walls with which her neighbours have surrounded her' and in 'doing away with the vexatious import and transit prohibitions', not by one country alone, but by Czechoslovakia, Hungary, Yugoslavia as well as Italy. The Austrian request to the League aimed at inducing it 'to put pressure on the Succession States to modify their tariff policy'. Britain in her turn would never agree to any preferential arrangement between Austria and the Succession States from which she would be excluded: 'into any change of tariffs we must come on a most-favoured-nation basis.' In an interview the head of the Commercial Department in the Foreign Division of the Austrian Chancellery complained violently 'that the high protection madness in Central Europe was continually getting worse'; the Poles had greatly increased their tariffs, now Yugoslavia had done the same, perhaps tomorrow Germany would follow suit: 'all countries concerned were suffering severely, but some could stand it much longer than others. . . . If the present rate of unemployment here would continue until next winter', the results would be very grave.[5]

Meanwhile the clamour of the civil servants for salary increases continued, inspired by the higher rates paid to the municipal employees in Vienna. The government tried to allay the agitation by stressing 'the necessity of submitting a new and "normal budget" to the Commissioner General and the League'. The British Legation emphasised the great difficulty of being unable to add to the expenditure 'which is already too heavy', while the senior officials were 'ludicrously underpaid and can scarcely make both ends meet'. In November 1925 the government adopted the curious solution of granting the officials 28 per cent of a month's salary as an advance which had to be paid back by the end of the year, so as not to effect the 1925 budget, and which was then to be repaid on 2 January 1926. Further salary increases were to be met by 'economies' of an unspecified nature, 'and quite unlikely to be realised'. Indignantly Sir Otto Niemeyer, the Controller of Finance, wrote from the Treasury:

> It is thus pretty clear that, as soon as the League has declared Austria 'financially stable', the Austrians will proceed to demonstrate the opposite. ... If ever a weak government have done their level best to intensify financial distrust of Austria at the moment when the contrary was most important, it is the Austrian.

In his opinion, financial control should be continued, but this was 'probably impossible at this stage'.[6] This proved to be correct. The Council of the League declared the control terminated, as the budget was balanced and the currency was 'stable and well-assured'. On 30 June 1926 the activities of the Commissioner General were concluded, but with the proviso that they could be resumed if a new crisis occurred.[7]

At the beginning of 1925 a correspondent had written that those banks which had survived the years of crisis 'are safe', especially the five leading banks. But in the summer of 1926 the Centralbank Deutscher Sparkassen – 'a sort of clearing house of most of the small savings banks of Austria' – collapsed at the same time as one of the banks serving the Christian Social Party.[8] The collapse of the latter was due to the failure of several local banks which it had taken over at the request of the government. Prominent among these was the Steirer Bank, founded after the war at the initiative of Dr Rintelen, the Governor of Styria, with himself as the President for life. It was run for the benefit of the local officials of the Christian Social Party, with ample credits granted to them. When the inflation boom came to an end, they could not repay the advances, and some of them incurred heavy losses in gambling on the Stock Exchange. To prevent a scandal, the Centralbank Deutscher Sparkassen was persuaded to take over the Steirer Bank, which was 'the more easily arranged as the chief shareholder of the Centralbank was a certain Wutte, an enterprising Styrian financier ... who was a close ally of Rintelen.' Two other banks were added to the burden the Centralbank had to carry, 'and the dead weight of these, together with gross mismanagement and exploitation by Wutte, made a complete collapse inevitable.'

Wutte's questionable practices had been 'facilitated by special administrative favours given to him by his other ally, Dr Ahrer, the Minister of Finance, against the advice of the permanent officials.' These unsavoury details were listed in the Annual Report of the Legation for 1926. Ahrer was another protégé of Rintelen; he was forced to resign and to emigrate, but nothing happened to Rintelen. In Parliament, the Social Democrats sharply attacked members of the government and accused them of 'jobbery and fraud'. The government was forced to guarantee the security of savings deposits of the Centralbank – a heavy loss estimated at more than £2,000,000.[9] Soon, another savings bank, the Postsparkasse, became involved in the collapse. Its Governor and Vice-Governor had to resign, and the President of the Austrian National Bank had to take over the management. He found a deficit of about 110 million Schillings,* or more than £3,000,000; 'there has, however, been no panic as the deposits enjoy a State guarantee.'[10] It was a sorry story, indicating corruption in high places and involving some of the most popular and well established banks.

In spite of these events the state revenue continued 'to be surprisingly high'. The 1927 budget envisaged a higher return from the existing taxes although income tax was reduced. The British Minister commented: 'The elasticity of the revenue is

---

*The Schilling was the new Austrian currency, introduced at the rate of 1 Schilling = 10,000 paper kronen, in the context of the Geneva agreement and the international loan.

indeed one of the most remarkable phenomena in the financial history of Austria since the Geneva scheme came into force, as it has persisted despite the great financial crisis and slump which began in 1924, and the severe unemployment of the last two years.' In November 1926 the new British Minister, Lord Chilston, was informed by Dr Rost van Tonningen, the financial expert employed in Vienna by the League, 'that the revenue is coming in so well that the Treasury is again accumulating new reserves, in spite of the losses of the Centralbank failure'; but the whole affair was bound 'to affect the already damaged prestige of the present regime' and to have serious 'moral and political effects'.[11] According to a memorandum by the Legation's commercial counsellor, the revenue from taxation rose by 5 per cent in 1926; while the yield of income tax and of the excise on wine declined, that of the monopolies, chiefly the tobacco one, rose by nearly 15 per cent owing to increased consumption; the yield of corporation tax, customs and turnover tax also exceeded the estimates. In the first six months of 1927 the receipts from taxation and monopolies were again higher than the estimates, in spite of a further growth in unemployment and in insolvencies. In his opinion, this indicated 'that these troubles are due to special circumstances and cannot be taken as an index to the condition of the country.' The government would 'find it very hard to carry through a programme of retrenchment now that the Commissioner General is no longer here'; several departments were planning to employ more officials, but some newspapers criticised these plans and advocated a reduction of taxes to 'facilitate the competition of Austrian manufactures on foreign markets.'[12]

Summing up the work of reconstruction under the auspices of the League, Lord Chilston described it as 'a remarkable success, when one considers how inflation was stopped, credit restored, a stable currency ensured and maintained and the budget balanced'. Unsatisfactory features were the 'excessively high budget' and the bad industrial situation. Parliament had not accepted the scheme of reform *in toto*, and it was soon found that with regard to expenditure the provinces and the city of Vienna could not be brought to tow the line. In spite of this, the government had carried out the greater part of the League's demands, 'and the result may be considered as a great achievement'. In another report it was admitted that Vienna and many provinces 'are far more extravagant than the closely watched Federal Government'; provincial rights were embedded in the Constitution, and the interests of the provinces were 'far more firmly established than interest in the new Confederation'; Vienna was rightly proud of the success of its administration and the 'popularity of the Socialist Municipal Government seems to be firmly established in spite of the high taxation.'[13] Undoubtedly, there was success, especially in the financial field, but it had been achieved at great social cost; as an Austrian historian has said: 'Inflation was more feared than unemployment.'[14]

Another bad sign was the collapse of long-established banks which were entrusted with the saving of countless small people, and the taint of corruption and bad management which it left at the expense of the ruling Christian Social Party. When the opposition vigorously attacked the practices of the Postsparkasse and its huge losses in Stock Exchange speculation, the Ministers of Finance and Commerce 'disclaimed all personal responsibility on the ground that they had been quite ignorant of what had been going on', and that during the inflation 'it had been impossible for it [the bank] to earn its expenses out of its normal business.'[15] The demand of the opposition that the guilty should be prosecuted or a parliamentary inquiry held was not heeded and neither of the responsible ministers resigned.

During the great crisis of the early 1930s more banks were to collapse, with even more disastrous results. The same of course happened in other countries, but as far as Austria was concerned, it indicated a weakness in the financial foundations as a permanent feature. Although the federal budget as a whole was balanced, that of the railways was not, and they still carried a large deficit. As Akers-Douglas wrote in 1926, 'it is well known that there are still far too many men employed on the railways and the axe could be freely used'; but this would be highly unpopular and very difficult to carry out.[16]

In the general election of 1923 the Christian Social Party, with 82 seats out of a total of 165, remained considerably stronger than the Social Democrats who gained 68 seats, but it failed to win an absolute majority and had to form a coalition government with some smaller parties, the German Nationalists or the Agrarian

League, who between them won 15 seats. Seipel remained at the head of the government. Akers-Douglas described him as 'a man of culture, tact and considerable subtlety, a good speaker, he had also the advantage of knowing how to control parties. By character and training a Conservative, he is not a reactionary.' Above all, Seipel was strongly anti-socialist and, allegedly because he was a cleric, the Social Democrats 'have not ceased to oppose him at every step and to pour every kind of abuse upon him.' At the end of 1923 the Minister reported that 'the Social Democrats are determined to go on harassing the unfortunate Premier until his fall if they can compass this'; their tactics had prevented any intensive work in Parliament, but recent negotiations between them and Seipel on financial and other matters, such as civil service salaries, resulted in a truce; after a few weeks, further concessions would be necessary, for the truce would only last a short time. This system of legislation by arrangement between the parties had been a characteristic of the pre-war Parliaments and governments: 'it means that long periods are spent in heated debate and then by concessions here and there to the Opposition in various matters of interest to them not necessarily connected with the matter before the House, the Government is enabled to get its Bill adopted at once.' In the present instance, the Social Democrats had complained bitterly about the unfair treatment of their supporters by several government departments which gave preference to non-socialists in appointments; on this and other points Seipel 'had to give some satisfaction, in word, if not in deed' to the Social Democrats.[17] Arrangements of this kind, so characteristic of Austria, allowed the opposition to exercise some influence on the conduct of affairs.

When a socialist deputy in Parliament attacked the 'terrorism' of the Italian fascist regime, Seipel objected to this interference in the 'internal matters of a foreign State' with which Austria maintained good relations, and the Foreign Minister even remarked 'that great progress has been made in Italy'. A few months later, in June 1924, Seipel was seriously wounded by an assailant; a bullet penetrated his lungs, but his condition was pronounced 'quite satisfactory'. As he suffered from diabetes, the doctors did not dare to try to extract the bullet, as this might endanger his life. He recovered and remained

Chancellor for another few months, but resigned because the provincial governments refused 'to become more subordinate to the Central Government in the matter of Federal expenditure'. When the government wanted to reduce the provinces' share of receipts from taxes they demanded compensation; if central and provincial government offices did the same work and the number of officials had to be cut (as the League demanded), the central government should give way and the provincial officials be retained. Provincial autonomy triumphed, and Dr Rudolf Ramek, a Christian Social politician from Salzburg, with little government experience,[18] became Chancellor after a crisis lasting two weeks.

Ramek remained Chancellor for almost two years. He was rather weak and more conciliatory than Seipel, who remained the real 'power behind the throne'. As *The Times* correspondent wrote privately, the Social Democrats claimed 'that Ramek was put in by Seipel who hoped in his vanity that this little country clerical from Salzburg would come a cropper and that the all-powerful Seipel would have to be recalled'. But Ramek enjoyed the confidence of the western powers and the League and did not inspire the hatred of the Social Democrats as Seipel did. Soon Vienna was full of rumours of intrigues against Ramek, allegedly emanating from Seipel and the Christian Social paper, the *Reichspost*. *The Times* correspondent, however, thought that if Seipel wanted Ramek to go, 'an intrigue seems quite unnecessary. An Order should suffice.'[19] In 1926 Ramek was succeeded, as the rumours had predicted, by Seipel who remained in office until the spring of 1929, still the dominating figure in Austrian politics, or, as he was described in a despatch from Vienna, by Allen Leeper, 'the most skilful and responsible statesman'.[20]

Speculation was sometimes expressed in the reports about whether the Social Democrats would persist in opposition or would enter a coalition government. At the end of 1925 Akers-Douglas thought 'that as soon as control is terminated the Socialists would change their attitude and could cease to fear the responsibility of either forming a Government themselves or of entering a Coalition'. They had realised 'that as long as Austria was dependent on the approval of the League of Nations, the control of Dr Zimmerman, and the need of foreign credits, it was impossible for them to take the reins of power.' He admitted at the same time that they were 'in a better position in Opposition than they would have been in power' and had 'succeeded remarkably well in securing most of their demands'. What he did not say was that the party held only 68 of the 165 seats in Parliament and that the formation of a coalition required a good deal of compromise on both sides. As the Christian Social Party was only one seat short of an absolute majority, their position was considerably stronger. In October 1926 the Minister reported that the opposition were preparing for elections and therefore 'they continue to press for searching examination of the bank scandals'. In contrast with the scandals they stressed 'the triumphs of the Social Democrat administration of Vienna'.[21] In the elections of 1927 the Social Democrats only increased their seats to 71 – a gain which did not change the position fundamentally.

As early as 1923 the Legation had pointed to the success of Vienna's 'clever financial Secretary Dr Breitner, in swelling the revenue by the collection of various dues', such as a tax on all visitors and higher electricity and gas tariffs; 'its financial administration has been much better run than that of the State', and the Mayor, Dr Seitz, 'is a capable administrator and a violent Socialist'. By 1926 the city was able to boast that the promise to build 25,000 flats in five years had been fulfilled in three, in addition to the construction for the community of 'innumerable schools, clinics, crèches, gardens, swimming-baths, playing grounds, etc.'. In its 1926 budget Vienna had set aside £5,517,000 for investments: 'its pride in the energy and efficiency of the Social Democrat Administration seems to be justified: undeniably they have laboured with success,' the Minister wrote.[22] In local elections in 1923 the Social Democrats increased their vote by 44 per cent and gained 78 seats on the Vienna Municipal Council, while their Christian Social rivals were reduced to 41, with one seat going to a Jewish party.

In Parliament by contrast, the Social Democrats were reduced to oratory. In the debate on the fascist regime in Italy, Otto Bauer distinguished between terror in Russia and terror in Italy: in Russia the great powers had launched an armed intervention but 'the same powers were in the closest friendship with the terrorist regime in Italy', besides being allied with the terrorist regimes of Romania and Yugoslavia. It was the right of every Member of Parliament, he maintained, to discuss the internal conditions of foreign countries.[23] There is no documented comment on this by any British diplomat, but it is quite clear that their sympathies were with Seipel and the government rather than with the Social Democrats.

Little attention was paid to the German Nationalists and other right-wing groups. But, as previously, the spread of anti-Semitism and the activities of the extreme right were noted from time to time. In February 1923 General Ludendorff of World War fame visited Austria, allegedly at the invitation of a peasants' league. He spoke in Klagenfurt, pleading for 'national unity' after the French march into the Ruhr; socialists who tried to interfere were said to have been beaten up. His journey from Carinthia to Vienna was 'watched by the Socialists, and outside Vienna the police had to defend the railway station from a mob which wished to drag him from his train.' The authorities then asked him to leave 'as his presence was not desirable' and popular feeling was against him. It was even reported that the crowd shouted: 'Down with the murderer of millions of men!' and 'To the gallows with him!' The Hitler Putsch in Munich in November 'had no repercussions in Austria'. The Austrian National Socialists were reported to be 'numerically weak, but making rapid progress', with about 2000 members in Vienna alone, a large number of sympathisers, and 'well disciplined'. After the expulsion of the moderates under Dr Riehl, who advocated participation in elections, the party was said to be directed by a committee of five, closely supervised by the German National Socialists, 'who insist on increased activity, complete abstention from voting etc. and enrolment of all members in the fighting units'.[24] The party also planned a mass demonstration to protest against the Treaties of St Germain and Versailles and the French occupation of the Ruhr, for which it would be able to draw on the support of many other right-wing organisations. The occupation of the Ruhr clearly provided all German Nationalists with a good subject for propaganda.

Another such opportunity was offered by the holding of an international Zionist congress in Vienna in 1925. According to the Legation, the *Hakenkreuzler* (Adherents of the Swastika) put up posters protesting against the congress and petitioned the government to prohibit the meeting. The government refused to do so, and the police 'took very special measures of protection'. The various right-wing associations announced a monster demonstration on the day that the congress was to open. This was prohibited by the government, but even the Christian Social *Reichspost* encouraged the 'Christian' population to demonstrate and severe disorders were reported. *The Times* correspondent vividly described the riots in the centre of Vienna: 'the police are in the centre, holding the mob in various sections on the outskirts of the disputed territory'; from time to time the demonstrators were dispersed by charges of the mounted police, but they reassembled quickly in the side streets with shouts of 'Clear out the Jews'. 'By 10.30 attacks on motorcars had become a regular feature of the traffic in the disturbed district, and attempts were being made to hold up tramcars and search them for Jews. The "severity" promised by the Police President seems to be entirely lacking.' Many of the demonstrators were students, 'but a large section seems to consist of persons on the lookout for a chance to plunder.' The correspondent himself had to use force 'to avoid being dragged out of his taxi-cab by crazy youths who clambered over the back armed with walking-sticks', and anyone driving along the Ring 'was liable to be stopped, hauled out and roughly handled.' Well over 100 people were arrested and many injured, among them 21 policemen.

The Legation subsequently attributed blame for the riots to 'Monarchist and Pan-German circles' who it was claimed had incited the students and others against the Jews with the aim of weakening the government and preparing the way for the Anschluss.[25] This was a questionable interpretation, for it seems very unlikely that the monarchists were involved, nor would they have been in favour of the Anschluss. Collaboration between the National Socialists and German Nationalists with the followers of the *Reichspost* and of the governing party was rather strange, but anti-Semitism was their common bond. In Vienna, a crowd could always be mustered for a good anti-Semitic riot.[26]

In November 1924 the National Socialists were also instrumental in bringing about a strike of the railwaymen. The three railway trade unions – Free, Christian and Nationalist – demanded higher wages as well as an increased 'dearness bonus' (cost of living bonus). In the negotiations with the management, the Deutsche Verkehrsgewerkschaft, which was under National Socialist control, put forward the most far-reaching demands and proved 'most intransigent', while the stronger Free trade union was more moderate. The strike lasted nearly five days and passed without any serious consequences; the mail was taken to the frontiers by a postal car service, and the unions let food be sent by rail to prevent any shortage; coal stocks proved sufficient to run the factories. The strike was settled when a compromise was reached: wages were increased by 6 per cent, instead of a maximum of 9 per cent demanded by some strikers, and the demand for a large 'dearness bonus' was also reduced. The settlement cost the railway board about £390,000 a year, while the full demand would have cost £500,000–£600,000. A demand by management for the right to discharge redundant employees was dropped. In the opinion of the British Minister the outcome was 'not a very satisfactory one from the point of view of the State', but at least the management proved 'that they are not compelled by the threat of a strike to grant all the Unions ask for'. A strike of the postal and telephone workers in 1923 lasted only three days and was also settled peacefully.[27] The *völkisch* trade unions had some influence among the public employees and white-collar workers, but virtually none in industry; they were a special feature of the Austrian scene and did not exist in Germany.

The metalworkers' strike in 1924 lasted ten days and was attributed to the influence of 'radical elements' linked to the communists. It was called against the wishes of the union leaders, but was declared official by them 'when they saw that they could not stop the movement'. In the end the employers agreed to a general wage increase of 10 per cent, and of 20 per cent for the lowest paid workers but the settlement was not binding on all employers. The radicals wanted to prevent the acceptance of these terms, and clashes occurred between them and the moderates who supported the union leaders. The employers' case was weakened by demands for the modification of the eight-hour day and of certain other rights won by the workers in 1918, but the demands had to be dropped. 'The result was a considerable victory for the workers,' the Legation commented.[28]

Austrian disarmament and the activities of the para-military associations continued to occupy the Allies' attention, and in July 1926 an Allied demand was put forward that the associations must stop their military activities. Confronted with the demand the Austrian representatives in Paris claimed that it was only the Republican Defence League of the Social Democrats 'which would give trouble', but that the Heimwehren and the other 'bourgeois' associations, including the National Socialists, 'would not make difficulties'. The British Legation doubted whether the government was strong enough to control the para-military associations; other, important internal problems had to be settled first, and the government and the opposition 'were hardly on speaking terms'.

The Republican Defence League (*Republikanischer Schutz-bund*) was founded in 1923 from the older Arbeiterwehren and squads of party stewards to give greater unity and vigour to the party's para-military efforts and it soon became of formidable organisation, uniformed and partly armed. When the British Minister interviewed Chancellor Ramek on the subject of the para-military associations, he replied 'that he himself would be glad if they did not exist at all; but that he was at a loss to see how he could possibly legislate for either disbandment or restriction of organisations which were entirely legal according to the Constitution.' When these organisations were started, he said, their purpose was protection against Bolshevism or, in the socialist case, against a Habsburg restoration. Many members were ex-soldiers, and that, rather than any current military training, probably accounted 'for the excellent bearing and discipline' shown by the Republican League in their march through Vienna in July, 'which was doubtless intended to impress the Government and people with the strength and importance of the Social Democrat organisation.' As to the others, the Chancellor claimed that the Heimwehr 'was gradually dissolving of itself' and that the *Frontkämpferverband* (Ex-servicemen's League) and the *Hakenkreuzler* (National Socialists) were of minor importance; they had 'no connection with the Ministry of War and they did no military training'. The first of these claims was probably quite correct, but the second much less so, for all para-military associations engaged in some form of military training.

Lord Chilston reported in 1926 that any step taken against the associations would certainly be regarded by the Social Democrats not as obeying a demand of the Allies, 'but as an attempt of the Government party to weaken its opponents and as a political move merely directed against them'. It was difficult to see how the government could bring about the dissolution of the associations; the Chancellor would fear that such a move would strengthen the socialists' influence and it would be misunderstood by the public.[29]

Allied pressure on the Austrian government, however, was sufficient to obtain a promise that all illegal military training would be stopped by legislative and administrative measures and that the associations would cease all military activities. A law to that effect was promulgated in December 1926 and reinforced by a decree three months later. The 'Organ of Liquidation' was to supervise the suppression, not of the associations themselves, but of their 'militaristic side' (whatever that might mean).[30] For the Austrian government this provided a welcome opportunity to move against the illegal arms depots of the Republican Defence League, which in any case were within easier reach than those of the right-wing associations. In March 1927 it took 'unexpectedly prompt action' to seize stores of arms hidden in the Vienna State Arsenal and to notify the 'Organ of Liquidation' of the seizure. These stores were considered their own by the Republican Defence League (clearly dating from much earlier times), but the police decided to remove them, broke into the Arsenal at night, and appealed for the army's assistance when they found themselves menaced by left-wing workers. Lord Chilston thought that the action 'seems to have been prompted partly by the desire to deprive the Social Democrats of these arms, partly to rouse public opinion before the elections to the danger of the Social Democrat semi-military organisation'. Naturally the Social Democrats were furious and protested against the 'burglary' in Parliament.[31] No similar action was taken against the Heimwehren or any other right-wing organisation.

When the 'Organ of Liquidation' demanded steps to be taken against the Heimwehren the government carefully concealed this from the public, so that among the Social Democrats the impression prevailed 'that the Allied Powers are mainly actuated by hostility towards Socialism' and that the Republican Defence League 'is the particular object of their dislike'; yet, in the opinion of the British Minister, it was as natural for the socialists to look at these bands 'as a menace to Socialist Vienna, which would be at their mercy, as for anti-Socialists to complain of the Schutzbund.' He also believed it was 'a practical impossibility' to obtain the dissolution of all the associations, 'unless under threat of serious sanctions', and such a step 'could hardly be in the interests of His Majesty's Government'. What was really needed were 'more tolerable relations between the two great factions', for 'a policy of reconciliation must be for the advantage of an independent and prosperous Austria. Unless Socialist Vienna and the Catholic provinces can learn if not to respect, at least to tolerate, one another, there seems little hope for this country's progress.' He therefore advocated 'a minimum of interference in internal affairs'.[32] In retrospect it seems doubtful whether this was the right course. And why was Allied pressure for the disbandment of the para-military associations 'a practical impossibility'? 'Serious sanctions' could have been threatened under the provisions of the Peace Treaty which Austria had accepted. The same, of course, applied to Germany where the para-military organisations also flourished.

The Frontkämpferverband which was mentioned in the discussions was not an armed association according to the British Legation. It did not admit socialists, communists or Jews, and it had a secret programme apart from its open one. It aimed at the union of all bourgeois forces against 'the red Jewish International' and considered the Jews promoters of Bolshevism. It wanted to organise resistance to any attempt at the overthrow of the bourgeois government and to any attempt at a *coup d'état*, whether it came from the left or even from the right. Its programme was stated to be similar to that of the Heimwehr but more strongly anti-Semitic.[33] But there was also an anti-Semitic component to the Heimwehr pronouncements, and at least in Styria its members wore the swastika and considered themselves part of the German *völkisch* movement.

Meanwhile the 'Organ of Liquidation' attempted to trace the manufacture of and the traffic in war material, a task which had occupied it for some years without conspicuous success. Renewed attention was drawn to this topic by a serious incident at the Hirtenberg arms factory in July 1924. When Allied officers wanted to inspect the factory, as they were entitled to do, they were refused entry although they had given the required 24 hours' notice of their visit. The Austrian government did not provide the required force to obtain entry and gave as the excuse 'the excited state of the workers at the factory and the desire to avoid an incident'; but it was suspected that the real reason was the illicit production of arms. The British War Office discussed the incident at some length with the Foreign Office. Both were 'anxious to find some means of bringing pressure to bear on the Austrian Government in order to induce them to put down the illegal manufacture and traffic in arms', with the Hirtenberg case as evidence.

In fact, manufacture was not only carried out at Hirtenberg, but also at Enzesfeld and Steyr, and visits of inspection by Allied officers to two military depots had discovered 'large quantities of surplus war material'. The officers also found 'two secret depots at Johannisberg and Muraumberg, the existence of which had not been notified to the Organ of Liquidation by the Austrian authorities', again with large quantities of war material. When arms were seized after such visits, it was claimed, 'the numbers actually handed over to the Organ of Liquidation for destruction have been inferior to the numbers actually reported as seized.' A memorandum on the subject drawn up by the Allied Military Committee of Versailles contained 29 typewritten pages.[34]

In April 1924 the Army Council listed three matters still outstanding in Austria. The first concerned hidden arms caches, but the Council considered 'that the amount of such material at present concealed in Austria is comparatively insignificant' and probably so out-of-date as to be of little military value. The second was the manufacture and export of weaponry; but in the opinion of the Army Council it would 'be impossible for the Organ of Liquidation itself under present circumstances to stop this illegal trade'. The final point was the manufacture of arms 'in a single state factory' according to art. 132 of the Treaty of St Germain, with which the Austrian government had not complied. The Council therefore stated 'that the Organ of Liquidation should not be withdrawn until the single State Factory is definitely established and in working order', which could be done within six months. Two months later, however, Austria was permitted 'to establish the various branches of the single State Factory in different localities' in virtue of her financial situation 'and the good faith shown by her in carrying out the military clauses of the Treaty of St Germain'.[35] It clearly was a retreat. Coming from the War Office it was also high praise and very different from its attitude to Germany where the violations of the military clauses of the Treaty of Versailles were of a far more serious order.

In Austria, the most serious problem from the British point of view was the second one on the War Office list – the manufacture and export of war material – which affected the whole area. In the Foreign Office Miles Lampson, the head of the Central European Department, minuted in August 1924: 'The gist of it is that Austria is again becoming the centre of the arms traffic in Central Europe which is not only contrary to her treaty obligations but to the interests of humanity. We should try to do what we can to stop her', but France and Italy were 'not blameless in the matter'. The Allies even knew of a highly confidential letter, sent by the Austrian War Minister Vaugoin to the Ministers of Commerce and Transport, that export licences for such munitions were issued declaring them as steel fittings and machinery: this traffic might place the government at any moment 'in an extremely awkward position'. In future, before accepting any orders from abroad, the factories were to inform the War Ministry, which would decide whether the contract could be signed and an export licence be granted. Some 64,000 boxes of ammunition had been sent from Hirtenberg to Poland and Romania, and that was only a small fraction of what had been produced there.[36]

In view of the passive resistance of the Austrian authorities and the negative results of visits to Steyr and other factories, the British officer of the 'Organ of Liquidation' suggested making 'any further loans ... dependent on the attitude of the Federal Government with regard to control', as this was the only argument which would carry weight with the Austrians.[37] In the Foreign Office it was recognised that 'some measure of this nature is the only lever, beyond that of force, which the Allies hold over Austria.' But the Prime Minister, Ramsay MacDonald, objected on the ground 'that the financial stability of the Central European States is a perquisite of the development and consolidation of that part of Europe' and that the measure suggested 'might destroy the work that has already been accomplished', especially in Austria, whose financial rehabilitation was largely due to the efforts of the British government. The Allies therefore possessed 'no immediate means ... of applying any drastic pressure on the Austrian Government'. All that happened in the end was that MacDonald wrote to Chancellor Seipel drawing his attention to the contraventions of the Peace Treaty, which were 'tacitly acquiesced in or even countenanced by the Federal Government' and to the damaging effects of these practices.

The letter, as the Austrian Foreign Minister Dr Grünberger admitted, caused 'a great fright' in Vienna. He declared repeatedly 'that the only thing which mattered for Austria was the goodwill of His Majesty's Government', and that he was determined to suppress any illicit arms traffic 'if there had been any'! The rather lame explanation he offered was that arms and ammunition on their way from Italy to Russia and from Czechoslovakia to Yugoslavia often passed through Austria in sealed waggons with false documents – a traffic which the Austrians could not intercept, as any such action 'might annoy their powerful neighbours'.[38] But this hardly answered the charge of the production of war material in Austrian factories; and there the matter rested.

The Austrian army remained at first at a strength of 30,000, and the failure to reduce its size was often criticised, especially by the High Commissioner of the League. The government, it was said in 1923, would be willing to do so, but the Social Democrats were opposed, and Seipel wanted to avoid a trial of strength on this issue. Indeed, Dr Zimmerman said 'he had some difficulty in accustoming his mind to the mentality of the Socialists who in Austria are the champions of the State and the Army', and who objected to the combination of the War Ministry and that of the Interior. It was also recognised that the War Ministry 'is most anxious to make the Wehrmacht non-political, and is indeed rapidly eliminating the "red" influence'; but now the German Nationalists and the National Socialists were trying very hard to influence the army and were quite successful in doing so.[39]

Early in 1924 Akers-Douglas referred to 'a constant struggle between the opposing parties, Christian Socialist and Social Democrat, to gain control of the army'; what it was still lacking was 'patriotism and a sense of duty'. What improvement there was was largely due to General Körner; it was a pity that he had remarked on 'the reactionary tendencies of the officers' and on the perpetuation of the differences between officers and other ranks. At the end of the year Akers-Douglas wrote that the War Minister, Vaugoin, was successfully 'weeding out the "red" elements and securing new recruits of an anti-socialist colour'. He had done much to improve the discipline, efficiency and prestige of the army in the face of violent attacks. Although its size had been reduced to some 20,000 it was regarded by 'almost all classes as an expensive luxury', and the middle classes still had doubts as to its reliability. In fact, only the socialists defended the present force and regarded it as an important asset.[40]

The Legation's Annual Report for 1926 stated that there had been 'a great improvement in the discipline of the Federal army'; the men were keener, more efficient and more interested in their duties than at any time since its formation. The junior officers displayed excellent discipline and bearing, and were 'far superior to those of previous years'. An inspection of the military academy at Enns showed that the discipline among the cadets was 'of an exceptionally high standard'.[41] This was clearly written by the military attaché and showed his appreciation of the changes introduced. But it might be questioned to what extent this was due to the systematic purges of the army carried out by Vaugoin, which were mentioned in several reports. An entirely different comment was made by *The Times* correspondent, himself a former Intelligence Officer, in 1925:

> Even the most vigilant of Control Commissions could hardly detect a threat to the peace of Europe in an army so far democratic that, in the middle of the band, a diminutive pony draws a small cart on which, before the drummer, reposes in all *Gemütlichkeit*, – the big drum.

The highest form of this Vienna *Gemütlichkeit* was in his opinion shown by a military detachment marching along the streets.[42] But this, of course, did not mean that the same spirit animated all the units.

From 1923 to 1927 some political stability and prosperity returned to Austria, at least superficially. But whatever advance had been made from the disasters of the war and its aftermath was to receive a rude jolt by the catastrophic events of July 1927, which opened up all the old wounds and once more proved the extreme fragility of the Austrian body politic.

Notes

1. G. E. R. Gedye, *The Times*, 18 August 1925; meetings of 14 January 1925 and 28 September 1926: Friends' Council for International Service, minutes 1921–25, and Minutes of the Vienna Sub-Committee of the Friends' Relief Council for 1923–27, Society of Friends' Library.
2. Akers-Douglas to Chamberlain, 2 January and 30 December 1925; memorandum by C. Howard Smith, 7 May 1925: FO 371, file 10660, fo. 3, file 10661, fo. 5, file 11211, fo. 5.
3. Akers-Douglas to MacDonald, 28 June 1924, and to Chamberlain, 2 January 1925: FO 371, file 9652, fos. 79–82, file 10660, fo. 3.
4. The same to Chamberlain, 27 January, 5 February and 15 April 1925: FO 371, file 10660, fos. 125, 142, 216.
5. Memorandum by Howard Smith, 7 May, and Akers-Douglas to Chamberlain, 3 July 1925: FO 371, file 10661, fos. 5–7, 62–4.
6. Akers-Douglas to MacDonald, 25 April 1924, and Niemeyer to Lampson at the FO, 18 November 1925: FO 371, file 9651, fo. 137 f., file 10661, fo. 196 f.
7. Chilston to Chamberlain, 19 June 1926: FO 371, file 11211, fo. 11.
8. Memorandum by Dr Tugendhat, s.d., and A. W. A. Leeper to Chamberlain, 7 July 1926: FO 120, files 1009 and 1013.
9. 'Austria. Annual Report, 1926'; Leeper to Chamberlain, 2 August, and Chilston to Chamberlain, 11 November 1926: FO 371, file 12078, fo. 139, FO 120, file 1013; Erich Zöllner, *Geschichte Österreichs*, p. 505.
10. Chilston to Chamberlain, 11 November 1926: FO 120, file 1013.
11. The same, 3 and 18 November 1926: FO 371, file 11211, fo. 44 f., file 11213, fo. 173 f.
12. Memorandum by O. S. Phillpotts, 18 August 1927: FO 371, file 12077, fos. 28–33.
13. Chilston to Chamberlain, 9 June 1926, and 'Austria. Annual Report, 1926': FO 371, file 11213, fo. 56, file 12078, fo. 131.
14. Zöllner, *Geschichte Österreichs*, p. 556.
15. Chilston to Chamberlain, 17 November 1926: FO 120, file 1013.
16. Akers-Douglas to Chamberlain, 3 November 1926: FO 371, file 11211, fo. 45.
17. 'Austria. Annual Report, 1922', p. 5. and Akers-Douglas to Curzon, 6 and 22 December 1923: FO 371, file 5843, fo. 45, file 8551, fo. 102, file 9645, fo. 167 ff.
18. Akers-Douglas to Curzon, 14 February and 6 June 1924, and to Chamberlain, 19 March 1925; 'Austria. Annual Report, 1924', p.

9: FO 371, file 9645, fos. 195, 205, file 10662, fo. 152.

19. Gedye to Harold Williams at *The Times*; 19 August 1925: Imperial War Museum, GERG 15.

20. Leeper to Chamberlain, 9 August 1927: FO 371, file 12074, fo. 194.

21. Akers-Douglas to Chamberlain, 30 December 1925 and 25 October 1926: FO 371, file 11211, fos. 4, 42.

22. Akers-Douglas to Curzon, 6 December 1923, and to Chamberlain, 25 October 1926: FO 371, file 8543, fo. 47, file 11211, fo. 42.

23. Keeling to Curzon, 26 October 1923, and Akers-Douglas to Curzon, 14 February 1924: FO 371, file 8553, fo. 145, file 9645, fo. 196.

24. 'Austria. Annual Report, 1923', p. 15: FO 371, file 9653, fo. 355; Agents' reports, 26 April and 21 September 1923: FO 120, file 1000.

25. Akers-Douglas to Chamberlain, 28 August 1925, and 'Austria. Annual Report, 1925': FO 371, file 10660, fo. 72, file 11215, fo. 99; *The Times*, 18 and 19 August 1925; G. E. R. Gedye, *Fallen Bastions* (London, 1939), p. 17.

26. For details see F. L. Carsten, *Fascist Movements in Austria* (London and Beverly Hills, 1977), p. 96.

27. Akers-Douglas to Curzon, 14 December 1923, and to FO, 13 November 1924: FO 371, file 8553, fo. 164, file 9646, fo. 231 f.

28. E.O. Coote to MacDonald, 20 September 1924: FO 120, file 946.

29. Phillpotts to Chilston, Paris, 16 July, and Chilston to Chamberlain, 20 July 1926: FO 371, file 11212, fos. 23 ff., 19 ff.

30. Sargent to Leeper, 29 July, and FO minute, 4 August 1927: FO 371, file 12074, fos. 165 f., 174.

31. Chilston to Chamberlain, 8 March 1927: FO 371, file 12074, fo. 106 f.

32. Leeper to Chamberlain, 9 August 1927: FO 371, file 12074, fo. 192 ff. For the arms depots at the Arsenal, see the Memoirs of Frank Vanry, *Der Zaungast*, Materialien zur Arbeiterbewegung, no. 27 (Vienna, 1983), pp. 126 ff.

33. Lindley to Curzon, 11 January 1921 (summary of a very long French report): FO 371, file 5770, fo. 78 f.

34. FO Memorandum 'Breaches of the Military Clauses of the Treaty of St Germain', s.d. (August 1924); Col. R.G. Finlayson, War Office, to British Section of Allied Military Committee of Versailles, 1 August 1924: FO 120, file 1005; WO 155, file 22.

35. B. B. White, War Office, to FO, 24 April, and H. J. Creedy, War Office, to FO, 28 June 1924: FO 371, file 9648, fos. 16, 128.

36. Minute by M.W. Lampson, 29 August, and Memorandum by

the British Section of the Allied Military Committee of Versailles, 29 August 1924: FO 371, file 9649, fo. 137, WO 155, file 22.

37. Lt.-Col. R. L. Sherbrooke to Director of Military Intelligence, 30 May 1924: WO 155, file 22.

38. Lampson to War Office, 13 August, MacDonald to Seipel, 12 September, and Keeling to MacDonald, 26 September 1924: WO 155, file 22, FO 120, file 1005.

39. Akers-Douglas to Curzon, 22 February, Keeling to Curzon, 29 March, and Agent's report, 26 April 1923: FO 371, files 8539, 8540, FO 120, file 1000.

40. Akers-Douglas to MacDonald, 31 January, and to Chamberlain, 9 December 1924: FO 120, file 939, FO 371, file 9646, fo. 269 f.

41. 'Austria. Annual Report, 1926': FO 371, file 12078, fo. 142.

42. Gedye on 'The New Vienna', *The Times*, 18 August 1925. *Gemütlichkeit* is rather difficult to translate: something between coziness, friendliness and easy-going.

4 The Vienna Riots and their Aftermath, 1927-29

For some years it seemed as if the para-military associations were satisfied with their weekend parades and uniformed marches, which usually passed peacefully; but from 1926 onwards serious rivalry developed between the Republican Defence League and the *Frontkämpferverband* in the Burgenland, the new province gained from Hungary in 1921. Both organisations tried to expand there and to found new local groups. Rival demonstrations soon led to clashes. For 30 January 1927 both planned demonstrations in Schattendorf, which the authorities did not prohibit in spite of considerable local tension. Both sides received reinforcements from outside, and members of the Republican League blockaded the local station to prevent the arrival of more *Frontkämpfer* units. Eventually they agreed to march from the station to the village where a Social Democrat meeting was taking place. Suddenly shots were fired into their ranks from a village inn, killing one man and a child, and wounding several marchers at the end of the column; there was no retaliation. Three men who had fired the fatal shots were arrested and tried in Vienna in July, not for murder but for 'criminal violence and attempted injury to life'. All three, however, were acquitted by the jury 'to the astonishment of everyone and to the indignation particularly of Socialist sympathisers'. As the British Minister reported, 'even the bourgeois papers have pronounced their strong condemnation of the injustice of the verdict'; it was an 'appalling verdict'.[1] Possibly the acquittal was caused by political sympathies with the accused, for no doubt existed that they had fired on what was to all extents and purposes a peaceful and legal demonstration, and there was no question of self-defence.

When the news of the acquittal spread to the Vienna factories
on 15 July the workers downed tools and marched to the centre to
protest against the verdict in front of Parliament. The electricity
works stopped and so did the trams and local railways. With
masses of demonstrators pouring into the centre the police tried
to protect public buildings and to hold back the angry crowds.
Clashes quickly broke out, the police charged, people were
wounded by sabre cuts, and the crowd retaliated by throwing
paving stones and other missiles. 'By the admission of the
Socialists themselves there were considerable "undisciplined"
elements in the crowd, that is to say Communists and extreme
agitators who were probably only too glad to attack the police.'
About noon, according to the Legation's report, 'the mob
stormed a police station and set it on fire after a fight with the
occupants.... Attacks were then made upon the Central Office
of the Householders' Union of Vienna and on the offices of the
Wiener Neueste Nachrichten, an anti-Socialist paper.' More and
more people poured in from the suburbs, 'and as the police
successfully barred the way to Parliament House the crowd was
forced round to the Palace of Justice'. This was held by a strong
police detachment which allegedly fired on the crowd. The
building was stormed and set on fire, and the files and documents
thrown onto the street and burned. The fire engines were unable
to reach the burning Palace. Strong police and military
reinforcements armed with rifles and machine-guns repeatedly
opened fire. 'The attitude of the crowd was so menacing at
various points that they were probably justified in firing when
they did,' the Minister commented; 'whether they were equally
justified in continuing to sweep the streets with rifle fire as long
as they did is another matter, but their conduct ... undoubtedly
saved Vienna from the extension of a spontaneous riot into a
fearful orgy of bloodshed and looting.' On the other hand, 'many
impartial persons consider that the action of the police in
charging the crowd was premature and much to be criticised.' At
the end of the day more than 80 people had been killed and more
than 400 wounded or injured, including about 100 policemen.[2]
Even in retrospect it is difficult to apportion blame. The
Legation's report tried to divide responsibility equally between
'the appalling verdict of acquittal ... shocking the feelings of the
masses' and the 'inflammatory speeches' of the socialists. It is

also clear from eye-witness accounts that the police continued to fire on fleeing demonstrators, and that in general it acted with undue severity.³

An entirely spontaneous demonstration had quickly become a riot. *The Times* correspondent stated accurately that 'the Social-Democratic leaders have lost control over the masses. When some of them tried to calm them they were nearly mobbed.' Detachments of the Republican Defence League appeared on the scene too late and then 'occupied strategic points in the city'. On this occasion, in contrast to the past, they were not able 'to handle the masses and to keep irresponsible elements in check'. *The Times* attributed this to the undoubted fact 'that there was, in fact, a Communist plot and that the Soviet Legation was implicated'. A communist by the name of Fiala, 'who is alleged to have fired the first shots', had been arrested.⁴ No evidence was produced for such a plot either then or later. The Austrian Minister in London, Franckenstein, sensibly stated that the outbreak was due 'to the tension which has existed for a long time past between the Social Democratic Defence Guard and the opposing bourgeois organisation, the Nationalist Front fighters, and was not in any way the result of a Communist plot.'

No surprisingly the 'plot' version found credence in Budapest and the Hungarian Foreign Minister, Lajos Walkó, told the British Minister there 'that Communist agitators in the pay of Moscow were responsible for the acts of violence committed. . . . The fate of Vienna was passing into the hands of Dr Seitz [the Mayor] and the extremists.' The Social Democrats from the outset disclaimed responsibility for the outrages and ascribed them to the communists, 'but their inability to control these shewed their helplessness under pressure from their Left', and in any case, although the present crisis would be tided over, 'the root of the evil would persist'. The British Minister in Budapest added that Hungarian opinion in general was 'inclined to exaggerate the sinister nature of all disturbances in Vienna and . . . invariably to attribute their origin and inception to the deliberate machinations of a communist minority within the Social Democrat party'. Whatever sympathy for Vienna and the Viennese might have existed previously, had been destroyed by the fact that communist refugees from Hungary 'have been allowed to foregather with impunity at Vienna and to foment acts of hostility to the present regime in Hungary'; riots 'were bound to occur sooner or later in a country whose leaders have for so long made a practice of playing with fire.'[5]

In London, the reactions were somewhat cooler, but the sympathies of the Foreign Office were clearly with the Seipel government and its policy of no negotiation with the opposition. Orme Sargent expressed his 'disappointment' to the Austrian Minister that such negotiations were taking place: 'it seemed to suggest that the Government did not feel themselves sufficiently strong to restore order without outside assistance which would probably have to be paid for pretty dearly.' The growth of the Heimwehren in consequence of the riots was equally attributed 'to the weakness of the central Government in the face of Socialist and trade union sabotage [sic]': their growth showed 'a close resemblance to the rise of Fascist organisations in Italy', and both 'have the same cause'.[6] The comparison was valid, but the explanation was quite unjustified and typical of the Foreign Office attitude at that time.

Allen Leeper, the new British Minister, on the other hand, wrote:

> Due credit must be given to the Socialist leaders (Seitz, Deutsch, and others) for their attempts, at great personal risk, to restrain the mob when it had got quite out of hand and to the efforts of the Schutzbund to rescue the police (whose numbers at first were lamentably small) and to assist the Fire Brigade.... For the sake of Vienna it is to be hoped that it will not be distorted by the foreign Press into an organised revolutionary outbreak (which it certainly was not) and that its importance will not be so magnified as to frighten away foreign visitors from a city which both financially and morally needs them badly.

He added that the members of the Republican Defence League who were present 'seem to have behaved well and endeavoured both to protect the police and innocent persons', but that the burning of the offices of the hated *Reichspost* was due to some of its members.[7]

On 20 July Leeper tried to assess the political effects of the riots and their suppression: the government certainly had shown itself 'able to stand firm and to enforce their will with a strong hand. The Social Democrat leaders, on the other hand ... were caught by surprise and were unable to restrain the large crowds

most of whom they would have considered as their adherents.'
On the same day *The Times* stated that, from the moment the
masses retreated from the Ringstrasse, they parted company
with the communists and became once more 'the docile tool' of
the leaders: 'It was this that made Dr Seipel's victory sure',
because the socialist leaders did not want a prolongation of the
crisis: 'it is difficult to resist coming to the conclusion that the
motive which directed them was fear – fear for the advanced
Socialist institutions of Vienna, for the Socialist monopoly of
municipal posts, for their reputation in international Socialist
circles'; they climbed down 'sooner than many people expected'.
The victory of the government over its opponents was certainly
welcomed in London, and not only by *The Times*. A first leader
of the paper even claimed that the Bolshevists 'have worked hard
to spread their doctrine among the Viennese themselves.
Friday's events are evidence that they have not laboured in vain',
and that the socialists 'have more or less prepared the way for the
Communists'.[8] How and why they should have done so was not
explained, and the bias was obvious.

On the evening of 15 July the Free trade unions proclaimed a
general strike to protest at the verdict and the violent clashes, but
after three days the strike collapsed, partly because of the forcible
intervention of the Heimwehren who had waited for such an
opportunity to arise. The Social Democrats gave up their
demand that Parliament should assemble and appoint a
committee of investigation into the conduct of the police, the
Legation reported. 'On this point the Government have
therefore won a complete victory and the immediate crisis is
over.' Seipel simply refused to summon Parliament until there
was a complete return to work. On 17 July 'the trams and taxi-
cabs reappeared in the streets'; on Monday the shops reopened,
and the strike of the railwaymen and postal workers was
terminated at midnight on 18 July. The *Manchester Guardian*
noted, 'the strike was never complete; food, gas and water
supplies, as well as all supplies to hospitals being maintained.'
Outside Vienna, the strike was much less effective.

The burnt-out Palace of Justice quickly became a tourist
attraction, and

> was surrounded by huge crowds.... Little but the foundations
> remain. The window frames are all burned, and only the bare iron

work of the right cupola rears its head into the blue summer sky. The doors have been burned, and all the artistic iron work of Renaissance style is twisted and destroyed, while inside the building are nothing but blackened and broken walls and heaps of plaster and rubble.... Remnants of the valuable judicial records are strewn all over the place.

The Times considered calling a general strike 'inevitable': 'It has occurred in Austria before and there is almost a tradition that it should occur when a crisis arises in which the trade unions have need to show their power.' As the socialists' aim was 'to gain control over the State ... it was natural that they should seek by any means to retrieve the loss of prestige which the disgraceful scenes on the Ringstrasse must have cost them.'[9]

Outside Vienna, *The Times* correspondent found the country districts retaining 'their usual tranquillity' and no sign of any disturbance, apart from a minor one in Wiener Neustadt. But on the following day he reported that in the Tyrol as well as in Vorarlberg the Heimwehren 'have compelled the railway and postal staffs to work. The same process has begun in Styria. ... The Heimwehren in Tyrol and the Vorarlberg have mobilised under the command of former officers and are being sworn in as if they had joined the colours.' In Styria, during the strike, 'some towns were held by Nationalist, others by Socialist, armed bands, and each, when it gained the ascendancy, promptly placed the members of the other under arrest.' The quick collapse of the strike was due to the action of the Heimwehren 'which occupied railway stations in Carinthia, Tirol and the Vorarlberg and compelled the staff to run trains by Sunday night.... The counter-movement which spread to Styria and the southern part of the Burgenland was such that there was a risk that Vienna might be beleaguered as in a similar crisis soon after the war, when the peasants cut off the supply of foodstuffs.'[10]

The Times correspondent was well informed about the development in the agrarian provinces where the Social Democrats had little influence and where the response to the call for a general strike was very patchy. One important result of the riots was a great upsurge of the Heimwehr movement which for years had fulminated against 'Red' Vienna and now saw all its suspicions confirmed. In September Lord Chilston reported:

'The feeling in the provinces against the Social Democrats appears to be growing in intensity and increasingly taking the form of strengthening the local "Heimatwehren". Last Sunday demonstrations of these anti-Socialist formations were held in various places', in Lower Austria, Styria and the Tyrol.[11] Soon the demonstrations became a regular weekend feature, and they provoked rival demonstrations of the Social Democrats.

On 20 July the Socialists staged an elaborate funeral in honour of those who had lost their lives in the riots. 'The wooden coffins painted in silver and supplied by the Socialist Party, were arranged in a half-circle on a raised dais', draped in black and decorated with red flags. After speeches by the Mayor and party leaders 'extolling the bravery of the dead', the coffins were carried into the cemetery and buried side by side. When the Austrian Parliament finally debated the events, Otto Bauer began with three confessions on behalf of his party:

> Perhaps they were to blame for not having organised the demonstration, for then it would have passed off in perfect order.... He could only say that they had not desired a demonstration, for the Schattendorf verdict could not be brought against the Government and they had no wish to abolish the jury system.

They had also failed in not having enough members of their Defence League on the spot to maintain order and being unable to assemble them quickly. Thirdly, they had been too slow in organising a municipal protection force. The Social Democrats' motion of no confidence in the government was lost, as was that for appointing a parliamentary committee of inquiry. A few weeks later Bauer even spoke of the 'catastrophe' of 15 July which 'had changed at one blow the whole atmosphere of Social Democrat progress, had enormously strengthened the self-confidence of the bourgeoisie, and was "the first reverse" experienced in a long time'; a few thousand demonstrators had abandoned 'the proper democratic political weapons and ... had thrown back the cause of the Social Democrats.'[12]

The outcome of the riots, according to the British Minister, was 'that there is now less likelihood of a general strike being declared at a time of crisis'; in the suburbs as well as in the provinces, the first signs could be observed of the formation of emergency services, to be used in case of another strike. In fact, when the attempt was repeated in February 1934, it was a complete failure (see below, p. 189). At the end of July the Legation's Commercial Secretary assessed the economic effects: 'Fortunately it does not appear that this is of a very serious character though in a country so largely dependent on international trade and finance as Austria anything calculated to disturb foreign confidence is injurious'; the bank rate was raised by 1 per cent, and the most popular holiday resorts were so full, 'largely with Germans, that it is impossible to get rooms in many of them.'[13] In the political field, however, the effects lasted much longer and they were much more detrimental.

The impression gained by *The Times* correspondent in Vienna after the riots was 'less that of a mutilated nation wrestling with insuperable disadvantages than of a nation which ... was hopelessly divided against itself' and where class war predominated. The Austrian press indulged in 'indiscriminate and inflammatory abuse ... on a scale which beggars comparison in Central Europe', and the courts 'have been drawn into the fighting zone'. The *Manchester Guardian*, on the other hand, connected the events with the prohibition of the Anschluss and the frustrations caused among the Austrians by foreign intervention: 'There is no doubt whatever that the programme corresponds to a deeply felt demand of the German national conscience, and to stand in the way of its realisation is to take a backward-looking view of Europe'; but France blocked the Anschluss, the Succession States blocked the Danubian Federation, and Italy blocked both. 'Austria will feel herself deprived of the right to live according to the best of her possibilities, which are not great; and this will not be the last time that a deep discontent flames up in the form of bloody clashes between two classes of Austrian', each blaming the other for 'this situation of impotent submission to the will of the foreigner.'[14] Frustration must have existed among the Viennese workers, about the high cost of living, political impotence, bureaucratic government, the strength of political Catholicism. It seems rather unlikely, however, that it was caused by 'the will of the foreigner' or the failure of the Anschluss.

From 1927 onwards the reports from Vienna had much to say about the Heimwehren and their links with other right-wing organisations in Austria and Germany. In September Lord Chilston wrote of a march of 3000 men in military formation from different points of the Inn valley, together with detachments of the Frontkämpfer and from Bavaria and Württemberg. They were reviewed not only by the Heimwehr leader Dr Steidle, but also by the Governor of the Tyrol, Dr Stumpf, who addressed them. At a time when Austria needed peace and order these speeches 'must have an inflammatory effect on thousands of ill-balanced minds'. In November he reported that the provincial self-defence organisations were trying to unite and were talking about 'a march on Vienna', if any attempt should be made to set up a Workers' Council or a 'red Dictatorship': they would reply to 'the challenge with the most radical methods'.[15]

In April 1928 Military Intelligence compiled a secret paper on the Austrian para-military associations. The Heimwehren were estimated to be 107,000 strong, with 40,000 in the Tyrol and 15,000 in Vienna, and supported by the Austrian industrialists. Their members were better trained than those of the Republican Defence League which had about 100,000 members, one-third of them in Vienna. Both possessed large quantities of rifles as well as some machine-guns, but 'the workmen are militarily far less trained than the peasants'. Their arms were said to be in bad condition and lacking ammunition. A reliable report on the Salzburg Heimwehr showed it to be 'well organised on military lines' and in 'complete understanding with the Army and Gendarmerie', with mobile detachments to act in support of the regular forces and a Technical Emergency Service, which was to take over the railways and public utilities in case of need and to guard important places. A political distinction was made between the units which were 'prepared to support the present government' under certain conditions, and 'the extreme or Fascist elements', especially the Frontkämpfer units, which did not believe in the stability of the government and were said 'to be preparing to seize power should the defeat of the latter result in the accession of a coalition', in other words should the Social Democrats again become members of the government.[16]

It seems doubtful, however, whether the Frontkämpferverband had a stronger tendency towards Fascism than the Heimwehren, for in these years the latter came increasingly under Italian and Hungarian influence and began to prepare for a seizure of power. The way to it they sought by 'provoking' the socialists, preferably by holding their Sunday parades in 'red' strongholds and hoping for violent clashes with their enemies. In September 1928 Sir Eric Phipps reported from Vienna that permission had been granted to the Heimwehren to hold a great rally in Wiener Neustadt on 7 October. Their leader Dr Steidle had chosen this 'red' town because he 'is convinced that an unexpectedly large number of his supporters will emerge from this Socialist stronghold.... The selection of Wiener Neustadt for this purpose is regarded by the Socialists as a direct provocation.' The socialists reacted by organising a counter-demonstration there on the same day. Steidle, the Minister thought, 'does not desire bloodshed, but ... feels strongly that it is now necessary to show the Socialists in an unmistakable manner that the Government intend to govern with a firm hand in spite of the awkward situation of Parliament surrounded as it is by a red Vienna.' The Vienna police Director, Schober, tried to persuade the Heimwehr leaders to postpone their parade by one week, but this they refused; 'indeed, encouraged, it is said by Vienna high finance, they are adopting a more and more uncompromising tone, for they feel that the whole strength of the police and of the army will be with them.' Two days before the rival demonstrations the scene at Wiener Neustadt was described by *The Times* correspondent as having 'the appearance of a military camp'; troops from Carinthia and the Tyrol as well as almost all the units from Vienna and its neighbourhood, together with artillery and machine-gun companies, were concentrated there; their total strength would be about 6000, and that of the police forces from all parts of Austria about 3000; and the communists were encouraging the workers to bring their weapons along for the occasion.[17]

On Sunday, 7 October, Phipps wrote: 'the Heimwehr, protected by large forces of military (horse, foot and guns) and gendarmerie ... marched early in the morning through the silent streets of the Socialist stronghold somewhat like the Duke of Alva's troops marched through those of the United Provinces.' Their march-past lasted only about one hour and was over before 11 a.m. instead of midday as had been arranged. The *Manchester Guardian* reported that only 13,000 men took part, not 18,000 as had been announced. 'When the Heimwehr reached bourgeois quarters they were received with enthusiastic cheers and flowers were thrown down on them.' When they had departed, Phipps continued, 'the military forces were withdrawn, and the town was given over to the Socialist Schutzbund leaders. Onlookers flocked to the windows, red flags were waved and some 35,000 Socialist regular and irregular marchers-by were cheered to the echo.'

The next day Seipel informed the British Minister 'that he had taken advantage of the fact that yesterday's proceedings had passed off peaceably to summon for October 11th a meeting of heads of parties to discuss the question of disarming both Heimwehr and Socialist organisations.' Phipps replied that his government would hear of this 'with great satisfaction'; he was particularly pleased by the news because he feared that such alarms 'would cause a most unfavourable impression on British financial circles and that a repetition thereof might even make them shy of participating in loans to Austria'. To London, however, he wrote that 'to put official pressure on the Government now might only weaken it without serving any useful purpose'; he had learned on good authority that the Heimwehr leaders 'declare that nothing will induce them to disarm', while the socialist seemed ready to do so if the other side did the same. Phipps advocated putting the financial screw 'on those who require capital and who encourage the Heimwehr to march and counter-march' because it was undoubtedly supported by financiers and industrialists. A few weeks later he heard that a committee was being formed which included 'a large number of Austrian financiers and industrialists' to support the Heimwehr.[18]

In the opinion of *The Times* correspondent, the Heimwehren were better trained and more widely spread than their socialist rivals. As to their composition and ideology, their organisation

> is based on the hatred of a conservative and deeply religious countryside for the godless and predatory Reds, but the impulse which has converted it into a disciplined armed force comes from the dispossessed official class which was the mainstay of the old Empire, but has no place in the new Republic. The employment and savings of this class have been swept away, and its sons, finding no opening to make careers, put their faith in reactionary conspiracies.

Some weeks previously the Heimwehren had closed a mountain area on the borders of Salzburg and Tyrol and conducted military manoeuvres which included shells fired by their own artillery. The correspondent feared that such activities and the adventurous element among their leaders might inspire them, 'even without provocation, to break the Socialist rule in Vienna by force of arms'. Steidle had spoken of a march on Vienna if the socialists continued their obstruction tactics in Parliament.

In November Phipps reported on clashes between the Heimwehr and the Republican Defence League in Innsbruck on the occasion of the tenth anniversary of the foundation of the Republic: 'order was finally established by the picketing of the town by a couple of armed Heimwehr battalions', which caused considerable friction between them and the local police chief.[19] In the Tyrol where the local government supported the Heimwehren, they more and more assumed the character of an auxiliary police force.

British interest focused, as it had done before, on the disarmament of the para-military associations and on the attitude of the government towards them. Indeed, it was absolutely clear that only very strong government pressure would be able to achieve anything, and by October 1928 Phipps was becoming doubtful of Seipel's policy and found it ambiguous: 'Till some months ago I have reason to believe that he viewed the Heimwehr movement without much enthusiasm, for it presented a potential threat to the Government'; its leaders spoke of the Chancellor as 'far too weak' and toyed with the plan 'of supplanting him by some more thorough-going reactionary'; possibly Seipel 'has been driven against his will by the strength of the Heimwehr movement . . . to take their part in the controversy over disarmament'. But there was reason to believe that he 'has become a wholehearted convert to the value of the Heimwehr as a political weapon.' In Phipps' opinion, the Heimwehr was now much stronger than the Republican Defence League, for the peasants made better soldiers than the urban workers; therefore, the socialists had 'become most genuinely converted to disarmament, simply from their fear of the Heimwehr.'

In the spring of 1929 Phipps pointed to a principal weakness of the movement – the personnel rivalries between its leaders which 'were as acute as ever'. There was growing opposition to the leadership of Steidle and his Chief of Staff, the German Major Waldemar Pabst. This was partly due to the 'irrepressible Dr Pfrimer', the leader in Styria, and partly to Prince Starhemberg,

the Upper Austrian leader, who was 'denouncing the irrespons-
ibility and the excesses of the cabal which at present aspires to
control the movement.'[20] The Heimwehr movement was never
able to overcome this weakness and it became the principal cause
of its later downfall. The members owed loyalty to a provincial
chieftain, but there was no efficient leadership, and wide ideological differences existed between the different local
organisations.

In August 1929 the British Minister reported that the
Heimwehren were making 'remarkable progress', not only in
Styria, the Tyrol and Upper Austria, but even in Vienna. He had
been told 'on good authority' that recently no fewer than 2500
Vienna tramway and electricity workers and 1500 engine drivers
and firemen of the railways had joined the movement, and that
public meetings in Vienna attracted 20,000 people. Significantly,
these gains were made in 'trades of vital national importance
which have hitherto been Socialist to a man'. It was by no means
impossible that 'by the autumn the Heimwehr may have secured
an overwhelming following in the country which might make its
voice heard in a general election or referendum'. Seipel (now no
longer Chancellor) was continuing to direct the destinies of the
movement, and it thus seemed unlikely that 'the military
adventurers, monarchists, anti-Semites, and Pan-Germans with
which the Heimwehr teems' would be able to undertake anything
'fanatical' or 'rash'. Another indication of Seipel's influence was
the anti-party slogan used by the movement. This had altered the
main issue and the effect was 'to rally the country as a whole against
parliament and the parliamentary system, rather than against
Socialism and the Social Democrat party'. But only four weeks
later the Minister recorded a change in Seipel's attitude: in an
interview given by him to a German newspaper 'he expressed a
sudden devotion to the cause of law and order . . . and ridiculed the
suggestion that the proposed constitutional reforms had a Fascist
flavour.' He also expressed himself in favour of an early general
election: 'it would seem that the ex-Chancellor is anxious now to
scramble back on to the fence from which he descended with such
an éclat a few months ago'; but such a feat 'would hardly be
calculated to enhance his reputation as a statesman of weight and
discernment.' The Heimwehr movement was 'losing
momentum'; Steidle 'is voluble, restless and suspicious, but

ineffectual as ever'; any delay was dangerous, and 'compromise would be a disaster'.

The Legation also reported a serious incident at St Lorenzen in Styria, where Heimwehr men occupied an inn which was the usual meeting-place of the socialists. When the socialists arrived, they decided to hold their meeting in the village square but were soon surrounded by their adversaries, and the police tried to break up the meeting as unauthorised. When the socialists delayed their departure the Heimwehr men threw missiles, and a member of the Republican Defence League then fired a shot. In the ensuing fight two people were killed and more than 30 seriously wounded.[21]

By the autumn of 1929 the Social Democrats were clearly worried by the rise of the Heimwehren and the threat to Vienna. When Herbert Morrison, Minister of Transport in the Labour government, visited Vienna in September, Bauer used the opportunity to give him a memorandum on 'The Aims of the Austrian Fascists' for the personal information of Arthur Henderson, the Foreign Secretary. This Morrison sent to London from Prague, not trusting the Austrian post office or the diplomatic bag, and mentioning the 'anxiety' among the Austrian comrades caused by the situation. 'It would be a great tragedy for Socialism if things went wrong, for fine work is being done in Vienna.' The comrades would consider it very useful if Henderson 'could drop a word to the Austrian Chancellor in Geneva & also if you could confer informally with Ministers from France (Briand) & Czecho-Slovakia.' Bauer was writing to Léon Blum, the French socialist leader, and others to enlist their help. For Henderson's benefit Morrison added: 'You may be sure that I have been non-committal, impressing Bauer with the fact that my department is Transport!'

Henderson was sufficiently moved by the memorandum to write to the new Austrian Chancellor, Ernst von Streeruwitz, about the rumours 'that there is going to be a coup d'état in Austria and that the Heimwehr formations are considering a march on socialist Vienna sometime between the end of the next month and December'. The leaders of the Labour Party 'are much interested in the fate of their friends in Vienna, and I have little doubt that if certain of the rumours to which I have alluded proved to be correct, a very embarrassing situation might arise', which would adversely affect the good relations between Britain and Austria.[22] Couched in polite diplomatic language, this was nevertheless a clear warning, addressed to a Chancellor who had himself close connections to the Heimwehr.

Bauer's memorandum distinguished between two groups controlling the Heimwehren: Austrian aristocrats and ex-officers of the Imperial army who aimed at the restoration of the monarchy; and German Nationalists, who hoped that a successful coup in Austria would be the signal for a nationalist and monarchist Putsch in Germany. The two Heimwehr leaders, Dr Steidle and Dr Pfrimer, belonged to the second group, and especially the German Major Pabst, the Chief of Staff of the movement. For the time being the two groups cooperated to achieve 'the suppression of the Austrian workers by force, the overthrow of the democratic constitution and the establishment of a fascist dictatorship'. A very important group of the Christian Social Party, headed by Seipel, tried to use the Heimwehren to force Parliament 'to agree to a reactionary revision of the Constitution'. The large sums put at the disposal of the Heimwehren were used to buy arms, and especially in Styria and the Tyrol they had depots of weapons in all villages. However, when they adopted a definitely fascist and putschist policy, the Austrian banks and industrialists stopped their subsidies, and only the Styrian steel and iron industry, which was controlled by the German Steel Trust, continued to subsidise them on a large scale, as did German Nationalist circles, and probably also Hungarian ones. The bulk of the trained members were the sons of peasants and petit bourgeois, under the command of former officers; workers only joined in considerable numbers in the Styrian industrial district, 'where they have been forced by the most rigid pressure and intimidation' on the part of the employers to join.

The memorandum warned that the workers who were in an excited mood would stand up to any Heimwehr armed pressure; 'once the fight breaks loose in any place it might spread over the whole country and become open civil war.' If pressed by the Allied powers, the Austrian government would move against the Republican Defence League and would take no efficient measures against the Heimwehren: 'A genuine disarmament of both sides would be possible only under a coalition government based on all the democratic forces of the country.' But Britain, France and Czechoslovakia should issue a confidential warning that they were going to demand the dissolution of all para-military associations, 'under proper guarantees for the impartiality and equality of the measure for both sides'. It would also be helpful if the powers intimated 'that Austria will hardly be able to get the foreign loan which she asks for so long as the peaceful democratic development of the country is not assured.'[23]

The memorandum showed how worried the socialist leaders were and how much they hoped for support from abroad. The German and Hungarian connections of the Heimwehr were mentioned, but strangely enough nothing was said about Italian influence and help which by this time was more important. In October 1929 the German Finance Minister, Dr Rudolf Hilfer-ding (an Austrian by birth) visited Vienna and suggested that something might be said to the Austrian Chancellor 'with a view to damping down the exaggerated attitude of the Heimwehr leaders'; a kind of *démarche* might be undertaken by the British and German diplomatic representatives. But the German Minister in Vienna objected that any such step 'would not only be useless but positively harmful ... and would defeat its own object' because it would be an interference in internal Austrian affairs. Phipps, when informed by his German colleague, thought it would be superfluous to preach moderation either to the Chancellor or to the socialist leaders who all 'desire a peaceful issue of the present "impasse" and who are well aware of the danger of incendiary speeches on both sides', but might find it difficult to control the rank and file. When Phipps saw Breitner, the City Treasurer of Vienna, Breitner told him the great danger was 'that the Heimwehr did not want an agreement'; it was financed and directed by right-wing German industrialists, such as Alfred Hugenberg, who did not care about Austria's condition; they wanted to crush the Austrian trade unions so as to gain experience of what they planned to do in Germany. For the officers of the old army who otherwise would be destitute and for the unemployed among the rank and file, the movement had created a vested interest; they were determined to lay their hands on government posts as the Italian Fascists had done.

Breitner's opinion was confirmed early in November when the

Heimwehr leaders issued a communiqué on the subject of disarmament:

> Every attempt to disarm our organisation either as a whole or in part must be met with our determined armed resistance, for the future interests of the nation and the State preclude us in any circumstances from tolerating such interference with our organisation, irrespective of the quarter in which it is initiated.

The communiqué concluded with a warning against misunderstanding the true aims of the Social Democrats so as to imagine that they sincerely desired internal peace. In the Foreign Office Hugh Dalton, the Under-Secretary for Foreign Affairs, minuted: 'The turbulence of the Heimwehr may only be a cloak for nervousness'[24] – hardly an intelligent remark in view of the seriousness of the situation and the strength of the Heimwehr.

The Legation's Annual Report for 1929 estimated the membership of the Heimwehren as 350,000 (of whom 120,000 were armed) and that of the Republican Defence League as 300,000 (90,000 armed). The former were now equipped 'not only with rifles and machine-guns, but with properly appointed transport, a few field guns, auxiliary services, and all the paraphernalia necessary for the prosecution of a full-dress campaign'. The men were organised in three categories: fully armed, armed only with sporting rifles, transport and auxiliaries. For a movement of such a size and pretensions, it was 'strikingly poor in leadership'; Steidle and Pabst were 'the centre of a small clique which has constituted itself the headquarters of the movement, but they are both men of dissipated habits, and do not command the personal respect compatible with such a function'. The Styrian leader, Pfrimer, was 'of sterner stuff', a fanatic whose fervent anti-Semitism was 'a source of embarrassment to the Federal leaders in their relations with the financial world, upon whose subsidies they depend'; but all of them 'are as wax in the hands of Mgr. Seipel, who ... is the only person who has so far contributed a first-class brain or ripe political experience to their councils.' It was understood that the Rothschilds and other financiers had made their support of the Heimwehr dependent on Seipel's endorsement of its programme; 'there can be little doubt that he is aiming at the creation of an Austrian Fascist State, and perhaps, ultimately, at a Monarchist restoration which would reinforce the waning influence of the Roman Catholic

Church in this country.' In general, finance and industry 'rallied
behind the movement', its numbers went up 'by leaps and
bounds', and an effective central organisation had been built up,
thanks largely to the efforts of Major Pabst: the Heimwehr had
become 'a political force'.[25]

An assessment by Military Intelligence of the same period
stated that the Heimwehr was supported by 'the great
industrialists and banks' as well as the German *Stahlhelm* (a large
right-wing veterans' association); the prospects of an upheaval
in Austria were 'seriously exercising the British Cabinet', but the
talk of such an upheaval had 'gone on for many months', and the
new Schober government 'is far stronger and more generally
respected than its predecessors'.[26] Some scepticism was clearly
justified, for the Heimwehr leaders always talked loudly but, in
spite of all Italian and Hungarian pressure to inspire them to take
more forceful action, seemed extremely reluctant to do so.

The British government meanwhile tried to promote
disarmament, in the hope that the new Chancellor, Johannes
Schober, would be able to square the circle. In October 1929 he
assured Phipps that in Vienna, Lower and Upper Austria the
paramilitary associations were not armed, as they were in
Carinthia, Styria, Tyrol and Vorarlberg, and in the Tyrol the
people had carried arms from time immemorial. He hoped to
bring about the disarmament of both sides 'in a not too distant
future'; the socialist leaders were showing every sign of 'being
reasonable and willing to compromise'. Schober had said
verbally: 'I want both parties to march up armed on to a bridge
and to lay down their arms in the middle of it, and, after saluting
each other, to retire.' Otto Bauer, on the other hand, told the
Minister that he 'would welcome immediate intervention by say
Great Britain, France and Germany with a view to ensuring
dissolution of illicit organisations. Disarmament could follow
later once their meetings and marchings were forbidden.'

In November Phipps wired to London that 'a wonderful
opportunity for obtaining disarmament of Austrian illegal
associations' had arisen: the head of J. P. Morgan & Co. in New
York had informed the Austrian Minister in Washington that an
Austrian loan could be floated 'if and when political situation in
Austria becomes stabilized'. Wall Street and the City should
make it clear 'that no loan will be forthcoming until associations

are dissolved and disarmed.' Yet only three days later another telegram was sent to London. It seemed that Schober 'has succumbed to the blandishments of Mussolini and has accepted an invitation to go to Rome' in December. He informed a friend of Phipps that the visit was necessary to obtain Italian consent to the loan, but the French Minister heard from the Austrian Foreign Ministry 'that Italian consent would probably be withheld unless [the] Chancellor undertook *not* to disarm Heimwehr.'[27]

In London, Arthur Henderson considered this a 'disastrous advice' and wanted to supply Schober with an argument to resist it. He therefore authorised Phipps 'to make immediate representations to Herr Schober' if he thought that some useful purpose would be served by it. Schober intended to transfer considerable numbers of Heimwehr men to the army: would he not 'lay himself open to the charge of making the latter a partisan body?', and could not members of the Republican Defence League be included at the same time? All that Phipps could reply was that he and the French Minister would make the desired representations to Schober when he next received the diplomatic corps; it was quite possible 'that Mussolini may support the Heimwehr openly as well as secretly'.

Some days later it was minuted in the Foreign Office that the representations had been 'well received' by Schober, and that there was 'no danger at the moment of Mussolini's openly championing the Heimwehr'.[28] Apparently it was no longer doubted that he was doing so secretly. A few weeks earlier Phipps had reported that machine-guns were sent into Austria from Italy via Switzerland, as he heard 'from a reliable source'.[29] Against the firm opposition of the Heimwehr leaders, backed by Mussolini and strengthened by Italian arms and funds, the whole policy of general disarmament stood hardly a chance, but no alternative policy seemed to exist.

Internal politics continued to be dominated by bitter conflicts between the Social Democrats and their Christian Social opponents, whose leader and guiding spirit was Seipel. In 1929 Breitner, at lunch with Phipps, declared him 'to be too big for this small country'; in Germany, he would make 'an admirable leader of the Centre Party', but in Austria, 'where a spirit of compromise is now so essential, ... he could only do harm', for compromise 'was not in him' and he was a man of vast ambition. In 1928 Phipps reported a speech made by Seipel at Graz, in which he paid tribute to the Heimwehren and surprisingly claimed that the movement 'was chiefly actuated by a yearning for true democracy' – that was why he trusted it. Its aims, he declared, were to prevent 'the Social Democrats from having the sole privilege of organising processions and demonstrations in the streets, for such a privilege would in the end be misused as a kind of weapon for a terrorist organisation.' Phipps thought that the speech indicated 'that he is so sure of his own strength that he intends to beat his Socialist adversaries to their knees.'[30] The spirit of reconciliation certainly was alien to this prelate of the Church.

In the same year Phipps remarked that 'the fear and distrust which the socialists feel for Monseigneur Seipel are indeed at times hysterical.' This was on the occasion of the election of the new President of the Republic, when the socialists feared that Seipel might be willing to stand 'and to pull the strings from that position of greater freedom and less responsibility of some puppet Chancellor of his own making'. The socialists were therefore willing to extend the term of office of President Hainisch for a second time, 'to prevent the election of a clerical candidate'. But this so annoyed the Deputies of the Christian Social Party that they opted for Wilhelm Miklas, one of their own members, who was duly elected by 94 Christian Social votes. The small bourgeois parties voted for Schober and the Social Democrats abstained, to prevent the election of either Seipel or Schober, whom they held responsible for the 'bloodbath' of 15 July 1927.[31]

When Schober became Chancellor for the second time in September 1929 this was welcomed in the Foreign Office as 'the best solution'; 'his appointment seems to be most opportune' in view of the demonstrations by the rival para-military associations. According to Phipps, Schober was honest and straightforward, but his 'besetting sin is vanity and he is far too much inclined to regard himself as the saviour of his country'; Schober was 'the last high card in the Austrian constitutional pack'; if he were to fail he would probably be succeeded by Vaugoin, 'a man of limited intelligence, boundless conceit and in the pocket of Monseigneur Seipel'. Seipel was now coming out definitely – but not publicly – against the Anschluss, as the socialists were its 'most ardent supporters'. Apart from this, Seipel 'shares with bulls alone a blind hatred for anything approaching red'; his 'efforts to fish in troubled waters' would be interesting to watch.

In a later despatch Phipps described 'Schober's surprising power of inspiring almost universal confidence', which he ascribed above all to two reasons: 'the welcome contrast that he forms to his over-subtle predecessor' Seipel, and 'his strength of character, rather than to any outstanding intellectual ability'. Schober was 'honest, plain and outspoken', 'his head is square and his body round', and 'he says what he means and he means what he says.' All the diplomats accredited in Vienna trusted him, 'from the representative of Fascist Italy to that of Socialist Czechoslovakia': he should be given by Britain 'all possible support as any change in the Chancellorship can only be for the worse.'[32]

This high opinion of Schober was shared in London. A Foreign Office memorandum of October 1929 stated: 'He has unique qualifications for acting as arbitrator in this crisis, the chief of which is that he belongs to no party and as former head of the Austrian police is solely interested in the maintenance of law and order. If he were to fall the general impression is that he would be succeeded by Herr Vaugoin, a reactionary hothead who would be capable of any folly.' Schober's sole objective in London's opinion was the simultaneous disarmament of the para-military associations, but he believed that the only means of achieving this was first to solve the constitutional problem. Schober's hand should not be weakened: any foreign intervention at this stage might undermine his position. Schober put forward a programme of constitutional reform which, after lengthy negotiations with the political parties, was eventually carried. The rights of the President were to be increased, and in future he was to be elected directly by the people (as the German President was). His conversations with the socialist leaders, Schober told Phipps in November, 'were very satisfactory and were being conducted in a most reasonable spirit'. When some of the Heimwehr leaders complained about the slow progress of the negotiations Schober enquired whether they wished him to use forceful measures against them, 'whereupon they had collapsed'.[33]

The German Chancellor, Hermann Müller, also declared that 'he was not anxious' as long as Schober was Chancellor of Austria. However, if he resigned and Vaugoin took office, Vaugoin might summon Parliament to Innsbruck or another town away from Vienna and proclaim a new Constitution; 'a kind of civil war' would then occur in which Hungary, Czechoslovakia and even Italy might intervene. When Phipps saw Schober early in 1930 at dinner he was still optimistic and thought he would succeed with his disarmament plans. Phipps asked whether he found the socialists 'unduly factious', but Schober denied this, and 'in fact he implied that the Socialists still eat out of his hand in private, whatever they may do in public for the gallery'. The day before they had walked out of Parliament, but sent a representative to talk to him afterwards. As Schober meanwhile had secured a large foreign loan, his 'prestige with the country at large stands very high indeed', and there was no sign as yet of 'any serious attempt by Seipel and Co. to overthrow him'. In Phipps' opinion, the danger to Schober 'certainly comes from the Right rather than from the Left, who in their heart of hearts wish him well' but did not dare to admit it, for it would have a 'disastrous effect' on the bourgeois parties.[34]

Reports on the policies and attitudes of the Social Democrats were frequently sent to London. In commenting on the Party Conference of 1927, Lord Chilston wrote that the Social Democrats 'appear relieved that any danger of a schism in the party has for the moment been averted. Both Right and Left wings were evidently conscious that a split would reduce them both to impotence. Internal differences have therefore been patched up.' Any forward move was rejected, and the party adopted 'a stationary attitude of defence and defiance against suspected Fascist attacks'. This was, in his opinion, satisfactory: 'it is to the good that the Social Democrats are thoroughly frightened of the possibility of civil war.... The country is sadly in need of quiet and of a return to constitutional methods.' The more moderate socialists, led by Renner, were in favour of a coalition government with the Christian Social Party, but the suggestion was vehemently rejected by members of the government and was 'impracticable at present'. The idea would also be opposed by the Socialist left wing 'of which Dr Otto Bauer is the ablest representative'.

In 1928 the British Minister described Bauer as 'an eloquent and ambitious Jew with all the temperament for arousing the masses but clever and tactful enough to get on well with all sections of the party; has an acute mind and is far ahead of most Austrian politicians in intelligence.' He added that Bauer was anti-Bolshevist 'and generally disapproves of the Soviet regime and of attempts at armed revolution which he sees are impracticable'. In September, Phipps reported as 'a fact, not generally known' that for the first time 'responsible leaders of the Social Democrats' were secretly negotiating with the communists with the aim of forming a united front against Fascism, and that the left wings of the German and the Austrian socialists were also in touch with each other for the same purpose.[35] Yet, given the size of the Austrian Communist Party, a united front with it was hardly practicable.

In 1929 Phipps made a sharp distinction between the views of Bauer, who was 'apt to see the future through the somewhat smoky glasses of pessimism' with regard to the rise of Fascism, and those of the City Treasurer, Breitner, who was 'hopeful that order will be maintained in Austria'. Breitner had been 'hopeful even in the most critical days of the recent crisis. . . . So lucid and orderly a mind instinctively recoils no doubt from visualising anything as alien as chaos'; to him, the future 'presents itself clear-cut and without over-emphasis on the shadows', and so far he 'has shown himself to be the better prophet.' In the Foreign Office it was minuted at about the same time that the Austrian Social Democrats hoped, if they were backed by the British government, 'to secure constitutional advantages' in the parliamentary negotiations on changes in the Constitution; but foreign support in a domestic quarrel would only 'increase the bitterness between political parties which is already the curse of Austria'. If the socialists called on democratic governments for support, their adversaries might 'appeal to Fascist Italy for assistance', which would 'prove much more effective than that which the British and French Governments could offer' and bring with it 'international dangers of a very real nature'.[36] The danger was clearly anticipated in London, and in 1934 the Austrian socialists were left to fight their battle without any support from the democracies.

Quite a different 'danger' was pointed out to Phipps by the

Papal Nuncio, Monsignor Sibilia - that of the growth of 'apostasy'. While in the years 1924–27 only about 7500 people a year had left the Church, during the first nine months of 1928 the number rose to 28,000. This the Nuncio attributed to 'keen Socialist propaganda', and in particular to the fact that the city of Vienna (in contrast with Austria as a whole) permitted and registered divorces and re-marriages. The Nuncio, Phipps wrote, 'makes no secret of his reactionary views', and the 'very word "Republic" is anathema to him'. When he addressed the President on the occasion of the tenth anniversary of the Republic, his speech contained the obnoxious word only once, and in his speech of congratulation to President Miklas when the latter received the diplomatic corps, Sibilia on purpose 'avoided any mention of that hated institution'.[37] Phipps apparently analysed his speech very carefully, and was convinced that the Nuncio favoured a Habsburg restoration - a possibility which otherwise hardly figures in the reports.

Little was said on the subject of the Austrian communists. After their tenth Party Conference in 1929 Phipps wrote: 'The Austrian Communist Party has become so weak, and internal discord among its leaders so sharp' that it had been unable to hold a conference for eighteen months. At the beginning of 1927 there had been 60 party cells in Vienna with 1044 members, and now there were only 34 cells with 454 members. In 1923 6000 copies of the *Rote Fahne* were printed; in 1926 this had fallen to 3000, and by 1929 only 1200 were put out.

The Deputy Director of the Vienna police sent the Legation a very detailed report on the Party Conference of February 1929, at which the Executive Committee of the Comintern had pressed the party strongly to adopt a more 'Bolshevist course' - a line which was completely victorious. As a result, the leaders of the so-called 'rightist', 'conciliatory' opposition had lost their places in the Central Committee, and the journalist Richard Schüller was coopted as a new member and Moscow's 'man of confidence'. He had spent several years in Moscow as a member of the Executive Committee of the Communist Youth International and had worked in France as a communist agitator. Allied with him were several protagonists of the Moscow line, including the party Secretary, Johann Koplenig, 'always a faithful servant of the dominant members of the Central

Committee'. On account of the party's 'aggressive course', its public meetings were usually prohibited by the police. The party slogans 'were no longer taken seriously not even by the party members' and the party lost all support among the working population. The depression among the party's supporters was reflected in a recent leaflet issued by former communist leaders which spoke of 'a complete organisational collapse of the party, brought about by the ultra-left course of the leadership'.[38] In fact, the fight against 'right-wing' and 'conciliatory' elements within the party reflected the general ultra-left line laid down by the leaders of the Communist International in Moscow after the 6th World Congress of the Comintern in 1928.

At the other end of the political spectrum, new anti-Semitic riots occurred at Vienna University and the city's academic and technical colleges. In June 1929 disturbances and clashes broke out at the university. When the authorities took disciplinary measures against rowdy anti-Semitic students, the National Socialist university students formed a 'German Committee' and demanded a full enquiry by the 'German' members of the Senate, the rescinding of all restrictive and disciplinary measures imposed by the Rector, the retirement of the university Secretary who had lost their confidence, and the entrusting of peace and order within the university to their own committee. When the Rector tried to address the students in the university aula he was hissed and shouted down. Later in the year right-wing students once more interrupted classes and mobbed Jewish students on their way to and from lectures. There were reprisals and socialist pamphlets were distributed, which caused new disturbances. When the rowdyism continued, all academic institutes in Vienna were closed for eleven days, according to the Annual Report of the Legation.[39]

For the time being the Anschluss was not practical politics. But this did not prevent Dr Dinghofer, Vice-Chancellor in the Seipel government, from addressing the nationalist students of Vienna in 1926 to declare: 'it was the duty of all Pan-Germans to bring about the realisation of their great ideal': the date might be uncertain, 'but no Power on earth will be able to prevent it in the long run.' Whereupon the French and the Italian Ministers expressed their surprise and asked how the Chancellor regarded these remarks. But when the Under-Secretary of State in the

Auswärtige Amt, Carl Schubert, visited Vienna in 1927, he assured the French Minister that this issue did not figure prominently in Berlin; the preoccupations of his government were the termination of the Allied occupation of the Rhineland, reparations and foreign debts, and the eastern frontiers (by which he meant the Polish Corridor), in that order of importance: the Anschluss figured low down the scale, if it were considered at all. Germany desired Austria's prosperity, and speeches on the subject of the Anschluss had no connection with official German policy. When the Austrian Chamber of Commerce in the same year appointed a member to investigate 'the possibilities of obtaining for Austria a wider economic field', he found 'little response' in Germany to the idea of an economic union, because it would impede the difficult commercial negotiations with other countries which Germany was conducting at the time.[40]

Only the manager of the 'Alpine Montangesellschaft', the great Styrian iron and steel company, stressed the necessity of union with Germany as 'an economic necessity of the first rank'. But this was hardly an Austrian firm. As the Commercial Secretary of the Legation reported in 1921, with the break-up of the monarchy, the supply of coke from Bohemia came to an end, perhaps because the Czechs wanted to terminate the interdependence of their country and Austria. Then the Italians acquired a controlling interest (250,000 shares) in the company, to secure supplies of iron and steel for the Fiat and other engineering works. They hoped to induce the Czechs to resume deliveries of coke, but they were disappointed. Their investment proved a failure and thus they accepted the offer of Hugo Stinnes, the German industrial magnate, to buy them out.

Stinnes hoped to replace Swedish iron ore by Styrian ore as Germany had lost Lorraine and was short of iron. At that time the exchange rate was 12 kronen to the mark, and this facilitated German economic penetration of Austria. The Czech policy of discouraging trade between the two countries helped to further this penetration. A report of 1922 added that at the time of the Stinnes takeover only one furnace out of six belonging to Alpine Montan was working in Styria; but now the works were expanding, and by the end of the year all six furnaces would be working again; coke supplies came from the German works controlled by Stinnes, and lignite from Czechoslovakia in exchange for steel. Grave discontent was caused by Stinnes' policy of replacing Austrian with German workers, and the attempt to introduce a 12-hour day and other measures seemed intended to provoke strikes, so as to justify the replacement of the Austrian workmen.[41] In fact, most of the firm's managers were also Germans, and after July 1927 they refused to hire workers organised in the Free trade unions, closed the union offices, and replaced union members by men who were members of the Heimwehr, or at least of the so-called 'independent' union which was in fact dependent on the management, so that strikes became a matter of the past.[42] Thus the events of July 1927 had far-reaching results in different fields, and the weakness of the Free unions was clearly demonstrated.

The socialists were further weakened by losing whatever influence they still wielded in the army. As a secret military memorandum put it in 1929, the army 'has been systematically purged of Social Democrats by Vaugoin during his long tenure of office as War Minister', and the party leaders were 'now thoroughly alarmed'. Phipps wrote in the same year: 'The Austrian Army is excellent', after the removal of 'subversive elements' by Vaugoin. The Vienna police too 'is admirable and in every way reliable'; both forces could be 'trusted to suppress any disorders or attempted uprisings, whether from the Right or from the Left.'[43]

In short, the political scene had fundamentally changed. The socialists and the Free trade unions were driven on the defensive and began to fear for their very survival. The Heimwehren were in the ascendant and threatened the existence of a democratic regime. The Republic might be able to survive, but it would be a very conservative one. 'Red' Vienna already seemed an island surrounded by hostile forces: and all this before the onset of the world economic crisis which elsewhere undermined the foundations of democracy. The tragedy that befell Austria in the 1930s was clearly foreshadowed in the 1920s.

Notes

1   Leeper to Chamberlain, 16 July 1927: FO 371, file 12079, fo. 211

f. For the tense situation in the Burgenland and the events in Schattendorf, see Carsten, *Fascist Movements in Austria*, pp. 109 f.

2. Leeper to Chamberlain, 15 and 20 July 1927: FO 371, file 12079, fos. 195, 211 f., 213, file 12080, fo. 25.
3. See, for example, Elias Canetti, *Die Fackel im Ohr* (Fischer paperback, 1982), p. 234 f.; or Frank Vanry, *Der Zaungast* (Vienna, 1983), p. 174 f.
4. *The Times* 16 and 18 July 1927, the second report was sent from Bratislava because of the strike.
5. Minute by Sargent, 18 July, and Sir Colville Barclay to Chamberlain, Budapest, 19 and 20 July 1927: FO 371, file 12079, fo. 230, file 12080, fos. 31 f., 35.
6. Minute by Sargent, 18 July, and FO minute, 27 September 1927: FO 371, file 12079, fo. 230, file 12080, fo. 111.
7. Leeper to Chamberlain, 18 July 1927: FO 371, file 12079, fo. 221 f.
8. The same, 20 July 1927: FO 371, file 12080, fo. 25f.; *The Times* 18 and 20 July 1927.
9. Leeper to Chamberlain, 18 July 1927: FO 371, file 12079, fo. 219 f.; *Manchester Guardian*, 18 July; *The Times*, 18 July 1927.
10. *The Times*, 18, 19 and 20 July 1927.
11. Chilston to Chamberlain, 5 October, and memorandum by 12080, fo. 112.
12. *The Times*, 21 July 1927; Leeper to Chamberlain, 27 July, and Chilston to Chamberlain, 5 October 1927: FO 371, file 12080, fos. 58, 116.
13. Chilston to Chamberlain, 5 October, and memorandum by Phillpotts, 31 July 1927: FO 371, file 12080, fos. 119 f., 91 f.
14. *The Times*, 3 August, and first leader of the *Manchester Guardian*, 18 July 1927: *Austria infelix*.
15. Chilston to Chamberlain, 21 September and 9 November 1927: FO 371, file 12080, fos. 112 f., 149 f.
16. M.I.3.b paper on 'Semi-Military Associations', 18 April 1928: FO 371, file 12849, fos. 120–35.
17. Phipps to Lord Cushendun, 13 and 26 September 1928: FO 371, file 12851, fos. 24 f., 98; *The Times*, 6 October 1928.
18. Phipps to Cushendun, 8 and 10 October and 22 November 1928: FO 371, file 12851, fos. 91, 107–11, 144 f.; *Manchester Guardian*, 8 October 1928.
19. *The Times*, 8 and 9 October 1928; Phipps to Cushendun, 22 November 1928: FO 371, file 12851, fo. 144.
20. Phipps to Cushendun, 17 October 1928, and to Chamberlain, 5 June 1929: FO 371, file 12851, fo. 120 ff., FO 120, file 1029.

21. J. H. Le Rougetel to Henderson, 8 and 21 August and 5 September 1929: FO 371, file 13563, fos. 199 f., 213, FO 120, files 1029 and 1034.

22. Morrison to Henderson, Vienna, 5 September, Henderson to Streeruwitz, 14 September 1929: FO 800, file 280, fo. 178, FO 371, file 13564, fo. 103.

23. 'The Aims of the Austrian Fascists', s.d.: FO 800, file 280, fos. 179–84; a copy in file 284, fos. 56–62. The memorandum was handed to Morrison by Otto Bauer, but it may not have been written by him. Cf. a very similar analysis of the Heimwehr movement in Borkenau, *Austria and After*, p. 234 f.

24. Phipps to Henderson, 19 and 30 October and 8 November 1929: FO 371, file 13564, fos. 75 f., 135 f., file 13566, fos. 79, 81 (minute signed H. D.).

25. 'Austria. Annual Report, 1929', pp. 11 f., 33: FO 371, file 14311, fo. 136.

26. M.I.3.b. memorandum, 14 November 1929: WO 190, file 73.

27. Phipps to Henderson, 17 October, 5, 24, 27 November 1929: DBFP, Series IA, vii, 1975, nos. 51, 53, 96, 97, 100, pp. 94 f., 180 f., 191.

28. Henderson to Phipps, 3 December, Phipps to Sargent, 5 December, and minute by Crowe, 11 December 1929: FO 371, file 13865, fos. 98 f., 111 ff.

29. Phipps to Henderson, 24 November 1929: DBFP, Series IA, vii, no. 95, p. 180.

30. The same, 29 December 1929, and to Chamberlain, 19 December 1928: DBFP, Series IA, vii, no. 155, p. 290; FO 120, file 1023.

31. Phipps to Chamberlain, 6 December 1928: FO 371, file 12850, fo. 105 f.

32. Minute by Howard Smith, 26 September, and Phipps to Henderson, 17 October and 17 December 1929: FO 371, file 13564, fo. 16; DBFP, Series IA, vii, nos. 25, 144, pp. 50 f., 265.

33. Memorandum by Sargent, 31 October; Phipps to Henderson, 29 October and 11 November 1929: DBFP, Series IA, vii, nos. 41, 43, 63, pp. 77, 83 f., 104. Cf. Zöllner, *Geschichte Österreichs*, p. 508.

34. Sir Horace Rumbold to Henderson, Berlin, 8 November 1929, and Phipps to Sargent, 13 March 1930: DBFP, Series IA, vii, no. 56, p. 99; FO 371, file 14305, fo. 242 f.

35. Chilston to Chamberlain, 2 November 1927, Leeper to Chamberlain, 1 August, and Phipps to Cushendun, 13 September 1928: FO 371, file 12080, fo. 144 ff., file 12850, fo. 253, file 12851, fo. 76.

36. Phipps to Henderson, 29 December, and FO memorandum by Sargent, 31 October 1929: DBFP, Series IA, vii, nos. 43, 155, pp. 83 f., 291.
37. Phipps to Cushendun, 3 October, and to Chamberlain, 13 December 1928: FO 371, file 12851, fos. 162, 261.
38. Phipps to Chamberlain, 2 April 1929, and report sent by Dr Pamer, 14 November 1929: FO 371, file 13563, fo. 124 f., FO 120, file 1031.
39. Phipps to Henderson, 13 and 24 June 1929, and 'Austria. Annual Report, 1929', p. 15: FO 120, file 1033, FO 371, file 14311, fo. 136.
40. Chilston to Chamberlain, 14 December 1926, 8 June and 24 February 1927: FO 371, file 11215, fo. 39 f., file 12081, fo. 21, file 12076, fo. 233.
41. Chilston to Chamberlain, 8 June 1927; report by Phillpotts, 10 March 1921; and secret report of 28 April 1922: FO 371, file 12081, fo. 22, file 5782, fo. 192 ff., FO 120, file 982.
42. See Carsten, *Fascist Movements in Austria*, pp. 122 f.
43. M.I.3.b memorandum, 'The Situation in Austria', 14 November, and Phipps to Henderson, 17 November 1929: WO 190, file 73; DBFP, Series IA, vii, no. 144, p. 267.

5 Last Years of Democratic Government, 1930–32

The world economic crisis which began in 1929 hit Austria with full force from 1930 onwards; a country so much dependent on trade with its neighbours saw its exports shrink alarmingly, with import restrictions and trade barriers mounting all over Europe. Early in 1930 Sir Eric Phipps wrote to London that at the end of January the number of unemployed receiving relief had risen to 273,000 – 'the highest figure yet recorded in Austria' – and it was estimated that the total number, including those not entitled to any relief and those receiving old age pensions because they were unemployed, reached 360,000. With a population of about 6,500,000, this equalled almost 6 per cent of the population. But unemployment was not evenly distributed. In the small industrial town of Steyr half the male population was unemployed.

Later that year the total number had dropped slightly to 230,000, according to the Minister of Social Welfare.[1] But by January 1933 the figure of those receiving unemployment benefit had climbed to 478,000 and the monthly average for that year was 406,000; 45 per cent of them were in Vienna alone. The Legation also stated that these figures did not include 'the increasing number of unemployed who have reached the end of the term during which they can hope for unemployment benefits, 'perhaps another 300,000 whose plight was by far the most serious.[2] And, of course, added to these figures must be the number of their dependants, which was very considerable. In 1933 the government spent 449 million Schilling on social benefits and the budget closed with a deficit of 241 million, which was only partly covered by a new loan 'and such reserves as could be marshalled to assist Austria'. The railways in particular were 'in a parlous state': the sum spent on upkeep of renewals was far below the figure declared necessary by two foreign experts for keeping them in proper order.[3]

The economic situation was very much aggravated by the collapse of the Austrian banks which assumed vast proportions. In the autumn of 1929 the Bodencreditanstalt collapsed and had to be incorporated in the Creditanstalt, the largest Austrian bank. As Phipps put it, the collapse was partly due to the 'wild talk' of the Heimwehr leaders and ought to be 'a warning to reactionary circles that their own fortunes would be endangered by a continuation of any exaggerated beating of the Heimwehr drum.'[4] By 1931, however, the Creditanstalt itself was in serious trouble, threatened by precipitate withdrawal of funds and the non-renewal of short-term credits by foreign lenders. These short-term credits amounted to about £15,500,000. A law passed by the Austrian Parliament in May 1931 to reassure the shareholders and the public had no effect. It thus became clear that the bank 'would have to close its doors within a few days, with disastrous results to international credit, not only in this and the neighbouring countries.' Consequently, a committee in London headed by Lionel Rothschild proposed an international guarantee to prevent the withdrawal of large foreign credits, and a new Bill was put before the Austrian Parliament empowering the Minister of Finance to guarantee credits granted by the Creditanstalt to enable it to continue its current business. During the debate the Social Democrat spokesman declared his party would vote for the Bill because its effect would be to provide Austrian industry with working capital; but he criticised the government for not changing the management of the bank and for not bringing to account those guilty of mismanagement. It was dangerous to give this guarantee unless drastic changes were made, and people were indignant that the heads of the Bodencreditanstalt received generous pensions instead of being held responsible.[5]

The withdrawals from the Creditanstalt, however, continued, as did the drain on the foreign exchange holdings of the Austrian National Bank, caused by withdrawal of foreign credits. The Austrian government tried to obtain new funds by the issue of Treasury Bonds and appealed to the Bank of England for an advance against this issue. In June 1931 Philip Snowden, the

British Chancellor of the Exchequer, wrote to the Bank of England after a visit of the Austrian Minister to the Treasury:

> I feel it only right to let you know that His Majesty's Government are deeply concerned at the dangers of the present crisis in Austria, which may at any moment disturb the stability of Germany and other countries in Central and Eastern Europe, and I need hardly emphasize to you the great importance in the public interest of providing financial assistance to Austria without delay.

As Austria had surmounted past difficulties so successfully, the bankers could 'rely on the good faith of the Austrian Government in regard to any international obligations' they might incur. The Bank of England accordingly advanced 150 million Schilling (about £5,500,000) to the Creditanstalt against the issue of Treasury Bonds, 'a very welcome increase' in the Austrian reserves of foreign currency. But the officials of the Austrian National Bank continued to be pessimistic about the Creditanstalt's future.[6] The Austrian request to the League for authority to issue Treasury Bonds to the value of 150 million Schilling was granted after a lengthy discussion and consultation with the Bank of International Settlements and an assurance that the Austrian government would 'not interfere with the commercial management of the industries of which it became a shareholder' through its guarantee. When the shares were sold the proceeds were to be used to redeem the new Treasury Bonds.[7]

This was not the end of the Creditanstalt affair. In August 1931 the Bank of England refused to renew beyond 11 August the credit of 150 million Schilling. The letter in which the Bank informed the Austrian Minister of this decision was forwarded by the Legation to its head, Franckenstein, who was holidaying at Evian-les-Bains and failed to reach the Austrian government. When the Bank received no reply within a week it contacted the Austrian chargé d'affaires who informed them that he had no copy of the letter and knew nothing about it. The Bank suggested as the best course that the Austrians should repay 50 million and ask for an extension of the remaining 100. The Austrian government disregarded this advice and Chancellor Schober made a personal appeal to Henderson: 'this decision if adhered to would lead to catastrophe with which Austrian Government could not cope'. As the British Legation reported, 'Schober practically threw himself upon the mercy of His Majesty's Government'; the credit had been used as cover by the National Bank and 100 million Schilling had been passed into the accounts of the Creditanstalt; the government was unable to repay it unless it could borrow the sum from other banks. All this made the officials of the Bank of England 'very cross', but they claimed this would not influence 'their handling of the question at issue', nor would they be influenced by a recent Austrian press campaign against British high finance. In the Foreign Office Sir Robert Vansittart minuted: 'The Austrians have behaved with their usual incompetence & unusual ingratitude'; the story of the letter of the Bank to the Austrian Minister 'is almost incredible'; and the Austrian Legation 'would seem to need a spring cleaning, if not a good sweep-out.'[8]

From Vienna Phipps reported in October that by the end of September the cash reserves of the government had fallen to 9 million Schilling and that the deficit for October was estimated at nearly 10 million, so that the liquid funds would be exhausted by the end of the month: 'consider cash position serious and energetic measures urgent.' At lunch with the Finance Minister he found him 'completely senile, but most amiable'. He told him 'an endless flow of anecdotage' which Phipps found 'physically exhausting', and claimed that 'the Schilling was as steady as a rock'. Phipps, on the other hand, considered the value of the Schilling 'purely fictitious': foreign currency was unobtainable, even for *bona fide* transactions, and there would be a steady flight from the Schilling 'if there were any real freedom in the foreign exchange market'. The Austrian Ministry of Finance admitted that it had no cash reserves, but declared that it would manage to carry on, and if the economies agreed on proved insufficient, further economies would have to be made.[9]

At the end of October 1931 the new Chancellor, Dr Karl Buresch, indicated that the government intended to proceed against one of the directors of the Creditanstalt 'for malversation of funds'; he was suspected as an intermediary 'through whom the Rothschilds managed somehow or other to spirit away a good part of their private monies' out of Austria. Phipps thought most of this might be gossip, 'but it reveals the unsavoury ingredients which have gone into the making of the Austrian broth and ... there is little hope of really cleansing the Augean stables of the

Creditanstalt', unless the matter were taken out of the hands of the government 'which could hardly be done without re-imposing foreign control'. A few weeks later Buresch declared publicly that nothing would persuade him to withdraw the government guarantee given to the Creditanstalt, nor would the state deal in purely commercial matters. 'His somewhat vague attempt to instil confidence,' Phipps commented, would unfortunately be offset by a statement by the directors of the Creditanstalt in reply to an accusation in the press that they had spent 300,000 Schilling after the beginning of the crisis 'to keep the Press from making known the serious situation of the bank'. The socialist adversaries of the bank and of the Rothschild family 'could hardly have received better ammunition' for their campaign against 'the corruption' fostered by the bank.[10]

In 1932 Phipps heard from 'a reliable source' that the Public Prosecutor had applied for the arrest of two former directors of the Creditanstalt, that the Cabinet considered the request on the same day but decided they should not be arrested. Two of its members who belonged to the Heimwehr (among them Rintelen) 'were particularly insistent that no action should be taken', for the suspects had paid large sums to their movement. The Austrian government also declined to ask for the extradition of one of the former directors from Portugal.[11]

The report of the Creditanstalt for the six months ending 1 July 1932 showed a further deficit of 34 million Schilling. According to the Legation, the bank was still 'within measurable distance of collapse unless it can set its house in order and settle on a moderate basis with its foreign creditors'. In July 1931 the reserves of the Vienna Savings Bank had been entrusted to it in return for a 'blanket' government guarantee, and these 'it now stoutly refuses to reimburse' in spite of all attempts by the socialist leaders of Vienna to withdraw them, because it could not possibly 'stand this further drain'. In addressing the association of the industrialists in July 1932 the new Chancellor, Engelbert Dollfuss, stated that, by baling out the Creditanstalt, the government was not only thinking of the needs of industry, but also of the 'hundreds of millions of savings banks monies' deposited in the bank; its collapse 'would involve similar consequences for the Austrian savings banks, almost without exception' and 'untold misery to private individuals'. The other three banks of any size – the Wiener Bankverein, the Niederösterreichische Escomptegesellschaft and the Merkurbank – were equally faced 'with overhead expenditure out of all proportion to receipts and profits', according to a report by the League representative in Vienna, Dr Rost van Tonningen. In the opinion of 'more than one reputable and independent observer' none of them 'could withstand the shock of compulsory liquidation of the Creditanstalt, upon which over 40 per cent of the larger industry of this country is to-day dependent.'[12]

By the end of 1932 the annual deficit of the Niederösterreichische Escomptegesellschaft came to 60 million Schilling (about £2,000,000) and that of the Wiener Bankverein to 19 million Schilling. The government therefore had to assist both so as 'to relieve part of the industries of this country of the load of indebtedness to these banks ... and to help some of the agrarian and communal enterprises dear to the heart of the supporters of the present Government.' Within a few days of March 1933 the sum of 5 million Schilling was withdrawn from the Central Savings Bank of Vienna. The government was faced by a new crisis and hastily summoned Rost van Tonningen in the middle of the night with the request that he must agree to an extra 40 million to be supplied by the Austrian National Bank, otherwise they would have to resign. 'Each member of the Cabinet,' Phipps wrote, 'had some of his supporters in adjoining rooms, in the shape of Peasants' Associations etc., hungrily waiting for some loot for themselves.'

Rost eventually agreed to the request, but only on condition 'that these millions should only be drawn upon with the special consent of Rost ... and so the extra 40 millions is to all intents and purposes non-existent,' Phipps commented. The purchase of the assets of the Niederösterreichische Escomptegesellschaft was to cost 90 millions, at the value shown in the balance sheet, and that of the assets of the Wiener Bankverein another 49 million Schilling, to save those banks 'from imminent danger of collapse'. The cost of baling out the Creditanstalt was much higher: nearly 1000 millions between 1931 and 1933. Its liabilities and assets had to be written down, salaries cut and many employees dismissed. By the summer of 1933 the bank was 'nominally in a position to start life again', the Minister wrote; 'it remains to be seen' whether it could become 'a living bank'. Thus three banks were kept alive artificially, while only one or at most two would be 'fully sufficient for the needs of present-day Austria'.[13] The Austrian government had to foot the bill - and that at a time of declining revenues and ever-increasing expenditure on social insurance.

Early in 1933 a British diplomat from Vienna visited peasants huts in the Tyrol near a well-known tourist centre and 'found them without exception in a miserable state inside, with a shortage in some cases even of bread'. The peasants in the mountains were too far from Vienna to sell meat and unable to grow their own cereals; they were 'in a bad way'. But in his opinion the peasants of Upper and Lower Austria benefited to some extent from import restrictions and the policy of the government. The owner of a large timber estate in Carinthia told him that no single estate could hope to pay its way in the current year, although his estate was close to the Italian frontier and well placed for export; in the mid-1920s the timber and wood industry had experienced prosperous years, but now it was 'almost ruined', and 'on this industry depends no small part of the Austrian peasantry'. In the writer's opinion, there was an urgent need to 'put an end to profiteering, to one-sided application of regulations and evasion of taxation by those well able to pay, and to chicanery of all sorts in every branch of trade and industry as well as in every grade of society': without such cleansing reforms were of little use, 'but who can force them thro' in Austria?'[14] It was a *cri de coeur* without much hope that it would be heard, for these evils were deeply ingrained in Austrian society.

What probably saved the Austrian government for the time being was another international loan, granted in 1932 through the League of Nations, of 300 million Schilling, to which Britain and France each contributed 100 million (£3,500,000). The French contribution was made on condition that Austria's economic position was rectified and that financial control by the League, withdrawn in 1926, was reimposed. The French informed the British privately that they also desired a renewal of the Austrian promise 'not to alienate Austrian independence', but this was opposed by the German and Italian governments. The Foreign Office favoured 'a strictly neutral attitude'. Britain 'should not be committed to supporting the French in trying to force political conditions through against German and Italian opposition', it would 'be most unfortunate' if the French proved adamant,[15] but they refused to budge. In the same year Phipps wrote from Vienna: 'the present clouds are not without a silver lining'; ever since the new Austria existed there had been 'the problem of retrenchment and reform in public administration'; a good deal of progress had been made under the control of the League, but the prosperous years which followed made it difficult to carry on the reform 'and there was a relapse into comparative extravagance'. Now necessity was forcing the government to tackle the problem once more. He also believed that 'the pre-war generation of Austrians can hardly be expected to become as hard-working as the Swiss', but their children were more promising and 'realise the necessity of work'; 'their sudden rush into economic life' was one cause of the severe unemployment. Since the war Austria had made 'very remarkable progress', until the effects of the world crisis and of the Heimwehr agitation became noticeable – in foreign trade, in production, in railway traffic, in the growth of savings, in the cover of the currency – more progress than most other countries could show and 'perhaps none in Europe', and 'the myth of Vienna being the hydrocephalous head which must ruin the body has been exploded.'[16] It was an optimistic view, but it served to put the Austrian economic crisis into a more general perspective. The slow economic recovery of the years after 1933 was to show that Phipps' optimism was not entirely unjustified.

Schober remained Chancellor for only twelve months, to September 1930, and was then replaced, as had been anticipated, by Vaugoin, whose term of office was even shorter lasting only a few months. One of Schober's principal aims remained the disarmament of the para-military associations, and this was probably why he enjoyed British confidence – more so than any other Chancellor – and perhaps also because he could truthfully claim that he did not act in any party's interest. When a compromise had been effected on a change of the Constitution at the end of 1929 Phipps wrote enthusiastically: 'Schober is really a wonderful man, pulling off this compromise. He has lost 20 pounds in weight since taking office!' In the spring of 1930 Arthur Henderson told his French counterpart Aristide Briand 'that Herr Schober had struck him as a man who desired to govern his country on enlightened and liberal lines, and wishes to maintain its independence'; Schober had assured him that he would 'deal effectively with the disarmament of the illegal associations'. Briand replied that his impressions were similar, and the two Foreign Ministers 'agreed that the position was satisfactory'. To a fellow Labour MP, Henderson wrote at the same time that he was 'carefully watching the situation in Austria' and that it had 'much improved during recent months'; Schober had informed the Secretary-General of the League that he intended to introduce a Bill 'to prohibit not merely the carrying, but the possession, of arms by unauthorized persons'; if this became law it would secure the disarmament of the Heimwehr as well as the Republican Defence League. Phipps, however, admitted that the proposals had 'unchained the fury of the extremists on both sides, but particularly of the Heimwehr'.[17] Without its weaponry the Heimwehr would be reduced to impotence.

In spite of all his sympathy Phipps noticed that Schober's 'undefeated optimism sometimes runs away with him and he promises more than he can perform'. He told the British as well as the French Minister that he wanted to have 'the whole loan at once' after the new international loan had been agreed to in principle; he felt his whole position would be compromised by any delay, 'for he rather imprudently announced openly that all would be successfully concluded by the end of June [1930]'. Phipps thought that Schober did not see the danger 'that the sinister Seipel may decide to overthrow Schober directly the loan is floated',[18] for Schober depended on the votes of the Christian Social Deputies in Parliament. And indeed three months later the Schober government did fall over a personal intrigue inspired by a leading Christian Social politician. But in the general election of November 1930 their party lost 7 seats and was reduced to 66, 6 fewer than the socialists, while the Heimwehren (which participated for the first time in an election) gained 8 seats.

At the end of 1930 yet another short-lived government was formed under the Governor of Vorarlberg, Dr Otto Ender, with Schober as Vice-Chancellor and Foreign Minister. It too fell after six months on account of the failure of the Creditanstalt and the ill-conceived plan of a customs union with Germany. This, as the Legation reported, 'took the business world by surprise as much as the politicians'; but the latter were more in favour than business circles; while merchants hoped for more trade in German goods, manufacturers and some bankers were rather sceptical. Some weeks later Phipps wrote that 'high finance continues to be unfavourably disposed', but that the bankers' influence in politics was 'small and only indirect'. The manufacturers were sharply divided: those engaged in mass production were 'mostly afraid of German competition', but those in whose work 'individual skill and taste plays a large role' were expecting 'to gain more from the opening of the German market than they lose from German competition'. Agriculture, on the other hand, was 'almost unanimously in favour of the customs union' as the German protective customs were higher than the Austrian ones, but the pig breeders were afraid of German competition.[19]

The proposal for a customs union aroused a storm of protest in France and the states of the Little Entente, and had to be renounced by Austria as a condition of new financial help. For the time being, Schober remained as Foreign Minister. In November 1931 Phipps reported: 'The Austrian Government cannot, by any stretch of the imagination, be described as a strong one, nor is it perhaps entirely free from corruption. Whilst Austrian public opinion is notoriously long-suffering, it is showing signs of impatience at the Government's slackness in coping satisfactorily with the grave financial and economic problems of the hour'; Schober was daily losing prestige and his continuation in office 'is not calculated to predispose the French in favour of Austria'.

According to an Intelligence assessment of the beginning of 1932, the internal situation was dominated by 'a duel between Schober and Seipel'. Although Seipel was not the Foreign Minister in the new Buresch government, he 'will probably exercise considerable influence behind the scenes'. This was also the opinion of Phipps, who wrote that Buresch had been forced at a Christian Social Party meeting to get rid of Schober and to form a government excluding the German Nationalists, so that the government did not possess a parliamentary majority; now it only remained for the latter to vote against the government and one of its proposals, 'and Mgr. Seipel will then have an opportunity to come forward and declare that the salvation of Austria under a parliamentary regime is obviously impossible.' If one asked why Seipel should desire a dictatorship so urgently when his task would be so extraordinarily difficult, 'the answer is that he cannot wait longer. He must be in the saddle before a Hitler regime comes in Germany, as otherwise Austria might be carried away on a National-Socialist wave.' Seipel wishes 'to pose as the saviour of Austria for the second time'. People in close touch with him had assured Phipps that he was in no hurry, and would prefer the present government to last for some months longer; but its weakness might make this impossible: 'a draught might blow it away and Vienna is a very draughty place just now.'[20]

In June 1931, when the Buresch government was threatened by the opposition of the German Nationalist Party 'over the vexed question of the taxation of officials' salaries', Phipps went so far as to approach the German Minister in Vienna, Dr Rieth, and to impress on him 'the folly of their behaviour', for any new Cabinet crisis would have a deplorable effect on the general and financial situation of Austria. Phipps asked Rieth 'to take an early opportunity of using his undoubted influence with the leaders [of the party]' to induce them 'to be more reasonable and to consent to reach some compromise with the Government'. Rieth promised to do what he could, and on the next day the press announced that a satisfactory compromise had been reached between the government and the Nationalists. But this government too resigned after a few months, in May 1932.

The new government was not formed by Seipel (who died in the same year), but by Engelbert Dollfuss, hitherto the Minister of Agriculture and Forestry. As the German Nationalists remained in opposition, the new government had a majority of only one seat, and it was with the greatest difficulty that it obtained parliamentary approval of the conditions attached to the new loan of 300 million Schilling, which *inter alia* included new prohibitions on the Anschluss and a customs union with Germany, in spite of British opposition.[21] There had been a quick succession of governments, none providing stability or showing a way out of the political and economic impasse. The question was whether the Dollfuss government would prove any stronger, at a time when Austria was threatened not only by the fascist Heimwehren, but also by the rise of German National Socialism.

The Austrian National Socialists were considerably weaker than their German comrades; in the election of November 1930 the party polled only 3 per cent of the vote, half of the Heimwehr poll, and did not win a single seat. At the same time, the German NSDAP gained more than 18 per cent of the total vote and became the second strongest party. But, under the influence of the German successes, the Austrian National Socialists experienced a remarkable change of fortune, in particular in 1932. In May, Phipps reported that in the previous year 'the Nazi movement was, comparatively speaking, unheeded in the country' and 'its leaders almost unknown to the public'; but now a 'noticeable change' had occurred and 'the Nazi party is steadily acquiring an increasing hold over a section of the electorate'; its meetings, even in Vienna, were well attended, 'its placards numerous, its speakers vehement and liberal in their promises to the discontented, disappointed and bitter elements'. Its Austrian leader, Eduard Frauenfeld (in fact only the *Gauleiter* of Vienna) was 'looked upon as a mysterious and able organiser' and the movement had apparently come to stay. It offered 'a promise of excitement' and, as in Germany, it exploited strong anti-Jewish feeling. If there were a general election, the party would win 25–40 seats at the expense of the established parties. Some people, however, maintained that in Austria enthusiasm of this kind could only last a certain time and 'that the inherently placid character of this population robs Hitlerism in Austria of much of the potential danger that it possesses in Germany.'

An Intelligence report of the same month mentioned the quick growth of the movement in Vienna, where 'a procession of 20,000 strong was received with great enthusiasm' and some 5000 of them appeared in military formation. The National Socialists made great capital out of the financial crisis, the collapse of the Creditanstalt and the weakness shown by the German and Austrian governments concerning the plan of the customs union. They gained many followers from the ranks of the para-military associations, especially the Heimwehr, and were helped by the vacillations of its leaders between a pro-German policy and legitimism. In local elections about 25 per cent of the soldiers had voted National Socialist and the rank and file of the army 'are coming more and more under the influence of Nazi propaganda', as did many of the junior officers:

> Born of disillusionment and discontent with the parties led by the generation that made the last war, the Nazi movement in Austria is essentially an appeal to youth; it cuts across the old party distinctions, drawing its strength from the rising generation, while its opponents, both Christian Socialist and Social Democrats are mainly men of middle and later life. It is violently anti-Semitic and anti-communist.[22]

It was a shrewd analysis, but it did not provide any insight into the social basis of the movement. The Annual Report of the Legation gave this as 'the large army of middle-class unemployed'. It also mentioned the growing strength of National Socialism in the army where 'one or two sporadic outbreaks of militant National Socialism' had occurred. When Soldiers' Councils were elected in August, on the other hand, only nine National Socialists were elected compared to 225 on the Christian Social list; but this was ascribed to the fact that the ballot was 'by no means as secret as it is supposed to be'; if it were the National Socialists would have won about 25 per cent of the soldiers' vote. When municipal elections were held in Vienna in April 1932 the Party obtained 201,000 votes and 15 seats.[23]

Part of the success of National Socialism was ascribed to their propaganda efforts, 'particularly among Government servants and in the middle and salaried classes'; part also to their 'exploits', such as free fights at the university and 'an attack with tear-gas bombs on a big store during the Christmas shopping week'. Another consisted of an attack on a golf club at Lainz near Vienna which had a large Jewish and foreign membership. At the weekly dance, a band of youths, some in Nazi uniforms, 'rushed out of the darkness upon the astonished guests, overturned the tables and did some damage to the furniture and window-panes, shouted Nazi war-cries and, at a given signal, departed.' The Legation's Annual Report for 1932 nevertheless predicted a decline of support for the movement which 'has not the support of Protestant sentiment against Roman Catholicism, of which it is largely the outward sign in Germany'; its doctrines would not be 'permanently acceptable in Austria. A party which is "anti-Marxist", anti-Semite and anti-Clerical is unlikely to commend itself to a country where everyone who is not a Jew or a Socialist is a Catholic.'[24]

This was perhaps true up to a point in Vienna, but especially in Carinthia and Styria there were large areas which had a very different tradition, nationalist and not Catholic. The Annual Report for 1933 stated more correctly that 'the twin Nazi doctrines of "more work" and anti-Semitism find a fertile field in the inherently anti-Semitic and impoverished youth of Austria'. It pointed to 'the hopeless economic future which faces the majority of adolescents as they grow up into manhood'. The professions were not only overcrowded but suffered from growing competition by Jewish and women students. Many active National Socialists were also found 'among the business classes, small traders, factory-owners, and hotel-keepers', doctors, dentists and lawyers 'whose livelihood becomes each year more precarious and who attribute their difficulties largely to Jewish competition', as well as among officials and teachers.[25] This was quite correct, and it largely corresponded to the analysis made then and later of the National Socialist movement in Germany. In the small towns and villages of Austria, the local 'intelligentsia' – doctors, lawyers, teachers and the like – had an anti-clerical, nationalist and pan-German tradition, which was the main force behind the German Nationalist Party. Its adherents now deserted en masse to the National Socialists. In Styria, Carinthia and elsewhere the local Heimwehr provided the National Socialists with a militant following.[26]

Several reports recorded outbreaks of anti-Semitism in Vienna which may have been inspired by National Socialists. As in Germany, the showing of the film 'All Quiet on the Western Front' at the beginning of 1931 led to violent demonstrations. 'The theatre in question was isolated by a police cordon, through which only those who had tickets for the performance ... were allowed to penetrate. The shopkeepers in the vicinity closed their shutters and the whole quarter presented the appearance of a beleaguered city'. Crowds of demonstrators sang 'Deutschland über Alles' or shouted 'Down with the Jews!' The mounted police tried to disperse them and about thirty people were arrested. The Minister of the Interior asked the Mayor of Vienna to secure order. When this request was disregarded, he issued an emergency decree banning the film throughout Austria. In 1930 the Senate of Vienna University decided to grant official recognition to 'societies of students of the same nationality and language'; the 'Deutsche Studentenschaft' was expressly recognized as the representative of all 'German' students – an aim it had long pursued. Only the societies of socialist and Jewish students protested against this partisan recognition, while the Christian Social *Reichspost* stated that the 'Deutsche Studentenschaft' included all 'German' students except only the 'Marxists', implying that this was quite a satisfactory solution. Yet in the following year the Constitutional Court decided that the Senate declaration was illegal. No sooner was this known than disorders broke out in the university with the cry 'Down with the Jews', and an anti-Semitic demonstration took place 'under police supervision'.[27] What the Legation failed to mention was the fact that the 'Deutsche Studentenschaft' had long adopted the 'Aryan' principle which excluded Jews and other 'non-Aryans' from membership: the action of the Senate implied a recognition of this principle.

At the end of 1930 the Legation confidently stated: 'The year 1929 saw the Heimwehr at the zenith of its power and the year 1930 its decline.' The main reason given for this was that 'the leaders of the movement were not of the necessary calibre to guide it once it became really strong', so that it 'degenerated into a weak and divided political party'.[28] This indeed was its most obvious weakness, apart from the ideological differences which separated the various local organisations and finally caused a split. This 'centrifugal tendency' was described in many reports from Vienna. At the beginning of 1930 it was noticed that the 'ruthless and uncompromising methods' used by the German Major Pabst, who was in charge of the technical and military side, antagonised many other leaders, in particular Vincent Schumy, the then Minister of the Interior.

Shortly after his arrival in Austria in 1920 Pabst was naturalised under an assumed name (he was a fugitive from German justice), and Schumy was determined to get hold of the papers and to prove their invalidity. The authorities of the Tyrol refused to hand over the documents, Pabst retaliated by securing Schumy's expulsion from the Carinthian Heimwehr, and he was backed by the Tyrolese and federal leader, Dr Steidle, who branded Schumy's Agrarian Association as traitors to the movement. Schumy demanded an unreserved apology but attempts at reconciliation failed. The leaders of the Agrarian Association expressed their solidarity with Schumy, condemned the attainment of political ends by force, Fascism as well as Bolshevism, and declared they would support the Heimwehr only 'in so far as its purpose was defensive'. Some local leaders demanded that, in opposition to the Heimwehr, a *Bauernwehr* (special peasant unit) should be organised. This caused an outcry on the Heimwehr side, which branded it as 'rank treachery' and declared open war on 'all persons who may attempt to foster such movements'; the assembled Heimwehr leaders desperately tried to settle their personal differences and the criticisms directed at Steidle's conduct.[29]

In opposition to Steidle and Pabst there appeared the much younger Upper Austrian Heimwehr leader, the aristocratic Prince Starhemberg, who 'has already built up a semi-independent position for himself on feudal lines', as Phipps noted in April 1930. In May Steidle, attempting to surmount the internal conflicts, 'declared himself openly a supporter of Fascism' and proclaimed at Korneuburg: 'we reject the Western Parliamentary system', thus throwing out a challenge to the Christian Social Deputies 'to choose between their allegiance to the party and to the Heimwehr'. The assembled Heimwehr leaders had to take an oath rejecting the parliamentary system and the party state. Among the Christian Social Deputies this oath caused protracted discussions, sometimes with and sometimes without the Heimwehr leaders, to devise a formula which would allow them to remain members of both organisations – discussions which were ended by the adoption of a 'remarkably empty resolution', Phipps wrote. Soon after the Schober government took action, Pabst was arrested and expelled from Austria; in Phipps' opinion he was 'the real organiser of the Heimwehr' and 'a great loss to that body'.[30] He further reported that 'the big guns of the Heimwehr' had conferred with numerous leaders of the German Stahlhelm veterans' association, headed by a veritable prince of the House of Hohenzollern, and a member of the Italian Legation at Budapest on the subject of Fascism and on cooperation between the para-military associations of Austria, Germany and Hungary – news which Phipps considered rather 'disquieting'.[31]

In May, on the eve of the introduction of the Disarmament Bill, the Heimwehr leaders issued a manifesto, stating the terms on which they were willing to help the government: they were to be permitted to collaborate in the seizure of arms depots of the socialists, and one of their leaders was to be made Minister of the Interior (to obtain control of the police). These terms were rejected by the government, and the Bill was passed by Parliament. In September Schober told Phipps 'that he hoped for early and favourable developments in the Heimwehr situation, beginning with the eclipse of Dr Steidle'. On the following day the assembled leaders, after a heated discussion, elected Starhemberg as their sole leader, allegedly with a majority of one vote, and Steidle was forced to resign as federal leader with his whole staff. Soon after Starhemberg was appointed Minister of the Interior in the new Vaugoin government, and one of the Heimwehr aims seemed achieved. It was now his task to enforce the Disarmament Bill; the measures taken were exclusively directed against the Republican Defence League, but 'even so the result appears to have been meagre', the Foreign Office commented. In November 1931 it stated 'that no present or future Austrian Government was likely to be strong enough to carry out any real measure of disarmament'.[32] That was the end of all earlier hopes.

In public the new Minister of the Interior exclaimed at a meeting of his uniformed followers: 'I will give the Viennese a good slogan for the elections; they should direct their electoral campaign against Breitner. Only when the head of this Asiatic rolls upon the ground will the victory be ours.' But later Starhemberg denied the correctness of his outburst against the popular City Treasurer. As Phipps remarked, the Heimwehr was 'at sixes and sevens as to what policy to follow during the elections': some leaders wanted a place on the list of the Christian Social Party, some desired a separate list, and the moderates 'are now genuinely alarmed at the behaviour of this member of the Government'. Phipps also tried to calm the 'exaggerated fears' of the *Manchester Guardian* correspondent, 'for after all the whole *raison d'être* of the Heimwehr is tall talk, and their utterances must not be taken literally.' In November he reported the triumphant return of Pabst from Italy to the Tyrol: 'As he set foot on Austrian territory flags were dipped and a band struck up.... At Innsbruck several thousand members of the Heimwehr gathered in the streets and escorted Major Pabst to his home with a torchlight procession. In the evening a reception was held at the Town Hall and the usual inflammatory speeches were delivered by Dr Steidle, Major Pabst and others.'[33] The exile had been very brief.

In the same month the Legation reported new dissensions: the provincial leader of the Heimwehr in Lower Austria, the Deputy Julius Raab, refused to recognise Starhemberg's authority and formed a Catholic movement of his own. In the provinces a tendency was growing 'which may lead to the detachment of the Heimwehr in each province from the control of the Federal leaders'; in Vorarlberg this had already happened; many people who had been enthusiastic supporters a short time ago 'now scoff openly at the whole organisation and at Starhemberg in particular'; they were alienated by 'Starhemberg's childish conduct while Minister of the Interior and his open sympathy with the National Socialists'. An Intelligence report of the same time stated that Starhemberg was 'in close touch with Hitler and all, at any rate of the militant elements of the Heimwehr are united under his leadership'. If they attempted a coup, it was impossible to say what the army might do, but any action 'against the Heimwehr is out of the question, and the troops would certainly lend the Heimwehr active support against the Social Democrats'; it would certainly make 'a strong bid for power, whether by constitutional or unconstitutional means', and the situation was 'extremely grave'.[34]

The long-expected coup took place in September 1931, but it was an isolated affair limited to Styria and some feeble support in Upper Austria. 'The Heimwehr began its attempt to seize power,' *The Times* reported, 'by occupying Government and municipal offices, railway stations and public schools in a large number of towns in Upper Styria'. Proclamations informed the inhabitants that Dr Pfrimer 'had assumed the reins of government, the people "in their dire distress" having installed him as "guardian of their rights".' He also issued a manifesto which suspended the Constitution and announced a new provisional one. By the afternoon, however, his armed followers retired from many towns; they still occupied seven Styrian towns, 'but the Government is convinced they will withdraw before nightfall.' The *Manchester Guardian* announced that two workers had been killed and two fatally wounded; order was restored by the gendarmerie and the army, but the Heimwehr units were not disarmed. When the correspondent visited its headquarters at Bruck and at Kapfenberg he noticed machine-guns and rifles. On the following day the paper mentioned that the leaders, including Starhemberg, had been arrested; their forces were financed 'by the German and Styrian heavy industries'. According to *The Times*, secret correspondence compromising Starhemberg was seized on Heimwehr premises at Judenburg; Pfrimer had issued an appeal to his men that they should return peacefully to their homes.[35]

The British Legation reported that the Putsch collapsed through the inertia and divided counsels of the leaders and that 'the Heimwehr movement is on the decline', but that its disarmament 'is likely to prove impossible so long as distrust of "red Vienna" persists in the cut-off and backward districts of rural Austria'. The causes of the failure of 'the comic opera that has been played during the last 48 hours' were: 'the jealousy and divisions among the leaders', 'the lack of unanimity between the Royalist, Christian-Socialist, and Pan-German adherents', the weakness in 'organisation, training and arms'. These features made any attempt at a 'seizure of the reins of government seem grotesque'. The failure had proved right those 'who laid stress on all these weaknesses among the Heimwehr leaders, even though it underrated their power of self-delusion and aggrandisement'.

In November another report stated that the Heimwehr was split into two main groups, those 'who wish to combine with the Hitler party in Germany' and the weaker legitimist section. Starhemberg 'tries to balance himself on these two divergent steeds; he takes money from the German Hitlerites, but assures his Legitimist friends that at heart he is with them.' His more intelligent friends were aware of his limitations, but also of 'his wonderful popularity with the peasants, etc., a popularity which has been considerably increased by the few days which he spent in prison last September'. From a 'trustworthy source' it was learned that the German National Socialists were paying 5000 marks a month and 100,000 marks down on condition that Starhemberg remained at the head of the movement. Why they should do so was difficult to imagine, unless 'they know full well that he is so weak and stupid that they can always be sure of dominating him completely'.[36]

The Legation's Annual Report for 1931 gave the maximum armed strength of the Heimwehr as 40,000; 10,000 in Styria, 'reasonably well armed and organised'; 3500 each in Carinthia and the Tyrol, 'in fair shape'; and in Vorarlberg 'an efficient little force' of 1000; the remainder 'are probably of little value'. The supplies of ammunition were very short; during the recent Putsch the men had only 50 rounds per rifle and in many cases much less, and the machine-guns a maximum of two belts. The Republican Defence League by comparison had a maximum strength of perhaps 25,000: 15,000 were organised in twelve 'battalions' in Vienna and thirteen more in the provinces. Considerable defections had occurred to the National Socialists and communists. The arms of both associations consisted largely of war-time rifles in poor conditions; both possessed a limited number of machine-guns which were old and suffering from neglect. Many officers of the army sympathised with the Heimwehr and 'would be prepared to back any "Putsch" from the Right, provided a good leader appeared to carry it through', but no such leader was visible.[37]

During the following months there were more reports about dissension and disorganisation in the Heimwehr ranks, and its own leaders began to worry about the growing rate of desertion to the National Socialists. In July 1932 Starhemberg, at dinner with the British military attaché, frankly admitted 'that the Nazi movement has taken away a considerable number of the Heimwehr men'; but he claimed rather optimistically 'that the movement is probably now nearing its zenith . . . as it has nothing essentially Austrian about it'; many of its more moderate adherents had left it on account of recent outrages.

In the spring of 1933, however, Starhemberg and several other guests of the military attaché 'made no secret of the fact that they had underestimated the strength of the wave of National Socialism and that they had been caught to a certain extent napping'. They mentioned 'widespread defections from the Heimwehr in Tirol' and the recent agreement between the National Socialists and the Styrian Heimwehr 'which left no doubt as to the gravity of the situation'. The Minister of Commerce added that in his own village in the Tyrol 'the whole population including his own men servants ... had all gone across to the Nazis'. If it were still possible to rescue the Heimwehr this could only be done by vigorous action and a popular slogan 'to rally their wavering supporters', such as raising the cry 'Save Austria from foreign domination'. 'All spoke of the situation in the most pessimistic terms,' the attaché informed the War Office.[38]

In May 1933, Phipps wrote that the Styrian Heimwehr, which was entirely independent of Starhemberg and had 'long shown hankerings after union with National Socialism', had accepted the leadership of Hitler and would wear the swastika on its steel helmets, but would retain its separate organisation and uniform. The final impulse to the agreement came when the German Steel Trust ordered its affiliate, the 'Alpine Montangesellschaft' of Styria, to withhold funds from the Heimwehr until it agreed to the conditions. In the same month the Heimwehren celebrated the defeat of the Turks outside Vienna 250 years earlier by a parade at the palace of Schönbrunn. The military attaché counted 25,000 men taking part in the march-past and 'his impression was distinctly favourable'. Four hundred National Socialists who tried to interfere were arrested by the police. The Legation's Annual Report for 1933 once more mentioned large defections from the Heimwehr ranks, especially in Carinthia and Styria, but also 'a revival in recruiting'; the attraction was a uniform and rifle as well as pay when on duty or participating in a demonstration, but 'the reliability of many units is very questionable'. The principal strength was in Lower Austria and the Tyrol, 'and the training of units is quite sufficient to render them of substantial value for dealing with internal disorder'.[39]

The original connections of the Heimwehr had been with Bavaria and its para-military associations, and later it received large funds from other parts of Germany. But these ceased when the movement began to adopt a more 'Austrian' policy line and came out in support of the Dollfuss government. Always short of money and weaponry, from about 1928 onwards it enjoyed strong Italian support, usually via the right-wing government of Hungary. (In 1932 the British Legation recorded rumours of a 'public fusion of the Fascist Parties of Italy, Austria and Hungary'.) An informant claimed that the Heimwehr had recently received 2 million Schilling as the result of a personal appeal to Mussolini; it also enjoyed the public support of the Dollfuss government and was otherwise 'dipping into' public funds, so that its 'chronic shortage of funds cannot be as acute' as it had been before.[40]

The Italian links were again in evidence at the beginning of 1933 when the Social Democrats denounced the smuggling of 100,000 war-time rifles from Italy to Hungary through Austria, which were discovered at Hirtenberg where they were to be overhauled: 30,000 of them were to be supplied with new bolts at the Steyr armament works and 15,000 were destined for the Heimwehr, Phipps reported. When he protested against this clear violation of the Treaty of St Germain, he was told by the Secretary General of the Foreign Ministry that the arms were merely in transit. Phipps replied 'that Austria did not exactly facilitate the task of those who were anxious to help her'. When he met Renner at a lunch party the former Chancellor remarked that the mistake was due to the youth and inexperience of Dollfuss, 'for he had not a sufficiently tight hold over his Heimwehr ministers, who were primarily responsible for the whole business'. The arms were under strong protection as they were surrounded by a Heimwehr cordon who in turn were surrounded by the Republican Defence League; but Phipps thought under Austrian conditions any practised gun-runner would be able to move the rifles through both cordons.

The British and French governments now intervened and invited the Austrians 'to return or destroy the arms', but did not mention any sanctions if they did not comply. Austrian collusion was proved when the Director of the Austrian railways offered a bribe of 15,000 Schilling for getting the rifles smuggled into Hungary, where the empty vans were to be sealed and returned to Italy. The Italian press gave publicity to the affair and started a campaign against foreign intervention in Austria, claiming that she was treated 'like a negro colony'. When the French Minister informed Dollfuss that the French tranche of the new loan might not materialise before the affair was settled, the Chancellor too told Phipps that Austria was treated like a colony and was being humiliated: 'the loan was being dangled before her eyes like a carrot, with new conditions being continually attached'; Austria had 'behaved in an altogether exemplary manner, and this was her reward.'[41] In the end, a company of the army was sent to guard the weapons until they could be sent back – a step that might have been taken much earlier.

With regard to the political allegiance of the army, General Jansa told the military attaché in 1932 that only a minority of the officers and other ranks sympathised with National Socialism and that the overwhelming majority favoured the Christian Social Party. But the attaché was doubtful and estimated that about 30 per cent would vote National Socialist in a free poll, only 50 per cent for the ruling party, and the remainder for the Social Democrats, while the majority of the senior officers sympathised with the Heimwehr. When the attaché had a similar conversation with two other senior officers in 1933 they informed him that the government's policy was 'unpopular with the Army as a whole'; the average officer would prefer an independent Austria to the Anschluss, but 'if it comes to a straight choice between Germany on the one hand and Italy and the Jews [sic!] on the other', popular opinion in the army would favour Germany (where Hitler had become Chancellor). The officers also mentioned that 'little love is lost' between the senior officers and the Heimwehr whose influence was for 'ever increasing'.[42]

It is difficult to form any definitive opinion from these remarks by a few senior officers but it seems noteworthy that in 1934 the army fulfilled its duty not only against the socialists, but equally against the National Socialists, apparently without any hesitation. It is also true that by then its ranks had been purged of active National Socialists and that the Social Democrats had long lost their influence in the army. The Inter-Allied Military Control Commission had fixed the strength of the police and gendarmerie at 9782 men, but on account of the internal security requirements Austria was permitted to exceed this figure as the army was kept below the permitted strength of 30,000. In May 1933 it numbered only 19,837 men, and the two police forces had 12,778.[43]

If the loyalty of the army was somewhat doubtful, there is no question where the Church stood. Before the election of November 1930 the Cardinal Archbishop of Vienna and the bishops of the Austrian sees issued a pastoral letter. It specifically condemned the separation of Church and state, divorce, free love and the 'catchwords' of 'unlimited freedom of the Press' and 'absolute sovereignty of the people', as well as 'heathenish nationalism', 'ruthless Liberalism' and 'the materialistic Socialist State'. There was no possibility of a compromise between Christ and his enemies; all good Christians were instructed to vote for the 'Christian Party', and prayers were to be held in the churches for a good outcome of the election. There was, of course, not the slightest doubt what was meant by the 'Christian Party', which nevertheless lost seven seats in that election. At least one of the bishops, Dr Johannes Gföllner of Linz, also published a pastoral letter attacking the National Socialist creed. The nationalism of the National Socialists, he declared, was unnatural and un-Christian; any idea of a specific German People's Church was anti-Catholic; it was anti-Christian 'to hate the Jews for being Jews'; but there was a certain type of Jewry which, together with Freemasonry, exercised an evil influence on modern life and was the 'supporter of mammonistic capitalism and the founder and apostle of Socialism and Communism, the forerunners of Bolshevism': this evil influence must be fought. The letter concluded by stating that it was impossible to be a good Catholic and a real National Socialist at the same time.[44] In Rome Cardinal Pacelli told the British Minister 'that he was much impressed with the energy and determination of Dr Dollfuss'; the Austrian government 'had the will and the power to deal drastically with their opponents', but much would depend on the support given by Britain, France and Italy.[45]

The Vienna police directorate continued to supply the Legation with detailed information on the Austrian Communist Party which, in spite of the economic crisis, showed no sign of growth, in contrast to the German Communist Party. In 1930 the police stated the most characteristic trait of the communist movement was the fight against social democracy, in the hope to become a 'uniform Communist mass party', for the Social Democrats had betrayed the interests of the proletariat and cooperated in the establishment of a 'Fascist regime'. The communists had succeeded in forming a 'Committee of Revolutionary Social Democrats' from discontented socialists, which was led by Dr Wilhelm Reich (of later fame). He had a following among the young socialists through his lectures on sexual freedom and his advice in such matters; the meetings called by the Committee were well attended and usually addressed by Reich and members of the Central Committee of the Communist Party. In the elections of November 1930, however, the communists only obtained 20,879 votes out of a total of 3,688,566 (or about 0.6 per cent); this showed 'the internal weakness and unimportance' of the party, which was fully admitted by its leaders. On Mayday 1931 2800 people participated in the communist demonstration in Vienna and 200 in Graz, while in Linz the figure was a mere 50.[46] Even in Vienna the party was of no importance.

The severe economic crisis of 1930–33 brought political instability to Austria – shown in the ever-changing governments and the near impossibility of obtaining a parliamentary majority. The Heimwehr no longer posed a serious danger; it was rent by internal differences and paralysed by the fatal split in Styria and Carinthia. There the movement turned towards the rising star of National Socialism, and there were many defections from its ranks also in the other provinces. But the National Socialists depended on German support and were lagging behind the German party. The real question was whether the Dollfuss government would be able to maintain itself in power and what methods it would use to do so. Dollfuss was threatened by the Socialists on his left and by the National Socialists on his right, and he leant heavily on some of the para-military associations. All the efforts to achieve at least their disarmament ended in failure, and this was finally admitted by the Foreign Office. Even a small country so dependent on foreign help was able to flout the provisions of the Peace Treaty. It was a bad omen.

Notes

1. Phipps to Henderson, 9 January, 5 and 12 February and 31 August 1930: FO 371, file 14304, fo. 178, file 14311, fos. 2, 9, 42.
2. Selby to Simon, 21 July 1934: FO 371, file 18342, fo. 114.
3. Hadow to Simon, 21 July 1934: ibid., fos. 227-30.
4. Phipps to Henderson, 19 and 29 October 1929: FO 371, file 13564, fo. 76; DBFP, series IA, vii, no. 41, p. 77.
5. Phipps to Henderson, 29 May 1931: FO 371, file 15150, fo. 74 ff.
6. Snowden to Governor Bank of England, 15 June, Phipps to Henderson, 18 June, and minute by Sargent, 2 July 1931: FO 371, file 15151, fos. 9, 25 f.

7. Sir Frederick Leith Ross to FO, 28 May 1931: FO 371, file 15165, fo. 65 f.
8. Hadow to Sargent, 9 August, Sargent to Hadow, 11 August, and minute by Vansittart, 11 August 1931: FO 371, file 15152, fos. 59, 61, 67 ff.
9. Phipps to Sargent, 1 and 13 October, and to FO, 13 October 1931: FO 371, file 15153, fos. 168, 194, file 15154, fo. 11.
10. Phipps to Sargent, 27 October, and to Simon, 23 November 1931: FO 371, file 15154, fo. 109 ff., file 15155, fo. 31 f.
11. Phipps to Vansittart, 27 June, and to Simon, 5 February 1932: FO 120, files 1058 and 1059.
12. Phipps to Simon, 5 July, and Hadow to Simon, 5 September 1932: FO 371, file 15889, fo. 362, file 15890, fo. 124.
13. Phipps to FO, 20 July, and to Sargent, 21 March 1933: FO 371, file 16627, fos. 209 f., 218 ff.
14. Selby to Simon, 20 July 1933, and unsigned draft (presumably written by H. H. Hadow), 8 February 1933: FO 120, file 1072.
15. Leith Ross, Treasury, to FO, 10 June 1932: FO 800, file 287, fo. 100 ff.
16. Phipps to Simon, 20 February 1932: FO 371, file 15892, fos. 35–8.
17. Phipps to Sargent, 5 December 1929, discussion Henderson-Briand, 9 May, Henderson to Ayles (Labour MP), 5 May, and Phipps to Sargent, 22 May 1930: FO 371, file 13565, fo. 114, FO 120, file 1041, FO 800, file 281, fo. 216, FO 120, file 1037.
18. Phipps to Sargent, 12 June 1930: FO 120, file 1039.
19. Hadow to Henderson, 25 March, and Phipps to Henderson, 7 May 1931: FO 371, file 15159, fos. 24, 29, file 15162, fo. 28 ff. Cf. Zöllner, *Geschichte Österreichs*, pp. 509 f.
20. Phipps to Simon, 12 November 1931 and 8 February 1932; M.I.3.b. note of 1 February 1932: FO 120, file 1050, FO 371, file 15888, fo. 94 ff., WO 190, file 137.
21. Phipps to Henderson, 27 June 1931: FO 371, file 15151, fo. 39 f. In general, Zöllner, *Geschichte Österreichs*, p. 511.
22. Phipps to Simon, 30 May, and M.I.3.b report, 31 May 1932: FO 371, file 15888, fos. 118–22, WO 190, file 148.
23. 'Austria. Annual Report, 1932', pp. 14, 32; Phipps to Simon, 26 April 1932: FO 371, file 16640, fo. 2, file 15888, fo. 99 f.
24. Phipps to Simon, 26 April and 2 July 1932; 'Austria. Annual Report, 1932', p. 14: FO 120, file 1065, FO 371, file 15888, fo. 101, file 16640, fo. 2.
25. 'Austria. Annual Report, 1933', pp. 1–2: FO 371, file 18366, fo. 48.
26. 'Austria. Annual Report, 1933', p. 31: FO 371, file, 18366, fo. 48;

Carsten, *Fascist Movements in Austria*, pp. 196 f., 200 f., 220 f., 183 f., 214, 217.

27. Phipps to Henderson, 10 January 1931, 14 April 1930 and 26 June 1931: FO 120, file 1048, file 1043, FO 371, file 15166, fo. 76 f.

28. 'Austria. Annual Report, 1930', pp. 7–8: FO 371; file 15163, fo. 244.

29. Le Rougetel to Henderson, 6, 9, 16 and 22 January 1930: FO 120, file 1037, FO 371, file 14304, fos. 168 f., 207 f.

30. Phipps to Henderson, 2 April, 20 May 5 and 16 June 1930: FO 371, file 14305, fo. 267, file 14306, fos. 52, 122 f., 152.

31. Phipps to Sargent, 22 May 1930: FO 120, file 1037.

32. M.I.3.b report, 22 July; Phipps to Henderson, 4 September; memorandum by D. J. Cowan, 5 November, and Sargent to Phipps, 10 November 1931: WO 190, file 83, FO 371, file 14307, fo. 246 ff., FO 120, file 1055.

33. Phipps to Henderson, 6 and 23 October, and 14 November 1930: FO 371, file 14307, fo. 359 f., file 14308, fos. 52, 172 f.

34. Le Rougetel to Sargent, 11 December, and M.I.3.b report of 10 October 1930: FO 120, file 1046, WO 190, file 83.

35. *The Times*, 14–15 September; *Manchester Guardian*, 14–15 September 1931.

36. Hadow to Henderson, 14 September, to Lord Reading, 22 September, to Sargent, 4 November, and to Simon, 12 November 1931: FO 371, file 15156, fos. 94 f., 115, 152, 156.

37. 'Austria. Annual Report, 1931', pp. 35 ff.: FO 371, file 15892, fo. 153.

38. Reports by Lt.-Col. F. M. Mason-MacFarlane, 12 July 1932 and 28 April 1933: FO 120, files 1060 and 1073.

39. Phipps to Simon, 2 and 15 May 1933; 'Austria. Annual Report, 1933', p. 31: FO 371, file 16637, fos. 304 f., 376 f., file 18366, fo. 48.

40. Unsigned memorandum, 14 December 1932: FO 120, file 1067.

41. Phipps to Simon, 20 and 24 January, to Sargent, 23 January, to Simon, 11 February and minute by Vansittart, 27 February 1933: FO 371, file 16631, fos. 169 f., 172, 181 f., file 16633, fo. 452 f., file 16634, fo. 200 ff.

42. Reports by Lt.-Col. MacFarlane, 9 November 1932 and 30 September 1933: FO 120, files 1062 and 1071.

43. M.I.3.b comments on Austria, 23 September 1931 and 2–3 May 1933: WO 190, files 128, 191, 192.

44. Phipps to Henderson, 30 October 1930, and to Simon, 30 January 1933: FO 120, files 1040 and 1069.

45. Kirkpatrick to Vansittart, The Vatican, 19 August 1933: DBFP,

2nd series, v, 1956, no. 342, p. 524.

46.   Information on Austrian Communist Party, sent 28 July 1930, 11 April and 22 October 1931: FO 120, files 1045 and 1053.

6 Austria under Dollfuss, 1933-34

On 4 March 1933 parliamentary government came to an end in Austria - not by any deliberate act on the part of the Dollfuss government, but as if by accident. A special session of Parliament was called to discuss disciplinary measures against railwaymen who had taken part in a strike during the previous week. A socialist motion that they should not be punished was lost, and then a resolution put forward by the German Nationalists that they be treated leniently was declared carried by a majority of one vote by the chairman, Dr Renner. The government, however, wished to mete out severe punishments to the strikers and claimed that one vote was cast irregularly by a Socialist Deputy who had voted on behalf of an absent colleague and had to be disallowed. When Renner announced his decision such an uproar broke out that he resigned as chairman, and this was followed by the resignation of the two vice-chairmen who belonged to the bourgeois parties. As Phipps commented,

> this unique case of a triple hara-kiri by all its Presidents has placed the Chamber in a most awkward state of suspended animation, from which the legal luminaries of the Republic are now busily seeking to awaken it. Let us hope that they will evolve some graceful and constitutional solution whereby these successive suicides may perhaps be cancelled and parliamentary work resumed.

The emphasis may have been on the word 'perhaps', and the Minister's apprehension was only too justified. Five weeks before, Hitler had become Chancellor of Germany and Dollfuss was eager, not to find the solution desired by Phipps, but to exploit the opportunity that after the three resignations no one was entitled to summon Parliament. He intended to rid himself of an institution where his government depended on a majority of one, and to which he had to account for his measures: a requirement very much against his own inclinations. A few days later the government published a proclamation which suspended certain provisions of the Constitution and indicated that parliamentary government had come to an end – if not for good, at least for the time being.[1] This was followed by a decree banning all political meetings, and a further eleven decrees on economic and financial matters. As *The Times* put it, 'these measures show that it is in no hurry to return to parliamentary forms.'[2]

The decrees were promulgated on the basis of an enabling Act of 1917 which had not been revoked, and which clearly applied to the very different, war-time conditions. On 14 March a Foreign Office memorandum stated that

> Dollfuss has in effect carried through a *coup d'état* – though in such a way that with the usual adroitness of Austrian politicians he could no doubt easily make a return to normal Parliamentary procedure and merely claim that the Austrian Parliament had by its own folly stultified itself.

But the possibility existed that Hitler's advent to power (eight days later parliamentary government in Germany came to an end) 'will prove infectious to Austria' and that the Austrian National Socialists might stage a coup of their own, which would 'have the effect of bringing about such a close state of co-operation between the two countries as to be in practice indistinguishable from a legally constituted Anschluss', in which Mussolini 'in his infatuation for Herr Hitler might now be disposed to acquiesce'. Dollfuss was trying to rule without Parliament, relying on the army and the Heimwehr, apart from the moral support he received from his party, 'and the overriding fact that he hopes to obtain the promised Loan'. Would that support be sufficient 'if a sudden demand for the Anschluss were encouraged from abroad?'

At the end of March another government decree declared the Republican Defence League dissolved throughout Austria. The Vienna garrison paraded in strength through the streets, Phipps reported, 'but there was no disturbance of any kind'; and Hankey minuted that the socialists were 'of course in a weak position, because any physical opposition on their part would have played into the hands of the Nazis, whom they hate far worse than the

Government.' In April yet another emergency decree deprived the city of Vienna 'at one stroke of 22 million Schilling which, the latter body assert, is legally theirs'. The proportion according to which the proceeds of the 'common taxes' were divided between the central government and the provinces was fixed by law, but the decree reduced Vienna's share from 85 million provided for in the 1933 budget to 63 million Schilling – a measure which found the strong approval of the economic expert of the League, Rost van Tonningen, as essential for the maintenance of a balanced budget. As Phipps heard, the municipality appealed to the constitutional court against the decree.[3] Nine months previously the Social Democratic government of Prussia had appealed to the German constitutional court against its forcible removal from office by the von Papen government. It was a futile gesture, showing how helpless the Social Democrats were against a government determined to use force against them.

What the Austrian Social Democrats did do was to try to mobilise British and French support to achieve a convening of Parliament. When Walter Citrine, General Secretary of the TUC, visited Vienna to attend a socialist conference, he told Phipps that the French government intended to inform the Austrians 'that unless the Austrian Parliament were reassembled in full session without delay there would be no loan for Austria as far as France was concerned.' Paul-Boncour, the French Foreign Minister, was dictating a telegram to that effect when by chance the French Minister in Vienna walked into his office and was 'able to dissuade him from sending any such disastrous instructions'. Citrine, however, hoped that similar instructions would be sent by the British government, but Phipps 'pointed out what a grave error this would be'.

After his return to London Citrine wrote to Sir John Simon urging him to use his 'great influence with a view to inducing the Government to reassemble Parliament there and thus set working again the machinery of political democracy'. He also asked Simon to receive a small delegation from the TUC General Council, but this Simon declined to do. According to a Foreign Office minute, 'Phipps deprecates any intervention in Austrian affairs as likely to play into the hands of the Nazis & undermine the authority of Dr Dollfuss. It seems impossible to question the correctness of these views.'

In the autumn of 1933 the National Joint Council of the Labour Party and the trade unions recommended that 'the Governments should urge upon the Austrian Chancellor the due observance of the provisions of the peace treaties which guarantee freedom of association for the workers', and Citrine renewed his efforts to induce the British government to do something for the Austrian Social Democrats. But the Foreign Office opposed any such move. In a conversation with Citrine, Sargent, the head of the Central Department, impressed upon him

> the danger of British Socialists giving any encouragement in present circumstances to what might easily develop into a civil war in Austria.... The Austrian Socialists had to choose between the danger of a gradual whittling away of their rights and privileges by Dollfuss, or the prospect of a complete annihilation by Hitler.

If Dollfuss placated the socialists, 'he would lose the far more concrete support which he is at present receiving from Mussolini' who insisted on an anti-socialist policy: 'in his struggle to maintain the independence of Austria' Dollfuss should not be weakened. If the British left wanted to be helpful, 'the line they ought to take would be to work in favour of building a bridge between Dollfuss and the Austrian Socialists'. As Sargent noted, Citrine 'showed himself extremely reasonable and understanding'.[4] Given the growing influence of Mussolini in Austrian affairs, little could be done by British socialists or the Foreign Office to achieve a return to more democratic forms of government.

If the Foreign Office advised the Labour Party 'to work in favour of building a bridge between Dollfuss and the Austrian Socialists', the attempt would have been very one-sided: the question was whether Dollfuss was in favour of such a course. In June 1933 Phipps wrote: Dollfuss must resist 'the siren-like Socialist appeals' for a coalition or some form of collaboration, even if they were supported by President Miklas.

> Any serious flirtation with the hated Marxists would cause Dr Dollfuss' speedy downfall, for not only would it split his party, but it would cost him the loss of Italian support. It is noteworthy, in this connection, that my Italian colleague still regards the Socialists rather than the Nazis as the Chancellor's chief enemies, and the ones against whom his most vigorous blows should be directed.

Nor should Dollfuss follow the promptings of the Heimwehr and take unnecessarily violent measures against Socialist Vienna; he 'must not cease to regard with distrust the National Socialists', even if they offered concessions, 'honey to the Austrian fly':

> Thus we find Dr Dollfuss cast for an heroic part in an unheroic land, and surrounded by many unheroic friends. The path he treads narrows as he proceeds, the thorns grow thicker and the nettles, ambushes abound and sirens beckon on either side.

Some weeks earlier Phipps found Dollfuss preoccupied by the bad relations between Germany and Austria, and 'determined to show no weakness'. He dismissed his Minister of Education, Dr Rintelen, because he intrigued with the National Socialists; his successor would deal firmly with all students causing trouble. Dollfuss was determined to maintain order and was convinced that he could do so. The National Socialist Party and its affiliated organisations were dissolved, their offices occupied by the police, and all German agitators expelled from Austria. Among them was Theo Habicht, a prominent German National Socialist, who had been the effective head of the Austrian party;[5] as late as May, Dollfuss had negotiated with him about the possible entry of a few National Socialists into his government.

The most dangerous measure for Austria was the introduction by the Hitler government of a visa costing 1000 marks for all Germans visiting Austria, with the aim of ruining her vital tourist industry: the hoped-for result was the collapse of the Austrian economy and government. Shops were bombed, prominent politicians were physically assaulted, and acts of sabotage were organised. Yet in July 1933 Dollfuss assured the new British Minister, Sir Walford Selby (Phipps had been transferred to Berlin), 'that he had the Nazi movement in Austria itself well under control, and if it were not for the constant agitation from without, he would be relieved of all apprehension.' He felt convinced that, if Germany undertook 'anything in the nature of a "Putsch" against Austria', Mussolini would intervene. In the same month Dollfuss came to London and spoke to Vansittart about 'the persistent attempts of Germany to undermine Austrian independence'. These were taking three forms: 'extensive terrorism, dropping of seditious leaflets from German aeroplanes over Austrian territory, and persistent subversive broadcasting - particularly from Munich - inciting the Austrian people to resist the present Government'. The Austrian government felt entitled to ask for support: Britain should officially draw the attention of the German government to these outrages and ask it to stop them. An Intelligence report also stated that Dollfuss's position was weakened by the delay caused by the French government in the issue of the new loan by the League: 'Unless Dr Dollfuss can show some tangible results in the economic sphere, he can hardly hope to maintain his hold on the country.' The longer the elections were delayed, the more certain was a National Socialist victory, 'if the Hitler regime in Germany proves a success', unless there was a considerable improvement 'in Austria's fundamentally unsound economic situation'. Dollfuss was 'fighting with his back to the wall'. Yet another commentator from Military Intelligence found this assessment of Dollfuss's chances 'unduly rosy', for 'a general election today would probably return the Nazis to power' – a large number of the police sympathised with them, as did many junior officers and other ranks of the army: 'if Dollfuss is expecting National Socialism soon to be discredited in Germany, he is taking an extraordinarily unrealistic view of the situation.'[6]

In a memorandum written for the Cabinet, Sir John Simon also stated that Dollfuss intended 'to rule until the National Socialists have discredited themselves in Germany (which he hopes will be soon) and to put off holding new elections till then.' The position was complicated by the fact that the French socialists had persuaded their government to tell Dollfuss that the loan would not be forthcoming unless he reintroduced parliamentary government; but more recently they were beginning to relax their opposition to the loan, for they saw that this would play into the National Socialists' hands. On 7 June the French government decided to agree to the issue of the French tranche, but they still wished to give priority to certain credit operations of their own and hoped to issue the Austrian loan later, possibly only in the autumn. If Dollfuss did not secure the promised loan soon, 'the survival of his Government for any length of time is, to say the least, problematical.' If his government fell, in the turmoil the National Socialists would probably gain power either through an election or by other means.

To assist Dollfuss the British government desired a tripartite approach to Berlin, and in July a note was sent to Paris and Rome suggesting mediation of the three powers in the Austro-German conflict. The British government was seriously worried about Germany's attitude towards Austria, its aim was to strengthen the confidence in peace, and to terminate the present state of insecurity and the inciting of the Austrian people against their government. Mussolini, however, opposed such a joint *démarche* and instructed his ambassador in Berlin to communicate the text of the British note confidentially to the Auswärtige Amt. What Mussolini had in mind, the ambassador said, was a German assurance that the activities listed in the British note would be stopped, possibly by an arrangement between Germany and Austria. Any joint pressure in Berlin was thus out of the question, and when the Anglo-French *démarche* finally took place in August 1933 it was rejected by the Hitler government.[7]

In the same month the British chargé d'affaires reported from Vienna that it was difficult to judge 'the shifting trends of sympathy among the peasant and small town population, whose main characteristic ... is antagonism to everything savouring of "red" Vienna'. The official press carried accounts of enthusiastic receptions of Dollfuss and other members of the government, 'but even in Vienna there is a feeling of nervous unrest', and in Salzburg the authorities had to resort to 'increasingly stern measures', apparently 'against a very considerable proportion of the population'. This was borne out by the severe sentences 'meted out for any form of National-Socialist activity', or for 'activities subversive of the Roman Catholic Church' – a new offence which had been added to the previous list. The opposition claimed that this policy of repression was 'alienating the sympathy of increasing numbers of the population'.

When the report reached London it was considered in the Foreign Office as 'hardly encouraging'; 'its perusal leads one to wonder whether the battle for Austria is not lost from the start.' Another official minuted: 'This is an unpromising picture. I have always felt we were backing a loser.' A week later the chargé d'affaires added that the Dollfuss government could not 'be said to govern by consent of the governed'; the most that could be said was that a considerable percentage was apathetic, while at least 60–75 per cent (Socialists and National Socialists in about equal numbers) were 'secretly hostile but can be cowed if no outside assistance can reach them'. Dollfuss had to be considered 'as

Fascist linked for the time being to Italy'; he would attempt to organise the Heimwehr on the lines of a fascist militia, with arms and instruction provided by Italy. This was supported by the League's representative in Austria, Rost van Tonningen, 'who is now an ardent and avowed Fascist' and who was implicitly trusted by Dollfuss.[8]

The British military attaché in Vienna told the Foreign Office officials at the same time that there was 'no enthusiasm for the Dollfuss régime'; originally Dollfuss relied on the support of the peasants throughout Austria, but it was doubtful whether this was still the case, in particular with regard to the younger peasants and to those who were suffering from the consequences of cutting off German tourism and from the German boycott of Austrian timber. But when Dollfuss met Sir John Simon at Geneva in September, he was full of optimism, and stated rather surprisingly 'that he now felt he could depend on the support of the youth of his country; in particular a large section of the younger supporters of the Christian Socialist Party had transferred their allegiance to him.' When the Foreign Secretary mentioned reports in the British press that the regime was developing into a dictatorship which would diminish his support in Britain, Dollfuss replied that he 'was obliged to make the fullest use of all the forces at his disposal' in the battle he was fighting. He begged Simon to use his influence and not to attach too much importance 'to the details of his policy, i.e., whether they represented a tendency somewhat more to the Right one day or somewhat more to the Left another'.

Dollfuss's claim was echoed by Mussolini: until now the older generation were all for Dollfuss, but now he 'made a special appeal' to the younger generation, the students and others, and 'had greatly reinforced his position by [the] new form of government he had installed'. In supporting him, Mussolini asserted, the powers were not necessarily fighting a 'losing battle'. But the new 'corporative' form of government remained a scheme on paper only. When Mussolini received the Zionist leader, Chaim Weizmann, he was 'openly and strongly anti-German' and 'very resentful of Hitler's persecution of the Jews'. According to a British diplomat's report he even told Weizmann that, by persecuting the Jews, Hitler was 'equally attacking the roots of Christianity.'[9]

Meanwhile Mussolini's influence was growing in Austria and the pressure to take action against Vienna and the socialists was increasing. In late August 1933 Selby wrote: 'Dr Dollfuss has returned from his visit to Riccione [where he had met Mussolini] in a very optimistic mood, an optimism which is justified so far as Italy is concerned.' By agreement with Mussolini, Dr Rintelen, 'a very lukewarm and uncertain supporter', was removed to Rome; internally, 'the danger might be lest Dr Dollfuss at Italian inspiration should be led into taking measures against the Socialists'. The steps so far taken against the municipality of Vienna could be justified 'on grounds of purely economic necessity', but any exceptional measures taken against the Social Democrat Party might drive the young into the arms of the National Socialists. It would be a great mistake if Dollfuss, under the influence of Mussolini, made concessions to Germany, for the support he enjoyed in Austria 'lies in the fact that he stands for Austrian independence of "Prussia", an age-long bone of contention between Berlin and Vienna'. Two weeks later, Selby noted that the reception given to Dollfuss at every recent public appearance was 'most deeply impressive, foreigners and English who have mixed with the crowds being ready to testify to the spontaneity of the welcome'. He thought this was partly due to Dollfuss's personality, partly to the support given by the Catholic Church and the close association with a Catholic festival, partly to the fact that he held the reins of government and the powerful backing he was credited with. All this would 'lead to the surmise that the same crowds who have so acclaimed Dr Dollfuss might be ready to cry "Heil Hitler" with equal enthusiasm were Germany to be generally believed to be the winning horse.' Five years later this prophecy was to be proved true.

When the British Minister met Renner at about the same time the latter confirmed 'that it was Italy who at the moment constituted the danger'; she was 'assisting the constitution of a Fascist-Hitlerite bloc across Europe', which ultimately would lead to war. Renner also affirmed that, if the government continued its anti-socialist policy, 'the only effect must be to drive a large section of the adherents of the Socialist party into the ranks of the Nazis'. All that his party asked for was to be left alone, yet the government took one measure after the other against Vienna; it seemed bent on 'driving the Socialists to desperation', and the 'feeling among the workers was becoming embittered in the extreme'.[10]

Yet Dollfuss never wavered from his anti-socialist course. Like the Church, he saw 'Marxism' as his principal enemy and was oblivious of the fact that his policy was bound to weaken any common stand against the German threat. At the beginning of 1934 Selby learned 'from a reliable source' that Dollfuss intended to appoint a government commission for Vienna and to suppress the Social Democratic Party and trade unions, but was unable to obtain confirmation of this from either the French or the Czechoslovak Legation. A few days later he went with Edgar Granville, Simon's Parliamentary Private Secretary, to see Dollfuss, and Granville reminded Dollfuss of Simon's remarks at Geneva on the subject of the Austrian socialists in which the Labour Party took a strong interest. Dollfuss replied 'that the Nazis would be the only beneficiaries' if he tried at this moment to reach a compromise with the socialists. The Labour Party was 'a national party'; it did not see the difference between them and the Austrian socialists who 'were far more extreme than their British sympathisers, cared in reality little for the independence of their country, and were anti-religious and subversive from every point of view.' He expressly thanked Granville for Simon's statement in the House of Commons in December that the British government did not intend to interfere in Austrian internal affairs which 'had given him great satisfaction'. Selby declared that his government wished to give him the fullest support possible and did not want to weaken that support by a division in British public opinion; he 'was grateful to the Chancellor ... for the moderation which ... he had endeavoured to display in dealing with his Austrian Socialist opponents.' Granville added that Dollfuss 'need not be unduly alarmed' about the attitude of the Labour Party, for the principal concern of all British parties was 'that nothing should be allowed to occur which would be detrimental to the interests of Austria'. This was giving Dollfuss the green light for any further measures against the socialists contemplated by him, although that may not have been the intention of his visitors.

Selby was fully aware of Dollfuss's 'deep-seated and personal dislike – due in part to his peasant origin and country connections – for "red" Vienna. He wrote at the same time: 'In view of the uncompromising hostility of the peasantry and Heimwehr' to anything savouring of socialism, any agreement Dollfuss might reach with the socialists would mean 'committing political suicide'. What he might achieve would be to draw some of them into his 'Patriotic Front', instead of letting them drift into the Nazi camp – which was what his opponents claimed.[11] What was never mentioned was the likelihood that some ardent socialists might join the Communist Party.

In January 1934 Fulvio Suvich, Under-Secretary of State in the Italian Foreign Office, visited Vienna and told Selby that he regarded the present political system in Austria 'as out of date': 'it must be "renovated" and a new basis found.' The Italians held that Austrian independence must be defended; it would be threatened whether Hitler directly established his authority in Vienna, or 'through pressure ... brought into power Austrian Nazi administration'. Another British diplomat was informed by Suvich a few days later that the socialist administration of Vienna was one of the causes of Austria's weakness – a view shared by the representative of the League, Rost van Tonningen. This institution ought to be removed. Suvich 'considered that it was absolutely necessary for Herr Dollfuss to move towards the Right'. From other sources we know that Suvich insisted on the elimination of political parties and 'red' Vienna and a constitutional reform after the Italian model, while Dollfuss was still hesitating.[12] The scene was set for the events of February 1934.

On 12 February 1934 units of the Republican Defence League in Linz repelled a search for weapons by the police, the socialists proclaimed a general strike, and fierce fighting broke out in Vienna, Linz, Steyr and the towns of Upper Styria, between their para-military units and government forces supported by the Heimwehr. But the general strike was a complete failure and the fighting remained limited to a few towns, where the army and police quickly gained the upper hand. As *The Times* correspondent reported from Vienna on the next day, 'except when prevented by fighting round their homes or by the absence of trams, the bulk of public and private employees went quietly to work. The electricity supply was restored to all private consumers by mid-day.' The *Manchester Guardian* stated that railway and telephone services had been restored, but the streets were in darkness and the theatres and cafés closed.

The next day Dollfuss told the British Minister that he had been taken completely by surprise; in the morning he heard of the trouble at Linz, but of the declaration of the general strike only at midday: 'thereafter government had no alternative but to meet the challenge.' In Berlin Hitler informed the French Ambassador that 'Dr Dollfuss has behaved with criminal stupidity in firing on Socialist workmen and women and children. His hands were now stained with the blood of his own people and he would very soon fall and be replaced by a National Socialist Government.'[13] By 15 February order had been restored in Vienna; 'even Floridsdorf, the scene of the fiercest fighting of all, is now outwardly calm, with its shops open, its streets full, and its trams running.'[14]

The government proclaimed martial law. The Social Democratic Party was declared illegal and the party's control of Vienna was terminated, the municipal council and the Vienna district councils were dissolved. The green and white Heimwehr flag was hoisted on the Town Hall. This was followed by the dissolution of the Free trade unions, of all socialist professional and educational societies, cooperatives and banks, sports and singing clubs, and social and welfare organisations. Their funds were confiscated and continuation of their activities declared illegal, as *The Times* reported. A leader in the paper stated that Dollfuss's journey to Budapest seemed to present to his fascist supporters 'a favourable opportunity for pressing for changes which the Chancellor is known to have been reluctant to make': 'in various places, as if by a concerted signal', the Heimwehr forces had demanded 'authoritarian' government, and in four provinces they raised the specific demand that all political parties must disappear. It was the deliberate policy of the Heimwehr leaders to eliminate the socialists, 'just as they had been eliminated in Italy and Germany'. A leader in the *Manchester Guardian* declared that Dolfuss had 'sold himself to a minute and violent faction'

that faction may rejoice in its victory for Austro-Fascism; it may not know it, but it has struck a great blow for Nazidom.... The search at Linz succeeded, and the Heimwehr have attained their aim.... But when these 'Putschists' have achieved their Pyrrhic victory, where is Austria?[15]

In the Foreign Office it was stated that Selby 'tells us the facts
... but he does not tell us what we want to know viz. (1) Have
Austrian Government received assurances of moral and material
support from Italians for this campaign against the Socialists? (2)
Has Dr Dollfuss completely capitulated to the Heimwehr?' E. H.
Carr (later renowned as an historian) added another minute:

> It is now possible to form some idea of the genesis of the Vienna
> Putsch. It has been evident for some time that the Heimwehr, and in
> particular the Vice-Chancellor, Fey, were bent on action.... It
> seems, therefore, clear that the Italian Government, which for two or
> three months has been lukewarm about the Heimwehr and had cut
> off most of its subsidies, recently changed its mind again and decided
> to put its money on the Heimwehr. The present events in Vienna are
> probably the direct consequence of this decision.

It seemed to be established 'with reasonable certainty' that the
Italians were responsible for the events, that the measures had
been 'in course of preparation for some days or even weeks and
had nothing to do with the alleged declaration of a general strike
or other provocation received from the Socialists on February
12th.'[16] This was quite true.

With regard to the fighting itself, a memorandum by the
Legation's First Secretary written from personal observation
stated that the bombardment was restricted 'to small portions of
the immense area covered by each of the blocks of flats' and that
there had been no 'rain of shells', as had been claimed. On the
other hand, 'the flats were in no sense fortresses or even able to
resist the most modest shelling from mountain guns', and
'resistance was sporadic and easily overcome once shelling
started'. The exceptional thinness of the walls of the Goethehof
'afforded so little cover as to render the flats quite untenable
when shelled'; its defendants apparently had 'no taste for
fighting and no knowledge whatever of machine-gun strategy or
methods of fighting and emplacement'. Yet the Goethehof was
the scene of the strongest resistance. The British military attaché
also visited the Vienna 'fronts' and found damage 'confined to
the big modern socialist tenements'. He thought the 'conduct of
Bundesheer and police exemplary but Heimwehr considerably
less valuable'. The disturbances in the provinces, at Linz, Graz,

Bruck, etc., 'never assumed serious proportions'; in his opinion, the people in the provinces were 'on the whole well pleased at the downfall of the Reds.'

The British consul at Innsbruck confirmed 'that the Government's position in the Provinces has been strengthened for the time being by their drastic onslaught' upon the socialists. The only fighting in the Tyrol had been at Wörgl, where a detachment of the Republican Defence League resisted a search for weapons by the gendarmes. In Innsbruck the Social Democrats attempted to proclaim a general strike, but 'the vast majority of the workers shewed no sympathy with the project and the police arrested the ringleaders'; business life was normal. In Carinthia there were no disturbances at all and the Social Democrats' attitude was 'wholly constitutional'; the mayor of Klagenfurt and another prominent socialist had resigned from the party declaring that they could not associate themselves 'with any policy disturbing public order'.

The annual Report of the Legation for 1934 stated that the 'greater part of the real work of restoring order had been carried out by the regular army and police'. In spite of this, the Heimwehr forces were 'able to arrogate to themselves most of the publicity and the glory', but earned the bitter hatred of their opponents by 'their harsh methods'. Workmen 'whose political orthodoxy was open to suspicion were liable to instant dismissal without compensation', and the Socialist Workmen's Bank was liquidated by methods 'which hit its investors very hard'.[17]

Before the fighting in Vienna had ended Ramsay MacDonald and Sir John Simon instructed Selby to see Dollfuss and to impress upon him 'the bad effect likely to be produced on British public opinion by the excesses against Socialists', for example, by the use of artillery against blocks of flats. Dollfuss claimed 'that he was demonstrating to the German Nazis that he could keep order' in his own country, but in the eyes of the British government he had become involved in civil strife. In the House of Commons Simon emphasised once more that the government 'had no intention whatever of interfering in the internal affairs of another country.' But in the British press there was an outcry which completely bewildered Dollfuss. The Secretaries of the Labour Party and the TUC, Henderson and Citrine, called on Simon to discuss the events in Austria and were informed that the government had expressed the earnest hope that a policy of clemency and appeasement would be adopted.[18]

The expression of this pious hope did not prevent the execution of savage sentences against those caught fighting. As *The Times* put it, 'with the crushing of the Socialists Austria is now set on a Fascist course.' The paper explained the recent events by 'the utter incompatibility between a Vienna governed by advanced free-thinking Socialists and an Austrian countryside dominated by pious Roman Catholics and other equally staunch enemies of Marxism. The two are poles apart; they have never met and never could meet.'[19]

In the Foreign Office later in February, E. H. Carr wrote a memorandum, 'The Austrian Problem', in which he stated: 'the present Heimwehr, the sole effective authority remaining in Austria, is in effect, a force of mercenaries in Italian pay. It is difficult to see how a régime established on this basis can either be stable or durable.' He concluded:

> Independent Austria is dead, and the heir to her estate must be either Italy or Germany.... In Austria itself, the Italian solution is supported only by the machine-guns of the mercenary Heimwehr, and cannot therefore have the stability of the German solution.... If the German solution is recognised as eventually inevitable, the sooner it comes the better.

Economically, neither the one nor the other solution 'would, in all probability, be inimical to British interests', but economically too 'the German solution offers in the long run the greater prospects of stability.'

Several senior officials, however, added minutes criticising these conclusions. Sargent did not believe in the inevitability of Austria's absorption by Germany: Carr had not taken into account the 'strong forces working against it', and he referred to the example of Belgium 'which was created in 1830 as a completely artificial entity' so that its absorption by France appeared 'inevitable' for a long time. The absorption of Austria, he continued, 'would constitute an absolutely new step forward in Germany's policy of aggression and a spectacular achievement'; it would result in 'a policy of truculence on the part of Germany and of truckling under on the part of the Powers of Central Europe, in which I would include Italy', and soon France and Britain would begin to feel its effects.

With this assessment Vansittart agreed: 'This picture of German hegemony is certainly a disquieting one. I remain one of those simple persons who prefer a 13 stone Germany to a 15 stone Germany – for she would put on another stone or two later on, on the strength of this.' Finally Sir John Simon wrote: 'I am not sure that a 17 stone Germany might not prove more ponderous & easy to deal with than a 13 stone & hungry Germany, but I don't relish the idea of all the satellite nations (including Italy) flocking to her assistance as the big boy who might then feel impelled to throw his weight about.'[20] All the anticipations were to be proved more or less correct within a few years, but there was no suggestion what Britian should do to prevent the growth of German power.

When Dollfuss visited Rome in March 1934, the Italian government spared no effort to make the visit a success, the British ambassador reported. In press interviews Dollfuss insisted that the large majority of Austrians 'regarded Parliament with ever-increasing distrust and often openly demanded a radical reform of the political system'. The Social Democrats had tried to oppose this general tendency and 'sought to seize power by violence', but this had only interrupted the government's work for a few days; 'the new constitution would be on a corporative basis' and there would be one single official trade union. From Vienna Selby commented that provincial autonomy had been effectively destroyed by the removal of all provincial governments and their replacement by authoritarian ones; the provincial governors elected with socialist support had been forced to resign; the new governors of Upper Austria and Burgenland were members of the 'Patriotic Front', with Deputies from the ranks of the Heimwehr, and such Deputies were also appointed in Lower Austria and Salzburg. In social questions the fascist trend was equally evident, and the trade unions were to be transformed along 'Christian, Patriotic Front lines'. The recruits joining the Heimwehren or the Christian Social *Ostmärkische Sturmscharen* were 'raw callow youths or obvious unemployed'. Only one thing seemed certain: 'for the moment Dr Dollfuss is, either willingly or unwillingly, in the hands of the Heimwehr and a tool of Fascism'; but he might gradually 'disentangle himself from an entanglement which he clearly knows is irksome to his people.... I see no other leader in Austria able or willing to continue the fight against Germany.' Selby therefore believed that it was to Britain's advantage 'to give him all possible and practical economic support', for Germany obviously relied on economic pressure to crush him without having to use arms. He doubted whether Italian support or the 'regeneration' of Austria along fascist lines could prevail for long against such economic pressure. But he was told that in his present embittered mood Dollfuss felt he could count on practical help only from Rome.[21]

Economic support for Austria had been discussed in London before the events of February, but the result was extremely meagre. In January 1934 the Austrian Minister addressed an urgent appeal to Simon on the basis of a request by his government: 'it is of the utmost importance that the economic position of the country should be improved and unemployment lessened' because every sign of distress was exploited by the government's enemies to weaken the confidence of the people: 'it is a matter of life and death for Austria that her trade should increase' as she had to pay by exports for her imports of raw materials and food. Franckenstein asked whether it would be possible to grant preference to Austria, on condition that the countries with which Britain had most-favoured-nation treaties raised no serious objections.

The Austrians proposed sending a very senior civil servant to London to discuss this, and Simon wrote to Walter Runciman, President of the Board of Trade, and pleaded for economic concessions to Austria. Runciman's reply was entirely negative. He was 'convinced that in fact there are definitely no tariff concessions of a generalised nature which our present commercial policy would allow us to offer to Austria.' He objected even more strongly to a preferential agreement with Austria which 'would put us completely at loggerheads with our industrialists ... and would be attacked by all critics of our policy of supporting Austria, and, I have no doubt, by the Dominions.' He could not agree 'to the Austrians being encouraged in any way to think that they will be able to negotiate an agreement with us'. If it was desirable for political reasons to receive the envoy from Vienna, he would not object 'on condition that he clearly understands that we see no possibility of the discussions with him or any subsequent discussions resulting in a trade agreement with Austria.' In the Foreign Office Sargent minuted: 'Mr Runciman does not budge a single inch on the question of tariff preference, and ignores our suggestion that as regards timber we might ask the Canadian Government to relax the strict letter of the Ottawa Agreement' to allow the import of Austrian timber. Meanwhile the Austrian envoy was sitting in Paris waiting for an invitation to come to London: 'I do not think we can possibly adopt Mr Runciman's suggestion and tell Baron Franckenstein that we have made up our minds, without even hearing the Austrian experts, that we can do nothing for Austria': the matter ought to be taken to the Cabinet. Vansittart added that this must be done immediately: 'we cannot consent to the risk of setting Central Europe alight, because the Board of Trade shrink from putting a reasonable point to the Canadian Government. Why should they?'[22]

On 31 January 1934 the matter was discussed by the Cabinet. Simon declared: 'It might be that the assistance we could give would not make much difference in the long run, but if Austria should turn Nazi we ought to be in a position to show that we had done all that was possible to avert it.' He had written to the French and Italian governments enquiring what they could do, and they asked 'the same question of us, pointing out that they had already done what they could.' He suggested that Canada might be willing to offer in a new agreement some relaxation on timber. The meeting was told, however, that no concession on timber would be of any use unless Austria was allowed a preferential tariff which would require Canadian consent. The agreement with Canada had been reached with great difficulty, and any concession to help Austria would require some further concession by Britain – 'Austrian timber was of not much use here, and the amount we could take would be so small as not to affect the question.' Runciman then said he could offer help only with regard to 'velour hats, which he mentioned to show how little could be done. Our imports from Austria were down to a very low level.' It sounded like a bad joke.

The Chancellor of the Exchequer, Neville Chamberlain, admitted that not much could be done but urged that something should be offered: 'We should express our willingness to waive our most-favoured-nation rights under any Treaty that Austria might make with any other Power, and especially Poland'; that 'would give some moral help, and set an example to France and Italy, who were in a position to do more, economically, than we could.' The burden could thus be shifted onto different shoulders. The Cabinet then agreed that the Austrian special envoy was to be invited to come, and that 'in certain circumstances and for a limited time our most-favoured-nation rights would not be claimed.'

The envoy was received at the Board of Trade early in February and made several suggestions. But the civil servants concerned explained to him 'the impracticability of the detailed suggestions put forward'. In the end he was asked whether he had 'any further suggestions which he would like us to consider and he indicated that he had not.' But he did not yet admit defeat and mentioned certain Austrian exports: if Britain agreed to grant to Austria preferences on these items, this would be communicated to the countries with which Britain had most-favoured-nation agreements; if they raised objections the agreement would lapse. This, Vansittart thought, was 'a fair proposal' which should be carefully considered. To Runciman he wrote that the envoy 'should at any rate not be sent away with a blank negative. If it is impossible to meet his desires at this stage, the door should at any rate not be closed to the resumption of negotiations at a future date.'[23] To this Runciman finally agreed. With that result the envoy had to return to Vienna, and the efforts of the Foreign Office came to an end.

During the same month the Cabinet also discussed what could be done for Austria in the political field – but with equally negative results. Simon explained how serious National Socialist propaganda was, and that there was 'a prospect of Austria becoming Nazi and of a union between the two States'. Britain had appealed to Mussolini for joint action, but he preferred to try his best in Berlin – without any result: 'the trouble was that we could do nothing concrete.' The Dominions Secretary, J. H. Thomas, suggested that more ought to be done to win the cooperation of Italy as her separate efforts in Berlin had failed. Could the French not be induced to do more?: 'It was no use bluffing the Germans, but public opinion here would not stand a war with Germany.' The Home Secretary, John Gilmour, said that 'if we were not getting France or Italy to march', nothing was to be done. Could they not be asked to consider a boycott or similar action? The Minister of Agriculture, W. Elliot, mentioned that the Committee of Imperial Defence were just finishing an inquiry into the question of a boycott of Germany by the League and that their conclusion was to doubt very strongly whether it would be effective. It would certainly be very costly to Britain, and sanctions 'could not be effective without belligerent operations'. Simon suggested the tourist traffic to Austria should be further encouraged: 'it was a very pleasant place for a holiday.' But MacDonald replied 'that the attempt to stimulate the tourist industry had not been a success, owing to the volume of the normal German tourist traffic' – which Hitler had stopped. The Prime Minister also asked: 'What would be the cost if the Austrian affair led to serious consequences? ... If political influence did not prove sufficient, what would?' All that emerged from the discussion was a suggestion that the problem should be explored further in the Foreign Office and that a draft note should be put before the Ministerial Committee on Disarmament.[24]

In a memorandum written at the same time, Simon stated that so far Dollfuss had 'always declared that he could not appeal to the League against his "brother German"'. That he now threatened to do so 'shows how desperate his position has suddenly become'. If Austria took the issue to Geneva, it could not be avoided 'however severe a strain it may put upon the League in its present debilitated condition'. But Simon was in favour of giving the Italians 'another chance, and if they refuse to co-operate the situation will have to be considered further on the basis of Anglo-French co-operation.'

All these documents show how helpless the government felt in the face of the German threat, how little it was prepared to do for Austria. In August 1933 Vansittart had written:

there can be little doubt that Dr Dollfuss, on whom Austrian independence now hangs, cannot survive the attacks of his opponents, within and without, nor check the demoralisation produced by the threats and intrigues of German agents in Austria, unless he can point to some economic improvement as the outward and visible sign of the support of his foreign sympathisers.[25]

But where were these visible signs? In July 1933 the Foreign Office was informed that Austria's foreign trade had 'decreased in value by almost exactly 50 per cent' since 1931.[26] Her survival must indeed have seemed doubtful, on political as well as on economic grounds.

Internally, the Austrian 'authoritarian' regime rested on three main pillars – the Church and its associations, the army and police, and the Heimwehr, in so far as its members had not joined the National Socialists. The Legation's Annual Report for 1934 stated succinctly: 'The pervading influence of the Roman Catholic Church in all branches of public life is one of the most striking characteristics of present-day Austria', but it was resented by the Heimwehr, 'particularly in the field of education, where the latter would prefer to see military and Fascist influences prevail.' In May, Selby reported on a 'severe "combing" of teachers' as a result of the Concordat which had recently been signed. Preference and promotion now depended on the endorsement of candidates by the Church. Medical experts complained 'that the profession of faith now takes preference over professional proficiency and that victimisation is rampant'. Similar 'murmurs' came from the legal profession; good evidence existed 'that this discontent is being exploited to its full by the Nazi propagandists.' Late in 1934 he wrote again about purges in the professions for 'political tendencies hostile to the Government', which, it was contended, 'is really part of the Catholic campaign for rooting out unorthodoxy and liberalism'. The government 'in its Catholicity' did not see the importance of conciliating these groups. The British consul at Innsbruck mentioned a conversation with a nationalist on local Catholic activity, who described it as 'part of the battle of the twentieth-century Counter-Reformation'. The struggle between the government and the Church in Germany was affecting western Austria, where pro-German feeling often went hand in hand with free-thinking.[27] But it also has to be remembered that the 'Catholicity' of the government rallied considerable support to it in the countryside.

Among the pro-governmental para-military associations the Heimwehr was still by far the strongest. A Military Intelligence note of September 1933 estimated its strength at 40,000, 'well armed, trained and organised', compared with about 6000 of the

Frontkämpferverband, about 1000 of the *Freiheitsbund* (linked to the official trade unions) and about 15,000 of the *Bauernwehren* (peasant units). No figure was given for the Christian Social *Ostmärkische Sturmscharen* which consisted of youths 'of or under university age'. The question, however, was how reliable the Heimwehr men were. Two senior army officers interviewed by the British military attaché were convinced that many of the 'rank and file were very unreliable and quoted many instances of Heimwehr men both in Vienna and Graz who were known... as being openly engaged in Nazi activities.'

Early in 1934 this opinion was surprisingly confirmed when the leader of the Lower Austrian Heimwehr, Count Alberti, whose 'Nazi intrigues... have long been notorious', was arrested in the flat of the National Socialist *Gauleiter* of Vienna, engaged in secret negotiations with a German diplomat. Starhemberg was forced to dismiss Alberti as provincial leader. As the Lower Austrian Heimwehr was 'one of the most important sections' of the Heimwehr and as Alberti had 'great influence' there, Selby considered this incident significant.

In February 1934 his own opinion was that the Heimwehr 'is a scattered, ill-disciplined, jealous conglomeration of ill-assorted elements very sensitive to local feeling'; if the rank and file should find their pro-Italian stance unpopular, as they were bound to do in the long run, neither they nor their leaders would make 'a stand for Rome against Munich', but 'like most Austrians, they have little stomach for Berlin'. From the British embassy in Rome it was reported in July 1933 that, 'as a result of Dr Dollfuss' visit to Rome', Italian contributions to the Heimwehr were resumed; no doubt Dollfuss had explained to Mussolini 'the full extent of the Nazi danger in Austria' and hence this decision. In August it was noted that the Italians were sending supplies of rifles and machine guns to the Heimwehr.[28] Indeed, the Italians had supported it for many years, but all their investments produced very poor results. Why they were continued nevertheless, has never been explained.

An issue which exercised British diplomats from time to time was whether the new Austrian regime was anti-Semitic. In August 1933 Neville Laski from the Board of Deputies of British Jews wrote to Vansittart that he had received information from three responsible members of the Vienna Jewish community that

Dollfuss was pursuing an anti-Semitic policy, although Jews had given 500,000 Schilling to his party. A *numerus clausus* was operating against Jewish doctors and medical students, and the *Reichspost* was advising patients not to go to Jewish doctors. From Vienna Selby confirmed in 1934 that the government's 'private and party funds, Heimwehr charities and endless similar organisations' depended on Jewish subscriptions – a fact giving 'an additional strength to Austrian Jewry'. Yet he also reported that Dollfuss was subject 'to strong anti-Jewish pressure by the more rabid clerical elements', and that in the provinces 'exaggerated murmurings' could be heard of the government having 'sold itself to Jewry'. These unfortunately blended 'with the unreasoning anti-Jewish hatred of the officer and other professional classes ... prone to believe any fantastic tale spread about by interested parties of the Jewish domination of the medical, dental, and legal profession.' Two members of the government, Major Fey and Prince Schönburg-Hartenstein, were 'violently anti-Jewish', as was Starhemberg, although he was indebted 'up to the neck' to Jews, and was a close friend of the industrialist Fritz Mandl. In the Vienna Heimwehr, on the other hand, there was 'a not unnoticeable sprinkling of Jews and the Jews have been successful, of late, in obtaining concessions such as the supply of medicines for public hospitals.' Most Jews were aware, the report continued, that 'the pivot of the Austrian merry-go-round is still the diminutive Chancellor'. The future of the Austrian Jews therefore depended largely upon his ability 'to retain office without having to compromise with Nazidom or with the blind elements of this country'.

In another report Selby stated that there was 'deep anxiety' in Jewish circles as to the government's intention to limit the percentage of Jews in the professions. Eventually the Foreign Office suggested Selby should use a favourable opportunity to draw the attention of the Austrian authorities to the strong sympathies of British Jews with the Jews in other countries and 'to the obvious fact that discrimination' against the Austrian Jews would weaken the sympathies with Austria in Britain and the support she was given. Unless that would seriously harm his influence in Vienna, 'it would be worth saying something on these lines'.[29]

No record seems to exist whether the mission was

accomplished in this form and, if so, with what results. But in November 1934 the First Secretary of the British Legation asked the Austrian Foreign Minister, Baron Berger-Waldenegg, to provide him with information on the policy of the government towards the Jews, which would also be of interest to Jewish circles in Britain, and particularly to Neville Laski. Berger-Waldenegg assured him 'that anti-Semitism was no part of the Government's programme' and asked him to invite Laski to visit Vienna and to discuss 'any further difficulties which might at any time preoccupy the Jewish community'. As the Secretary reported to London, the Foreign Minister was 'first and foremost a strong Heimwehr partisan' and he therefore saw in this invitation 'a hopeful sign of competition' between the Heimwehr and the Christian Social wing of the government for Jewish support. The Heimwehr leaders were 'frankly anti-Semitic and prejudiced', their 'upbringing, leanings and dependence upon Jewish money-lenders' had made many of them hostile to Jews, and the Jews had more to expect from the Christian Social side of the 'present coalition'. But anti-Semitism 'is apt to be fanned by the more bigoted authorities in this country, and is a convenient line of retreat for unscrupulous politicians who may desire to make their peace with Germany'. Jewish business men were 'subjected by needy politicians to every form of impost and unofficial exaction' and would suffer heavily, but on the other hand gain some benefit by being able 'to decrease wages and lengthen hours without possibility of effective protest from the working class'. Some of them accepted Heimwehr demands for the replacement of socialists by followers of the government, and for this the Jewish community 'will pay a heavy price in increased anti-Semitism among the working classes'. As far as the writer could judge, 'a hard time, therefore, lies ahead for the Jewish community.'

The Foreign Office passed on to Laski Berger-Waldenegg's 'cordial invitation ... to call upon him personally and expound frankly any difficulties' facing the Austrian Jews,[30] but there is no record of such a visit. As far as the Austrian government was concerned, the measures taken against the Jews were of a comparatively mild variety at a time when anti-Semitism in Germany was becoming violent, and when the Austrian National Socialists engaged in vicious anti-Semitic propaganda.

In June 1933 the Austrian National Socialist Party was proscribed and henceforth continued its activities in an 'underground' form. Even in German eyes it was not strong enough to seize power on its own; but Hitler was convinced that, if a general election took place, it would become the strongest party and that it was the aim of the Dollfuss government 'to drive the German national idea out of Austria and to replace it by the Austrian idea'. The danger existed that Germany would lose 6 million people who would 'undergo a process of Swissification', as he put it in a meeting of the German government in May 1933. Hence Germany took stringent economic measures to bring about the collapse of the Dollfuss government and at the same time continued to press for an early general election. From Munich violent denunciations were broadcast against the Austrian government, which was abused 'in an absolutely unbridled fashion' and accused of treason, as the Austrian Minister in London stated. The Austrian National Socialists were encouraged to 'resort to acts of civil disobedience', and the Austrian protests in Berlin against these actions were in vain.[31]

In July 1933 Franckenstein called at the Foreign Office accompanied by a senior civil servant from Vienna. He informed Vansittart that his government was doing its utmost 'to cope with the growing deeds of terrorism fomented by Germany', but that the strain was becoming too great for the very limited Austrian forces. The government therefore intended to recruit an auxiliary force of 8000 men; they had already approached the French and Italian governments and received favourable replies. Vansittart strongly approved: 'the maintenance of Austrian independence is a major European question. We cannot perpetually stimulate the Austrian people to maintain it and then fail to help them in any way whatever.' The Foreign Office accordingly wired to Rome that it agreed to the Austrian proposal, on condition that the strength of the force together with that of the army did not exceed the figure of 30,000 as stipulated in the Treaty of St Germain; that their service did not last longer than 12 months; and that the French and Italians approved. The French government made its consent dependent on the agreement of the states of the Little Entente. By 1934 the strength of the auxiliary corps recruited from the Heimwehr and other para-military associations reached 12,000, while that of the army was gradually increased to 40,000.[32] The German Minister in Vienna, on the other hand, strongly complained to Selby about the attitude of the Dollfuss government towards the National Socialists: its resistance was solely due to the fear of the parties supporting Dollfuss that their future would be in jeopardy if they made any concession to National Socialism. 'It was for that reason and that reason alone that Chancellor Dollfuss has rejected every offer of the Austrian Nazi leaders to co-operate with him', and they had only asked for two seats in the government – 'a moderate demand'. The German Minister also declared that 'it was intolerable' that a section so strongly represented in Austria 'should be debarred from having any voice in the direction of Austrian affairs'.[33] Selby might have replied that there was another section strongly represented in Austria which was equally excluded from participation – the Social Democrats – not to mention Germany, where by this time only one party was legal and all others totally suppressed.

Early in August 1933 Wickham Steed, former editor of *The Times*, informed Vansittart that National Socialist headquarters in Munich were inducing members of the Austrian SA to go to Lechfeld in Bavaria to form an Austrian legion 'for operations against Austria which are intended to begin by the end of August at the latest'. German propaganda was telling the Austrian people 'that economic and political collapse is imminent' and that there would be another inflation. The propaganda was having 'a certain effect and is keeping the people in a state of nervous anxiety'.

The Foreign Office received information that the Austrian legion planned a raid into the Tyrol, 'to take Innsbruck by surprise, occupy all government buildings, shoot at once all leaders of opposition parties, enforce an election' and threaten everyone not voting with dire consequences. The forces opposing such an attempt in the Tyrol were reported to be 'extremely ill-equipped, men lacking weapons and even boots'. The Legation in Vienna reported a police raid on 'a secret Nazi Head Quarters' where several journalists were arrested, as were a number of 'couriers'; some German newspaper correspondents were expelled or arrested. At a bridge near Salzburg sentries shot an Austrian National Socialist, and an Austrian frontier guard was killed near the Bavarian frontier. Stringent regulations were issued 'against Nazi sympathisers among the teaching profession'. Feelings on both sides were roused, and 'tension between the two countries cannot, therefore, be said to have relaxed to any extent'. From Munich the British consul telegraphed it was openly said there that the crisis would culminate in early September, as soon as the harvest was over; 'insurrections would be engineered by Austrians in the country itself and, when the attention of the authorities was centred on their suppression, a force of Austrian Nazis would cross from Bavaria and endeavour to seize Innsbruck.' The British consul there, however, doubted whether such an incursion 'would meet with universal or even widespread sympathy'; the Nazi cause had supporters at Kufstein and in the villages of the Inn valley, but the majority of the peasants were not National Socialists.[34]

In November 1933 the British consul wrote from Innsbruck that meanwhile anti-Nazi feeling in the Tyrol had become somewhat stronger; only eight men had left Kufstein (near the German frontier) to join the Austrian legion in Bavaria out of a population of about 6800, but 'the Nazi nuclei ... are still active and still receive German help'; their activities were continuing in Hall near Innsbruck, and in the small town of Kitzbühel – considered by the authorities 'the most unruly place in the province' – National Socialism was considerably stronger. In Vorarlberg the town of Dornbirn was described as the focus of National Socialism; a large percentage of its population depended on two cotton factories whose owners were well-known National Socialists, who believed that their profits would increase if they had free access to the German market. The members of the Agrarian Association had gone over to the National Socialists, as they had in Carinthia; there 'Nazi activity continues unabated', although local unemployment had declined by 20 per cent since August. In the consul's opinion, the majority of the people of Vorarlberg were National Socialists. He also recorded a conversation with a senior army officer in Innsbruck who told him: 'as the British are sprung from the same Teutonic stock as the Germans, they should be the natural friends of Germany'; the French constituted the greatest danger to the peace of Europe and he called them 'mad'. The consul suspected that this attitude 'prevails among the Innsbruck garrison more widely than appears on the surface' because 'the discipline and efficiency of Fascism' appealed 'to the military mind'.

A British officer visiting Austria at the time also noticed that 'Nazi influence had penetrated the ranks of the Army in one or two Austrian Provinces' and that desertions from it continued 'though probably on a very small scale'. In his opinion, National Socialism 'has taken a strong hold upon the peasants and upon the youth of the country'. In the countryside people greeted each other openly with the fascist salute although this was a punishable offence. The Dollfuss government was widely distrusted as 'playing into the hands of Austria's old enemies, France and Italy, and into the hands of the Jews, who . . . control the trade of the country.' The National Socialists were convinced that Hitler would 'guide the German nation to success and prosperity just as Mussolini did' in Italy.[35]

From Vienna Selby wrote that 'the main point of Nazi danger' was still Upper Styria; there the National Socialists possessed large stores of arms and enjoyed the support of the 'Alpine Montangesellschaft', Austria's 'most powerful industrial concern', which was controlled by German interests. In January 1934 he reported that hundreds of National Socialists had been arrested, including the former *Gauleiter* of Vienna Frauenfeld, that two National Socialists demonstrating in Klagenfurt were shot by the police, and that 'an unfortunate illiterate tramp' was hanged because he had burned a haystack ('for entirely non-political motives') 'as a warning to the Nazis that the Government would not hesitate to use the death penalty against them'.

A Foreign Office minute of the same month stated that the National Socialists profited by defection from every party, socialist as well as bourgeois: 'with the exception of the Social Democrats, there appears to be no Austrian party firm enough in its convictions to escape the self-immolation of Brüning's Catholic party in Germany. Christian-Socialists, Pan-Germans, Agrarians and Heimwehr will all within a short time be blissfully *gleichgeschaltet* if the Nazis established themselves as the real masters of Austria.'

From Innsbruck the British consul reported that since the end of 1933 the National Socialist movement had become much stronger. The moderate elements expressed themselves openly in favour of an understanding with Germany and against the repressive measures of the government; the more extreme National Socialists were fully aware of the serious effects of the 'thousand Mark ban' (the cost of a German visa) and 'growing far bolder'. Among the unemployed, hotel-keepers, merchants and students 'the abolition of the Austro-German frontier is coming to be regarded as a short-cut to the millenium.' In Carinthia, he continued, the National Socialists were using the voluntary labour camps as centres of propaganda. From the camps they marched into Klagenfurt and Villach 'with swastika armlets and behind a Nazi flag'. In short, 'the chances of the Austrian Government holding out in western Austria are poorer than at any time during the last five months.'[36]

In Vienna, the National Socialists used the occasion of a visit by the Under-Secretary in the Italian Foreign Office, Suvich, to stage violent demonstrations. A British correspondent trying to reach his flat described the scene as 'like getting through to a beleaguered city'. While Dollfuss was entertaining his guest that evening in the Burgtheater, bombs were detonated 'despite all police vigilance'. In June Selby mentioned 249 cases of 'attacks with explosives' which were listed in 'the regular Nazi broadsheet'. During the past 48 hours the Austrian papers had announced seven cases of dynamite attacks on the railways around Vienna, and others upon power stations and public buildings. The National Socialists, he added, were gleefully pointing to an early meeting of Hitler and Mussolini as 'proof positive' that the two would reach agreement on Austria and the elimination of Dollfuss. A Foreign Office official who travelled in Austria in the same month was impressed how carefully the outrages were planned. Between Linz and Salzburg a railway bridge had been blown up, but none of the passengers in his compartment showed any sign of indignation. More serious than the acts of sabotage – which so far had caused little loss of life – he found 'the apathy and complaisance of the general population who do not think that the fight against Nazism is worth making enemies over'; equally serious was 'the extent to which all the public services are contaminated by Nazi cells'. The regime 'was hated in Vienna as indeed almost everywhere except perhaps in Upper and Lower Austria', where Dollfuss enjoyed some personal popularity.[37]

Selby was informed at about the same time that the Ministry of Finance and those responsible for roads and railways were asking 'how long the budget can stand destruction of public property such as took place last week'. In May the railways had shown a record drop in earnings and the tourist traffic was quite unsatisfactory; the Germans were boycotting the Austrian apple crop; and trade with Czechoslovakia had declined markedly. Austrian exports to Germany decreased 'slightly but steadily' from 18 to 15 per cent of the total. The timber trade in particular suffered, and German agents declared Germany would again take 'the full capacity of Austrian production' as soon as political peace was restored between the two countries.

In 1933 there was a budget deficit of 241 million Schilling and for the first six months of 1934 it was confidentially estimated at 142 million. Unemployment, however, decreased slightly: in 1933 the average number of benefit payments was 329, 493, but in 1934 it fell to 288,037 – a decline of about 13 per cent. But the Legation considered that 14,000 men currently employed in voluntary labour camps should be added to the figure. It also did not include 'the increasing number of those no longer entitled to unemployment benefits ... or those who, for participation in political activities hostile to the Government, have for one reason or another been deprived of their employment yet receive no dole.' The para-military associations too 'have absorbed no small number of the unemployed.' Thus too much importance should not be attached to the official figures, Selby stated in October 1934.[38] It certainly was a very discouraging picture, and the stark facts of the economy added to the political difficulties facing the government. The German boycott was a very effective weapon, and all attempts to find other outlets for Austrian produce met with very little success at a time when the world economic crisis affected nearly all countries.

In August 1933 Vansittart wrote: 'At present – let us make no mistake about it – we are all backing a losing horse in Austria.'[39] Little happened during the following ten months to change that view. In July 1934, however, the long expected National Socialist Putsch was finally attempted, and its failure to some extent changed the whole situation, at least in the short run.

Notes

1. *The Times*, 6 March; Phipps to Simon, 6 March 1933: FO 371, file 16636, fo. 134 f.; G.E.R. Gedye, *Fallen Bastions* (London 1939), p. 82.
2. *The Times*, 11 and 13 March 1933: 'Decree Rule in Austria'.
3. FO memorandum by R. M. A. Hankey, 14 March, and Phipps to Simon, 1 and 18 April 1933: FO 371, file 16636, fos. 144–8, file 16637, fo. 234 f. (with minute of 10 April), file 16628, fo. 390 f.
4. Phipps to Simon, 17 April, minute by Hankey, 22 April, Citrine to Simon, 27 April, and Sargent to Eden, 13 October 1933: FO 371, file 16637, fos. 246, 251, 277, FO 120, file 1068.
5. Phipps to Simon, 23 May and 30 June 1933, and memorandum by Hankey, 13 June: FO 371, file 16638, fo. 60 f., file 16641, fos. 194, 272.
6. Memorandum by Hankey, 13 June, Selby to Simon, 10 July, Vansittart to Paris and Rome, 25 July, M.I.3.b note of 27 May, and comment by Major Whiteford, 26 June 1933: FO 371, file 16641, fo. 272; DBFP, 2nd series, v, nos. 245, 270, pp. 408, 445; WO 190, files 204 and 206.
7. Memorandum by Sir John Simon, 19 June, and minute by von Bülow, German Under-Secretary of State, 31 July 1933: PRO, Cab. 24, vol. 242; *Akten zur deutschen auswärtigen Politik 1918–1945*, series C, i, 2, 1971, no. 383, pp. 696 ff.; G. L. Weinberg, *The Foreign Policy of Hitler's Germany – Diplomatic Revolution in Europe 1933–36* (Chicago and London, 1970), p. 93.
8. Hadow to Simon, 17 and 24 August 1933, with minutes by J. V. Perowne and Vansittart (?) of 22–24 August: FO 371, file 16643, fo. 276 ff., file 16644, fo. 38 ff.
9. Sargent's minute of conversation with Col. Mason-MacFarlane, 2 September; conversation between Simon and Dollfuss at Geneva on 24 September; Graham to Vansittart, Rome, 28 September 1933; and Drummond to Vansittart, Rome, 19 February 1934: FO 371, file 16644, fo. 179; DBFP, 2nd series, v, nos. 414, 417, pp. 640, 646 f.; FO 371, file 18363, fo. 248.
10. Selby to Simon, 31 August, 14 and 21 September 1933: FO 800, file 288, fos. 298–302, FO 371, file 16645, fos. 213, 273 ff.
11. Selby to Simon, 9, 11 and 23 January 1934: FO 371, file 18344, fos. 17, 117 ff., file 18345, fo. 259.
12. Selby to FO, 20 January, and Eric Drummond to Simon, 25 January 1934: FO 371, file 18344, fo. 164, file 18345, fo. 320; W. Goldinger, *Geschichte der Republik Österreich* (Vienna, 1962), p. 189.
13. Selby to FO, 13 February, Phipps to FO, 17 February 1934: FO

371, file 18348, fos. 144, 237; *Manchester Guardian*, 13 February 1934.

14. *The Times*, 14 and 16 February, 1934.

15. *The Times*, 13 and 15 February; *Manchester Guardian*, 13 and 17 February 1934.

16. Minutes by R. A. Galby and E. H. Carr, 13–14 February 1934: FO 371, file 18347, fo. 68, file 18348, fo. 142 f.

17. Memorandum by Hadow, 3 March, Selby to FO, 15 February and 19 March, Ian L. Henderson to Selby, 13 February 1934, and 'Austria. Annual Report, 1934': FO 371, file 18348, fo. 179, file 18350, fos. 99, 355, FO 120, file 1083, FO 371, file 19843, fo. 266.

18. Conclusions of a Cabinet meeting, 14 February 1934: PRO, Cab. 23, vol. 78, p. 135 f.; Walford Selby, *Diplomatic Twilight 1930–1940* (London, 1953), pp. 22, 25.

19. *The Times*, 17 February 1934.

20. Memorandum by E. H. Carr, 26 February, with minutes by Sargent, 12 March, Vansittart, 18 March, and Simon, 20 March 1934: FO 371, file 18351, fos. 210 ff., 215 f., 245.

21. Drummond to Simon, 17 March, and Selby to Simon, 5 March 1934: FO 371, file 18363, fos. 390, 393; DBFP, 2nd series, vi, 1957, no. 332, pp. 424–9.

22. Franckenstein to Simon, 17 January, Runciman to Simon, 29 January, and minutes by Sargent and Vansittart, 30 January 1934: FO 371, file 18360, fos. 3 f., 9, 82 ff.

23. Conclusions of a Cabinet meeting, 31 January, Quintin Hill, Board of Trade, to Carr, 2 February, and Vansittart to Runciman, 3 February 1934 (draft): Cab. 23, vol. 78, pp. 62–66, FO 371, file 18360, fos. 69 f., 79, 81.

24. Conclusions of a Cabinet meeting, 24 January 1934: Cab. 23, vol. 78, pp. 47–54. The quotations come from the minutes in which the contributions of the participants appear in a very much abbreviated form.

25. Memorandum by Simon, 22 January 1934, and by Vansittart, 28 August 1933: Cab. 24, vol. 247; DBFP, 2nd series, v, no. 371, p. 554.

26. Selby to Vansittart, 20 July 1933: DBFP, 2nd series, v, no. 260, p. 435.

27. 'Austria. Annual Report, 1934', Selby to Simon, 28 May and 4 August, and Henderson to Hadow, 18 July 1934: FO 371, file 19843, fo. 268, file 18351, fo. 374 f., file 18354, fo. 84, file 18352, fo. 194.

28. M.I.3.b note on semi-military organisations, 22 September, report by Lt.-Col. MacFarlane, 30 September 1933, Selby to Simon, 13 January and 19 February 1934, Philip Nichols to

Wigram, Rome, 20 July, and Hadow to FO, 23 August 1933: WO 190, file 213, FO 120, file 1071, FO 371, file 18344, fo. 141 f., file 18349, fo. 113 f., file 16638, fo. 86, file 16646, fo. 41 f.

29. Neville Laski to Vansittart, 25 August 1933, Selby to Simon, 19 March and 14 May 1934, and O'Malley to Selby, 30 October 1934: FO 371, file 16638, fo. 141 f., file 18350, fo. 100, file 18367, fos. 286 ff., FO 120, file 1089. The Vienna Legation kept a special file on the Jewish problems.

30. Hadow to Simon, 9 November, and O'Malley to Laski, 6 December 1934: FO 120, file 1089.

31. *Akten zur deutschen auswärtigen Politik*, series C, i, 2, no. 262, p. 483; DBFP, 2nd series, v, nos. 215, 237, pp. 358, 401.

32. Minute by Vansittart, 24 July, FO wire to Rome, 1 August 1933, and secret M.I.3.b report, 11 December 1934: FO 371, file 16634, fo. 303, file 16635, fo. 324 f., WO 190, file 288.

33. Selby to Simon, 21 July 1933: DBFP, 2nd series, v, no. 264, pp. 438–41.

34. Wickham Steed to Vansittart, 3 August, FO wire to Rome, 18 August, Hayter to Simon, 8 August, memorandum by Perowne, 1 September, and Henderson to Legation Vienna, 11 September 1933: FO 371, file 16643, fos. 127 f., 217, 122 ff., file 16644, fo. 109, file 16645, fo. 259.

35. Henderson to Selby, 20 September, 7 and 17 November 1933, and memorandum by Group Captain Christie, s.d.: FO 371, file 16645, fo. 268, FO 120, file 1077 and 1078, FO 371, file 16644, fo. 165 f.

36. Selby to Simon, 16 October 1933 and 13 January 1934, FO minute, 18 January, and Henderson to Selby, 15 January 1934: FO 371, file 16639, fo. 274, file 18344, fos. 140 f., 148 f., file 18346, fos. 162–9.

37. Gedye, *Fallen Bastions*, p. 96; Selby to Simon, 11 June, and Notes by R. A. Gallop, 19 July 1934: DBFP, 2nd series, vi, no. 449, pp. 743 ff.; FO 371, file 18353, fos. 172 f., 178.

38. Selby to Simon, 16 April and 11 June, Hadow to Simon, 21 July, Selby to Simon, 30 October and 22 December 1934, 'Austria. Annual Report, 1934': FO 120, file 1081; DBFP, 2nd series, vi, no. 449, p. 744; FO 371, file 18342, fos. 227 ff., file 18343, fo. 139 f., file 18344, fo. 11, file 19843, fo. 277.

39. Vansittart's memorandum of 28 August 1933: DBFP, 2nd series, v, no. 371, p. 549.

7 Austria under Schuschnigg, 1934–37

On 26 July 1934 the British papers announced that the Austrian National Socialists had carried out their long expected coup d'état. Dollfuss had been shot, and it was broadcast from the Vienna radio station that the government had resigned and Dr Rintelen – the man who had long intrigued with the National Socialists, and been sent by Dollfuss to Rome as the Austrian Minister – was the new Chancellor. Martial law was proclaimed in Vienna, and the Minister of Education, Dr Kurt von Schuschnigg, was forming a new government. According to *The Times*, he was negotiating with the men who occupied the Chancellery, and they had agreed 'to let the members of the government who were prisoners go free on condition that they themselves were given safe conduct to Germany'. The *Manchester Guardian* reported that 'there is complete chaos'; the Chancellery, the police headquarters and the principal public buildings were surrounded by troops and armed Heimwehr men. 'Young Nazis go in batches of five to ten through the streets, easily recognizable by the leather trousers and white stockings.' The negotiations between the authorities and the National Socialists occupying the Chancellery were reported in great detail as was the role of Rintelen and that of Major Fey, the Minister for Public Safety. In its obituary *The Times* apostrophied Dollfuss as 'one of those who have had greatness thrust upon them':

> He was reviled and threatened by every device known to the Nazi propaganda machine, and at the same time involved in milder hostilities with the Social Democrats. But he stuck to his guns unflinchingly, declaring after a narrow escape from assassination that his motto had become *Jetzt erst recht*. With capable helpers he

was able, not only to pursue the fight against the Nazi lawlessness . . . with a vigour unlooked for in Austria, but also to conduct an intensive campaign and organise a wider following for the patriotic revival which he saw was necessary before he could hope to turn the Nazi tide. . . . The ruthlessness with which the outbreak [of February 1934] was suppressed and the leaders afterwards executed cost Herr Dollfuss much of the sympathy his stand against the bullying of Germany had aroused in foreign countries, and it left the Socialists so much embittered that some of them have of late been cooperating with the Nazis to overthrow the Government. . .'[1]

The next day, the *Manchester Guardian* stated that the majority of the population was 'enraged by the brutal and cold-blooded way in which the Nazis murdered the Chancellor'; they had carried across the German frontier 'the brutal practices by which they exterminated their former friends as well as their enemies on June 30 [1934].' Black flags were flying from the public buildings and from many private houses, and in many windows candles were burning. After a trip through the provinces the British military attaché reported that the mourning 'was genuine and widespread in Lower Austria and in most of Vienna', but lukewarm elsewhere and non-existent in Carinthia. The government was making much capital out of Dollfuss's death, and could 'definitely count on more support in the population than two months ago'. Its propaganda also benefited from the murder of Röhm, the other SA leaders, and many more on 30 June in Germany. From Rome the British embassy wired that the press was unanimous in its condemnation of the murder 'and openly attribute responsibility to National Socialist Germany'. The broadcast from Munich which deplored the crime 'is characterised as impudent and cynical'. The Italian press had never been 'so outspoken and violently anti-German' as it was on this occasion. The papers announced that Italian troops had been moved to the frontier.[2]

In March 1934 the British military attaché had written: 'The danger of an armed Nazi "Putsch" against the armed forces of the Government may now be considered to be non-existent. Hitler's present attitude and all available local evidence seem to prove this conclusively.' He also believed that 'the Nazis had never approached the military strength of the *Schutzbund* in organisation, training and armament', and yet the government forces quelled the revolt of February with only negligible assistance by the Heimwehr and other auxiliaries. But when the revolt of July spread to the provinces, especially Styria and Carinthia, severe fighting erupted which lasted for days, and considerable assistance was rendered to the army by Heimwehr and other para-military units.

On 28 July the *Manchester Guardian* reported that the insurgents had been cleared from the Enns valley and the Upper Styrian towns of Leoben and Donawitz, but they still occupied certain passes and mountain areas and heavy fighting was continuing. In Styria the Heimwehr had gone over to the National Socialists with their stores of weapons, and their units were better trained. *The Times* recorded severe fighting with loss of life in the two provinces, and on 27 July the First Secretary of the British Legation telephoned London that 'obstinate resistance' had to be overcome in Styria with 24 men killed on the government side: 'so far government seems to be master of the situation.'

A few days later the military attaché summed up: 'The Nazis – mostly extremist members of the peasant population – fought well.' He regarded any repetition of such a Putsch 'as quite out of the question'. Above all, 'thc Army has shown no outward sign of disaffection and once more performed all that was asked of it in an exemplary way.' He also mentioned that the Heimwehr leaders 'were quite in the dark as to the attitude the Army would adopt'. They thought that, if the rising had an initial success, the army would have changed sides and 'were frankly astonished at the exemplary way' in which it supported the government. The industrialist Mandl who had close connections with the Heimwehr told him that the Putsch 'had been very much a touch-and-go affair': if the insurgents had succeeded in capturing the whole Cabinet at the Ballhausplatz (as was their plan), 'they might have gained the day comparatively bloodlessly'. The total casualties on the government side were later given as 81 dead and 172 wounded.[3]

On 27 July *The Times* published a first leader entitled 'Policy by Murder':

> The truth seems to be that in Austria, as in the Saar and in Memel, there is a growing repugnance to being closely united with a State which is the home of the political gangster.... The subversive

literature distributed in Austria has been brought over from Germany; and on the very night of the Vienna *coup* our Munich correspondent reported mysterious movements of the Austrian legionaries who are camped and trained in Germany. On the facts of the case, and on account of her precepts and her example, Germany cannot be absolved of some moral responsibility.

The assessment of 'a growing repugnance' was rather optimistic, but the paper left no doubt of its loathing of National Socialism:

The Austrian Nazis have gone one better than their German fellows in allowing a man of Dr Dollfuss's position and religious convictions to bleed to death without the succour of the Church, which might easily have been made available. The full story, which has only gradually been revealed, is making the name of Nazi to stink in the nostrils of the world. A system which flourishes on such methods inspires loathing and disgust everywhere.

For a paper as sedate as *The Times* such words were exceptional and outspoken, but the practical consequences drawn in the British policy towards Germany did not correspond to them.

At the end of July a leader in the *Manchester Guardian* commented that, in choosing Schuschnigg, President Miklas had shown good judgement; he was the only one among Dr Dollfuss's former colleagues 'who has any chance of giving Austria what she needs – "concord and unity"', but there was no real 'unity among the Austrians who, for many different reasons, compose the "Fatherland façade", miscalled a "front" [the official organisation of the regime]'. The Heimwehr leaders were 'consoled with an increase of influence, but it is much that they should not have the whole Government in their hands'. Too many of them had joined the National Socialists or had negotiated with them, hence the real strength of the new government was with Dr Schuschnigg, and not with 'his inconvenient allies'.

This was a fair assessment, for the movement had long passed its peak, and two years later Schuschnigg was able to dissolve the Heimwehr without much difficulty. As far as the policy of the British government was concerned, the Foreign Secretary wrote to the Prime Minister in the same month: 'Our own policy is quite clear. We must keep out of trouble in Central Europe at all costs.' July 1914 'stands as an awful warning.... There are circumstances in which Italy might move troops into Austria. There are no circumstances in which we could ever dream of doing so.' Together with France and Italy, Britain 'desired to see Austrian independence continue, but this involved nothing military.'[4] The reference to July 1914 – an entirely different situation – was ominous: it clearly showed the trend of British policy towards Hitler's Germany. To 'keep out of trouble in Central Europe' was hardly realistic.

In August Selby reported on the severe sentences passed on the insurgents in Styria and Carinthia, 'varying from life to ten years'. Several hundred more, mostly youths, were still awaiting trial, as were most of the prisoners taken in Vienna. 'The Heimwehr have been particularly active in endeavouring to have sentences lengthened on the score that judges or juries were latently Nazi in their sympathy.' Of the socialist prisoners taken in February, about 1000 had been sentenced, many of them for a second or even a third time when the Public Prosecutor appealed against the first sentence, which was increased by twelve months on average.

The Legation also recorded that many employees of the Federal Chancellery had greeted the National Socialists who stormed the building with cries of 'Heil Hitler' and were now 'rueing their haste' in accepting the change of power: 'many more would probably have done so without a sigh on the first sign of insurgent success'; and the public was whispering that Major Fey had played exactly the same part in the negotiations in Vienna on 25 July. The memorandum further stated that the gentry and other responsible German Nationalist groups kept aloof from the uprising, either because they believed it 'to be foredoomed to failure', or out of dislike of the Austrian refugees in Munich who had authorised it.

From Innsbruck, on the other hand, the British consul wrote that the same circles – that is, businessmen, lawyers, doctors, etc. – regarded the recent violent purges in Germany 'as regrettable, but as in no way affecting the basic ideal of Teutonic racial patriotism'. They might 'even be gratified that the left wing of the movement appears to have been suppressed.' But Italy, according to the British ambassador, had never been 'so violently anti-German as since the 30 June massacre: the shock has been tremendous.' This, and the murder of Dollfuss, Vansittart thought, would allow Britain 'to widen the breach between Italy & Germany'; 'I hope,' he wrote to Simon, 'we shall not allow the opportunity to escape.' Simon replied that the opportunity would 'of course' be used but there was no hurry, for 'the breach between Germany & Italy is not going to be healed overnight.' And a personal message was sent to Mussolini endorsing his firm stand in all its aspects.[5]

During the years 1934–37 Austria's economic situation slowly began to improve as the world economic crisis abated and industrial recovery gained ground. In October 1935 Selby reported a 'favourable trend of receipts' so that the deficit was reduced by over 20 per cent compared to 1934. Industrial production was 'appreciably higher', and by the end of September unemployment was reduced by 16 per cent compared with the previous year. In October 1936 'signs on the whole of a steady improvement' were noticed, so that it was decided to dispense with the control exercised by a Financial Adviser of the League and 'a more indirect form of supervision from Geneva' was adopted.

The Legation's Annual Economic Report for 1936 stated that the total deficit in the budget was reduced from 157 million to 33 million Schilling, largely on account of a big reduction in extraordinary expenditure. The shock occasioned by the collapse of the Phoenix Life Insurance Company causing losses of some 250 million Schilling was overcome with ease without any external help: 'considering the magnitude of the failure and the very large number of the public who were affected', the visible effects 'were relatively small' and the reaction of the Stock Exchange 'comparatively slight and of short duration'.

The Annual Economic Report for 1937 added that the budget was balanced, many industries were fully employed, foreign trade had 'noticeably increased in both directions', savings deposits were steadily growing, and the number of registered unemployed had declined: 'indeed, the situation of the country today, when compared with even five years ago, is regarded by many foreign observers as being "little short of a miracle", and by the Austrians themselves as a matter of justified pride.' In July the military attaché wrote: 'A big factor working for the Government was the improved economic situation', for the average Austrian only wanted work 'to make him a contented and loyal citizen'. From Innsbruck the British consul recorded a slight, steady improvement even in the Alpine provinces. The Legation's monthly economic reports for 1937 registered further economic progress, especially in the iron and steel industry, and also in the paper and pulp industry, and to some extent in the cotton industry, the least satisfactory sector. The very important tourist industry too showed an upward tendency: in July 1937, 195,139 foreign tourists visited Austria, as against 158,337 the previous year, and in June 195,000 as against 184,000.[6] If the general improvement was not spectacular, it was nevertheless clearly noticeable.

The weak spot, however, was still unemployment, especially among the young. In February 1938 302,000 people were in receipt of unemployment benefit, 10,000 more than in January but 13,000 fewer than in February 1937; but to this would have to be added the very many 'who are not eligible for unemployment support' because their entitlement to receive benefits had expired, or because they had never been employed since leaving school, the Legation's commercial councillor recorded. According to a memorandum sent to London at the same time, some people estimated that of the youngsters who left school in the 1930s only 15–20 per cent had been able to find a job. Perhaps even more serious was the case of the white-collar youth; of the university and college graduates only a small number could hope to find a position in the professions, no new trading licences were issued, and no new business could be started under the terms of the 'trading prohibition'. These two groups were 'hypnotised by the glowing accounts that are forced on them of the high level of employment in Germany'.[7] High unemployment thus had political results and the position of the government remained unstable and insecure.

British trade with Austria continued to decline. Early in 1936 Selby wired that in 1931 Austria had exported goods to the value of 81 million Schilling to the United Kingdom, but during the first eleven months of 1935 their value fell to 30 million, and that of hats and hoods from nearly 8 million to a little more than 3 million Schilling. These items were of the 'greatest importance' to Austria, and he had received 'many complaints from both officials and business men of crippling effects, particularly on hat industry, of existing British duties'.

In October 1935, the Import Duties Advisory Committee recommended a significant increase of import duties on felt hats and felt shapes for making into hats. Eden, the new Foreign Secretary, protested 'that the political effect in Austria of any such action by the United Kingdom would be wholly deplorable, and would almost certainly outweigh any small economic advantage which might result for the British industries concerned.' The increase in the duty was in 'flat contradiction' with the British policy towards Austrian trade 'and will be interpreted as a douche of cold water'. But Runciman, the President of the Board of Trade, refused to agree to Eden's proposal that the recommendation to increase the duties should be rejected. He was supported by Neville Chamberlain, the Chancellor of the Exchequer, who argued: 'if the traders of this country were to be told that after their applications had passed all the tests applied to them by the Import Duties Advisory Committee they might be rejected at the last minute ... because we had political reasons to show favour to a particular country', an agitation against the government's foreign policy 'might render it so unpopular as to destroy the Government's support for it just when it was most needed.' The dangers foreseen by Eden, Chamberlain added, 'may perhaps turn out less serious than he anticipated'. On 26 February 1936 the Cabinet decided to accept the recommendations of the Import Duties Advisory Committee to increase the duties on felt hats and shapes, and the protest of the Foreign Office was overruled.[8] Once more the British government found it impossible to make a small concession to the Austrian manufacturers and to encourage Austrian exports, and any help on the political side was even more difficult.

At the beginning of 1935 a lecture on Austria given by an Intelligence Officer to British officers stated that the Austrian government 'exists by favour of the armed forces of the state and particularly the armed irregular formations which support the various leaders of the dictatorship'; there was strong rivalry between the clerical *Ostmärkische Sturmscharen* 'who wish to make Austria into a Catholic clerical state and the Heimwehr, the Austrian Fascists, who desire a corporate state on the Italian model'. But, the officer claimed, 'at least 50 per cent of the Austrian population probably desire a Nazi government', and it was therefore difficult to see how Austria could ultimately be prevented from joining 'her big German brother'.

Another Intelligence Officer discussed the Austrian situation with O'Malley, the head of the Southern Department of the Foreign Office, and 'said that we could see no method by which Austrian independence was likely to be maintained in the long run'; there was a desire for cooperation with Germany, particularly in the Austrian army, as well as 'extreme dislike of Italy'. It was difficult to see how 'the present non-representative Austrian Government could be kept in power'; ultimately an election would have to be held which 'we believed would show an overwhelming majority for cooperation with Germany'. O'Malley generally agreed and said that in his department they had no illusions as to 'any practical way to ensure the independence of Austria', but in the Foreign Office it was thought 'that one might as well keep Austria on her legs as long as possible', as the situation might improve.[9]

The pessimistic view of Austria's chances of survival was shared by the Foreign Office and Military Intelligence; but the latter seem to have overestimated the degree of National Socialist support and underestimated the two other principal currents – the socialists and the supporters of the government – who, in the aggregate, were probably as strong if not stronger than the followers of National Socialism. As there was no test of public opinion, no figures are available.

The information, however, was certainly correct about the continuing rivalry between the various para-military associations, which was one of the great weaknesses of the regime; and there was also strong rivalry between them and the army. In August 1934 E. H. Carr minuted 'that the Heimwehr are a mercenary force of doubtful reliability, that their fighting value, if it comes to the point, is very small, and that, since they are cordially disliked by the army and enjoy no popular support in the country, they are in the end bound to discredit rather than to uphold the cause.' In the view of the Foreign Office the government would be well advised to rely on the loyalty of the army and on some popular support 'which can only be increased by measures calculated to conciliate the Socialists and the Nationalists'.

In conversation at the Foreign Office the British military

attaché in Vienna confirmed that 'the army regard the Heimwehr as riff-raff and would not at any price desire to incorporate large chunks of it in its ranks'. The Heimwehr leaders in any case would not accept such incorporation 'except on terms which meant that they swallowed the army'; but a disbandment of the Heimwehr and the other para-military forces was not 'practical politics', because they formed the 'backbone' of the government. There was every reason to believe that Mussolini regarded the Heimwehr 'as the principal bulwark of Austria's independence', and his relations with Starhemberg were closer than with any other Austrian politician: to propose the disbandment of the Heimwehr was 'therefore, to run our head into a brick wall'. What the Foreign Office favoured was a course of 'moderation' or 'conciliation', in particular towards the arrested socialist leaders, such as the former mayor of Vienna, Dr Seitz.

From Vienna Selby wrote in August 1934 that the new Chancellor, Schuschnigg, and the Minister of Finance, Buresch, also believed in moderation, but between them and its fulfilment 'stood the Heimwehr party, triumphant and ready to "dictate" to the Government'; time had been lost and the more moderate ministers needed 'encouragement in this statesmanlike idea'.[10] Backed by Mussolini and triumphant after the victories over the hated socialists and National Socialists, the Heimwehr leaders were in no mood for any concession, but they considerably overestimated their own strength – and they were as disunited as ever.

Proof of disunity, 'of jealousy and mutual recrimination within the Heimwehr', was given to the military attaché later in the year when a close associate of Starhemberg accused the Vienna leader, Major Fey, of accepting a bribe of 300,000 Schilling from the Alpine Montangesellschaft in Styria in return for a promise to terminate the government control that had been imposed on the company because of its support of National Socialism and the July Putsch. According to the information, proof of this and 'of incredible bribery and corruption in Government circles' was withheld from Starhemberg 'in order not to aggravate the tense situation' between him and Fey. But, according to Selby, 'like Prince Starhemberg, Major Fey must keep his own Vienna Heimwehr going by accepting money where he can get it. From Prince Starhemberg he can hope for none.' The Heimwehr leaders also objected to any negotiations with Nationalist or Pan-German groups which, after the failure of the Putsch, were in a more conciliatory mood.

On 1 August 1934 the Foreign Office wired to the embassy in Rome that it hoped the Austrian government 'would recognise the wisdom of conciliating both Socialists and pan-German elements who might now be prepared to support the policy of Austrian independence'; but unfortunately a statement by Starhemberg showed that the government was 'continuing to antagonise all those elements on either wing which are not prepared to accept *in toto* the Heimwehr programme'; such a course was 'fraught with the gravest danger'. The ambassador should try to find out what Mussolini had said to Schuschnigg on the subject; this was a good moment for the British and French governments to support a policy of conciliation in Vienna.[11]

From Vienna itself, Selby reported that 'responsible pan-German elements', which feared the 'eventual triumph of irresponsible S.A. and S.S. elements directed from Munich', were at that moment seeking a compromise with the government on reasonable terms; but the government believed that the collapse of Hitlerism was at hand and was 'staking everything upon holding out for the next two or three months by an uncompromising show of force'. It was encouraged in this attitude by the Italian Minister 'who sees in compromise only a sign of weakness'. Selby suggested that the British, French and Italian governments should counsel Austria to adopt a policy of 'conciliating all responsible Nationalist (pan-German) and Socialist elements in Austria'. Carr minuted that he agreed with the suggestion: 'I confess that I am not sanguine about the success of any such move, but the situation is so bad that I should be inclined to try it.' Vansittart consented to 'take the suggested action at once... I too am not very sanguine about this, but we must try & try hard and without loss of time.'

The only possible solution that emerged during the following weeks was a proposal, allegedly made by Rintelen, that some German Nationalists should enter the government – an idea which might be acceptable to Germany. But this, as Carr noted, was unacceptable to Mussolini and 'is therefore not practical politics'. If this was the case, 'the only conclusion is that there is no solution.' Another Foreign Office official wrote that the suggestion 'postulated an amenable Germany, such as we are not likely to find for some time to come.'[12] In fact, neither Hitler nor Mussolini was likely to accept such a proposal and a British suggestion on these lines would not find approval in Vienna.

In October 1934 some German Nationalist leaders tried to reach an agreement with Schuschnigg on the basis of Austrian independence, and Schuschnigg had conversations with a former leader of the Agrarian Association, Anton Reinthaller (a 'moderate' National Socialist), which 'seemed for a time to be going surprisingly well'. At Schuschnigg's request Reinthaller produced a memorandum which showed willingness 'to work for an independent Germanic Austria' and to join the 'Patriotic Front', in which nationalist leaders acceptable to the government were to be given posts. But news of the negotiations leaked out, and the government had to publish a statement that Reinthaller had no following and that he and his associates must renounce their faith. Once more, Selby commented, 'the Heimwehr has been able to force its will upon the Chancellor', and the nationalist circles were left 'disconcerted and angry'. Clerical circles, on the other hand, 'still hanker after a Catholic State, with Austria as its centre and including South Germany, Croatia and other Roman Catholic lands'. Selby also learned 'on unimpeachable authority' that the Minister of Finance was 'unhappy at the endless demands made upon the Treasury by the Heimwehr and Ostmärkische Sturmscharen' and by other political 'relief works', which cancelled out any increase in revenue. Selby was equally critical of Starhemberg's support of the many schemes of his friend, the industrialist Mandl, to increase the armaments of the military and para-military forces.[13] As the two were close associates, what helped the one was to the advantage of the other.

The Legation's Annual Report for 1934 commented in detail on the para-military associations, estimating that the Heimwehr had 35,000 members, compared to 10,000 of the Sturmscharen and 3000 of the Freiheitsbund, who were armed during the revolts of February and July. Although the Heimwehr leaders had little support in the country 'outside the bayonets of their semi-military forces', Schuschnigg could not afford to alienate them. Their finances were in a bad way and foreign subsidies were considerable reduced, but recruiting was not difficult 'as the rates of pay and the easy conditions are an attractive bait in present circumstances'. The Ostmärkische Sturmscharen were becoming a serious rival of the Heimwehr. They were a Catholic organisation with ample clerical funds at their disposal – facts much resented by the Heimwehr. The Freiheitsbund was largely a labour organisation and recruited among former members of the Republican Defence League. Antipathy between these formations had caused serious disturbances. They were all represented in the *Schutzkorps*, a kind of fascist militia, with 'its separate party elements'.[14]

In October 1934 the editor of the *Neue Freie Presse* informed Selby that the Heimwehr had just forced the Creditanstalt Bank to grant them a credit of 15 million Schilling, and 'money was being squandered in every direction ... principally for armament'. The freedom of the press was more and more 'interfered with in the interests of the Government, or rather the Heimwehr influence in the Government ... Austrian life was being crushed between the upper millstone of Germany ... and the nether millstone of Italian Fascism'; but for the time being Italian Fascism 'was supreme in Austria'.

In November the British consul reported from Innsbruck that relations between the Heimwehr and the Sturmscharen had become so bad that a general was summoned from Vienna to 'organise a joint inspection and soothe the ruffled feelings on both sides'; now the relations were more peaceful 'but may become strained again at any time'. Meanwhile new antagonism developed to the Freiheitsbund which held large demonstrations in the Tyrol and Carinthia, improved its discipline and equipment and attracted many new recruits. In July 1935 the consul wrote it was 'freely whispered, apparently on good grounds' that the local Heimwehr no longer received subsidies from the Italians, pay was irregular and the rank and file were dissatisfied; a minority desired a Habsburg restoration, but the majority declared that the movement would be compromised if it were drawn into the legitimist camp. The whole 'Patriotic Front' in Innsbruck, as well as outside, was torn by 'petty dissensions and personal enmities', and the government's cause was 'weakened by mistrust and recrimination'.[15]

When E. H. Carr visited Austria in the autumn of 1934 he found that the basic problem was not an economic one and that it did not matter whether Austria was 'a possible economic unit'. The real trouble was

> that not enough people in Austria believe in Austria as an independent country.... No doubt if, by some economic miracle or by the pouring of money into Austria from outside, Austria could become an islet of economic prosperity in the midst of a sea of distress, her independence might be maintained for some time, just as a dying man can be kept alive by artificial supplies of oxygen.

But life under such conditions 'is not that of a healthy or natural organism'. To this Sargent added a minute agreeing 'that economics *alone* are not going to create an Austrian will to live'; he was beginning to wonder whether a Habsburg restoration 'may not be the only thing which will help to do so.'

In April 1935 Selby noticed a growing discontent among the people 'owing to the decreasing purchasing power' of the Schilling; those in authority were aware of it, and recently Starhemberg had attacked the Minister of Finance for his undue concern for the 'foreign debtors' of the country as opposed to the 'needs of the people'. This pressure on the government would exist whatever government was in power, and the best solution would be an underpinning of the economy by increasing Austria's foreign trade: that was the most important means of preserving Austrian independence.[16]

As to the system of government, Selby found striking similarities between Austria and Germany: parliamentary government had disappeared in both, the Social Democratic Party was suppressed, the press was subject to severe censorship; while the Jews were persecuted in Germany, a strong feeling existed in Austria 'that the Jews monopolise too great a proportion of posts which should be available to Christians'. The survival of the Austrian government was to a large extent due to Italian efforts to oppose the advance of Germany to the frontiers of Italy, but in fact she had 'only succeeded in many respects in approximating the system of government in Austria very nearly to the system which Herr Hitler has succeeded in imposing upon Germany.' E. H. Carr added a minute: 'Prophecy is dangerous; but it seems inconceivable that a regime so rotten internally (apart from external attack) can survive for long.' And Sir John Simon wrote: 'I am far from being persuaded that the preservation of this ramshackle regime is a positive gain – it is only tolerable "for fear of meeting something worse".[17] In retrospect, the differences between the National Socialist and the Austrian authoritarian regimes are perhaps more striking than the similarities, but at the time the parallels seemed very obvious, and not only to the diplomats.

In April 1935 the British consul at Innsbruck reported on the increasing demands of the Heimwehren. They objected 'to the continued existence of the party spirit', to 'the undue influence of the Roman Catholic Church', and to the fact that their members did not always receive preference in employment. The Deputy Governor of Salzburg expressed his sharp hostility to the Freiheitsbund and accused it of being 'Communists in disguise, who were attempting to sabotage the new Austrian Constitution'. The consul added that in western Austria the provincial governments contained 'some bitter opponents' of the Heimwehr, at Innsbruck as well as at Salzburg. When a new Austrian government was formed in October 1935 it contained, according to the Legation, four Heimwehr ministers – Starhemberg as Vice-Chancellor and the Ministers of Finance, Foreign Affairs, and Interior and Security – and six non-Heimwehr members. But the influence of the four 'would be out of proportion to their number', they were holding the key posts, several other ministers were 'very close' to the movement, and Schuschnigg as Chancellor was 'far from resolute'. The implication clearly was that he was not sufficiently resolute in curtailing the growing influence of the Heimwehr leaders.

A few days later Sargent replied: 'The more I look at the new Austrian Government the less I like it.... The Government seems to be composed entirely of the creatures of Starhemberg, and I find it hard, as probably you do, to have any confidence in that gentleman's judgment or policy.' The new government, he thought, was 'more completely under Italian influence than its predecessor' and would antagonise all those in Austria who were 'at the same time anti-Nazi and anti-Italian'. Particularly sinister was the removal of Buresch from the Ministry of Finance and his replacement by a creature of Starhemberg who would, if asked to do so by his chief, be 'prepared to play ducks and drakes with Austrian finances'. At about the same time Carr described the Austrian situation as 'fake and unreal'; and Selby mentioned the Italian decorations which 'have descended in a flock on Austrian officials': 'Italy is working the situation in this and other ways for all she is worth.' But in reality Italy was 'detested and despised by the great majority of Austrians'; recently several Austrians had expressed the hope to him that Britain would put Italy in her place. Ominously, Selby added that the 'real danger' was an accommodation between Germany and Italy 'which would directly affect the fate of Austria and its Government': such a development ought to be apprehended with the outbreak of war between Italy and Abyssinia,[18] which indeed changed the whole situation in Central Europe quite dramatically.

After the invasion of Abyssinia by Italy in October 1935 the Council as well as the General Assembly of the League decided to apply sanctions to the aggressor under Article XVI of the Covenant, but Austria, Hungary and Albania dissented and sided with Italy, their 'protector'. A few days later Selby saw Vansittart who told him that this would cause Britain to revise her attitude towards Austrian independence. Selby protested and replied that it was impossible to adopt such a line, and was then told by the Foreign Secretary that he should inform the Austrian government that their action at Geneva had caused 'some embarrassment' in London.

In November Sargent wrote to Selby: 'we cannot pretend to like either them [the Austrian Government] or their Geneva policy, and I doubt whether it will pay in the long run to give them any excuse for supposing that we do so'. It would not be a bad thing to let the Austrian Foreign Minister see 'the reverse side of the medal'; Britain would maintain her interest in Austrian independence as 'part of our general European and League policy, and not as a mark of favour to any particular Austrian Government'; if the new Austrian government desired British sympathy it should prove by deeds that it was no less satisfactory than its predecessor; this depended on the degree in which it would 'collaborate with the League, or at any rate not neutralise and defeat League action, in the matter of sanctions', and on its relations with the political parties not represented in the government. Collaboration with them would broaden 'the basis on which the government stands'. In any case, Selby should be 'quite explicit about the unfavourable reaction which recent developments in Austria may have' on British public opinon and government 'if the new Austrian Government do not mind their step'.[19] Indignation was clearly aroused by the Austrian vote at Geneva and the composition of the new Austrian government, but we do not know in what form Selby passed on these strictures to the Austrians.

British ire was aroused even more strongly when, after the Italian victories in Abyssinia, Starhemberg sent a fulsome message of praise to Mussolini:

> in my consciousness of Fascist unity ... I congratulate your Excellency with all my heart ... on the glorious and splendid victory of Italian Fascist arms over barbarism, the victory of the Fascist spirit over democratic duplicity and hypocrisy.... Long live the victory of Fascist thought in the world!

In London Vansittart put it to the Austrian Minister that 'a distinct coldness' was caused in Britain when Austria failed to do her duty as a member of the League; on top of this came Starhemberg's congratulation to Mussolini 'who was engaged in flouting the League'. Starhemberg would 'have done much better to have kept his mouth shut ... and for all the compliments lavished by Prince Starhemberg on Fascism, Italian supplies to Prince Starhemberg's Heimwehr had in fact completely dried up.' As Vansittart put it, it seemed 'an act of supreme folly to insult one's democratic benefactors, particularly as the supplies of cash elsewhere in the world were none too plentiful'. Franckenstein declared that he too was 'horrified to see the text of Prince Starhemberg's message' in the papers; he was 'exceedingly glad' to know Vansittart's opinion, for it would strengthen his own hand in informing his government. He asked whether anything might be done to counter the effect of the message, and Vansittart replied 'that was naturally for his Government to say'.

Perhaps it was Franckenstein's telegram to Vienna or the outcry in the western press which persuaded Schuschnigg to get rid of his eloquent Vice-Chancellor. Whatever the reason, a few days later Starhemberg was dismissed from his posts in the government and as leader of the 'Patriotic Front', and there was no resistance of any kind. As Selby wrote from Vienna, paradoxically enough the decay of Starhemberg's authority could be dated from the reconstruction of the government in the previous November. Contrary to all expectations, the new

Minister of Finance, one of Starhemberg's nominees, introduced strict economies which hit many Heimwehr members, and no fresh funds were provided for their growing needs by the Austrian exchequer. A few days later the political director of the Austrian Foreign Office explained to Selby that it was 'Starhemberg's inability to do any consistent office work which was the real cause' of his dismissal; the leaders of the 'Patriotic Front' and the Heimwehr 'were never able to "get hold of" Prince Starhemberg, as he was always absent from his office for one reason or another.' Berger-Waldenegg, the Foreign Minister, had not seen the telegram to Mussolini before it was sent and would never have approved of it; but after its publication he had no alternative but to resign from the government together with Starhemberg; when Schuschnigg saw the text 'his fury was unbounded', so Selby was informed.[20]

In March 1936 Selby reported that the Italians had stopped their subsidies to the Heimwehr and since the previous year, 'they have been living from hand to mouth'; the Minister of Finance refused to pay such large sums so that it was necessary to reduce the auxiliary *Schutzkorps* from about 12,500 to only 400 or 500 men. The main body of the Heimwehr, still had between 70,000 and 80,000 members; but, according to his information, neither Mussolini nor Starhemberg considered it of much further use because the army and police had been considerably strengthened and were quite capable of coping with any disorders. But this more modest role was resented in Heimwehr circles and caused severe criticism of Starhemberg and his leadership. According to another report, the whole grandiose scheme of creating a militia on fascist lines 'will require considerable modification in view of the straightened financial circumstances in which the whole Fascist movement finds itself'. The Austrian military authorities had never been enthusiastic about the plan, and their enthusiasm had waned further.

The outbreak of new fierce quarrels between the Heimwehr leaders, especially between Fey and Starhemberg, offered Schuschnigg the opportunity he had been waiting for. In October 1936 the government dissolved all para-military formations and incorporated them in the militia of the 'Patriotic Front', the only legal para-military assocation. This meant the end of the Heimwehr as a separate force and, as Selby commented, it also meant the end of the dualism which had existed since Dollfuss's death: 'Dr von Schuschnigg has now definitely established himself as sole leader.' A member of the Italian Legation contributed the information that Mussolini was 'tired' of Starhemberg and 'had placed the whole weight of his authority behind the Chancellor', for whom he had the highest regard, not only for his character 'but also for his capacity for work'[21] – a capacity which Starhemberg singularly lacked. In the opinion of the Legation, Schuschnigg was 'intensely serious and devout, an indefatigable worker', with a reputation for honesty 'as yet rare in Austria'. Since the disbandment of the various para-military associations he had steadily increased the strength of his position.[22]

On 10 July 1936 Selby wired London that the negotiations for an agreement which had been in progress for some time between von Papen, the German Minister, and Schuschnigg 'are approaching successful conclusion'; the Austrian conditions were the recognition of Austrian independence and of the principle of non-interference in internal affairs; National Socialism was neither a political factor nor a party with which agreements could be made and Austrian foreign policy would remain unchanged. The acceptance of these conditions by von Papen in the name of his government made the conclusion of a 'gentleman's agreement' possible. No change in the composition of the Austrian government was envisaged, but possibly one or two representatives of the 'national' circles would be admitted without a portfolio. In Selby's opinion, this step was taken 'without Austria abandoning a single one of the principles on which the present Austrian State is based or diverging in any way from the Dollfuss line'; Austria would now go 'her own cultural, political, social and economic way'.

The agreement was published on 11 July, and on the face of it its text confirmed the principles reported by Selby. In addition, Austria recognised that she was a 'German State', and it contained a secret clause according to which Schuschnigg promised 'a far-reaching political amnesty' for the arrested National Socialists and undertook to let 'representatives of the so-called "national opposition in Austria" partake in political responsibility' – a dangerous concession which could be interpreted in different ways.

A few days later the First Secretary of the Legation mentioned speculation about concessions which Schuschnigg 'may have made to Herr Hitler in return' for the agreement, but added that he was unable to obtain confirmation of such an undertaking. He also recorded the reactions in different Austrian circles: the 'underground' socialists and communists declared they would 'continue the struggle against the Fascist Dictatorship'; the Legitimists too were 'furious at what they consider the Chancellor's betrayal of his country'. The Jews as well as the extreme National Socialists were opposed to the agreement, but for different reasons; the latter felt 'that they have again been let down by Herr Hitler as in July 1934', but the 'moderate' National Socialists welcomed it. In general, he concluded, 'Dr von Schuschnigg seems to have achieved a striking success', although the socialists and extreme National Socialists were determined to continue their activities. From Innsbruck, the British consul added that 'the first cry of the Nazis was that they had been betrayed.' They distributed a pamphlet reminiscent of their praise of Röhm after his murder in June 1934. Another pamphlet was then smuggled across the frontier from Munich, extolling 'the beneficence and wisdom of the German Chancellor' and admonishing the National Socialists to 'a sense of their party loyalty'. During the recent visit to Salzburg the consul found 'senior Government officials sceptical and even despondent' about the agreement, while for the first few days those in Innsbruck had shown 'an exaggerated sense of triumph'. He concluded that the Austrian government had embarrassed or even failed 'its most valiant supporters' in the bureaucracy.[23]

The appreciation of the agreement in the Foreign Office was that at first sight it looked 'like a fine success for everyone except Germany'; but a closer look showed that this was not the case: 'the two countries are now so brought together that the result is already a sort of half-Anschluss'; the test was whether Germany would 'observe the spirit as well as the letter of the agreement'. Probably there would be a respite, but 'the *longer* view is less reassuring, and, on this basis, one can only incline to regard the agreement as a German victory.'[24] And so it was, especially with regard to the secret clause of which the British diplomats were unaware. With the growing rapprochement between Germany and Italy, Schuschnigg may have felt that he had no option but to make concessions, especially after Hitler's triumphant reoccupation of the Rhineland which met with no opposition from the western powers.

The reaction of the British press to the agreement differed a good deal. *The Times* had a first leader entitled 'A Welcome Agreement', which congratulated Hitler on 'another stroke of policy': the agreement would 'stabilize and pacify Central Europe, improve the economic conditions, and pave the way for a permanent settlement between the two main branches of the German race'. The advantage seemed to lie 'almost entirely with Austria': her independence was respected, the Austrian legion in Germany was to be dissolved, the agitation for the Anschluss, prompted from Berlin, was to be stopped, the 1000 mark tax on German visitors to Austria was to be rescinded; and in return Austria only conceded that Austrian National Socialists could join the 'Patriotic Front' and that a minister with German sympathies would enter the government. The agreement had clearly been concluded with the help of Mussolini who thus became more closely associated with Germany: Austria 'which has so long been an obstacle to better relations between Italy and Germany, has become a bridge between them.'

The leader of the *Manchester Guardian* was more critical. It stated that Hitler had three great aims: the Anschluss, the persecution of the Jews, and the overthrow of Bolshevism. He had not abandoned any of them, but with regard to the Anschluss he was 'willing to postpone it because he is sure that it will come in any case and because he thinks that a few years' delay will not matter'; the pronouncement by both Germans and Austrians that Austria was a 'Germanic State' was 'a recognition of Hitler's racial doctrine'. This was important, 'for the Germans have a habit of proclaiming abstract principles as a cover for their concrete demands – a "moral union" would give Germany the "right" (as Hitler would call it) to take a special interest in Austrian internal affairs. We shall hear more of this "right" later on.' The temporary abandonment of the union with Austria would give Hitler more freedom to pursue his two other aims: the persecution of the Jews was going on all the time 'and likely to grow even more severe'; the 'war against Bolshevism' would be pursued via Danzig, Memel and along the Baltic coast – and 'would the Western Powers ... intervene? These are the questions which Germany must be asking – and answering in a sense favourable to herself.'[25] The paper was quite correct both in claiming that Hitler would never give up his principal aims and in identifying three of them: he was to achieve two and to come more or less close to obtaining the third. It was a truly prophetic analysis.

That Hitler's aim with regard to Austria had not changed was shown only a few months later, in February 1937, when the German Foreign Minister, von Neurath, visited Vienna. All the way from the station to his residence he was greeted by large crowds which 'got completely out of hand', continuously shouting 'Heil Hitler'. In London the Austrian Minister called at the Foreign Office and explained 'that the German Government had abated nothing of their subversive and disruptive tactics, and Dr Schuschnigg was becoming weary of the incessant and disloyal intrigues'; Italy 'was proving an equally unreliable associate'. Vansittart replied 'that the sum and substance of his complaint was this: that Germany changed not at all, whereas Italy changed too much.'

To show von Neurath that they were still master in their own house the Austrian government on the day of his departure organised a mass demonstration all along the route by crowds shouting 'Heil Schuschnigg'. A diplomat present at the station heard the German military attaché mutter that Germany would never 'forget the insult'.

In April 1937 Hitler and Mussolini met at Venice. The official communiqué issued (as *The Times* reported from Vienna) gave a jolt to Austria because it failed to mention 'Italy's vital interest in Austria's independence', and Gayda, the editor of *Giornale d'Italia* (Mussolini's mouthpiece) stated that National Socialists were to enter the Austrian government. The article was suppressed in Austria but caused consternation in political circles which had 'barely recovered from the shock of the Austro-German truce of last July'. Schuschnigg, however, rejected the claim on the ground that 'coalition governments are excluded in Austria'. Selby added after a discussion with *The Times* correspondent that the Chancellor was 'still struggling to prevent himself from being subordinated completely to the Berlin/Rome axis'. He was convinced that Schuschnigg's difficulties would increase as a result of the Venice meeting; and everything ought to be done, 'especially at this moment to avoid [the] impression that Germany and Italy are having it all their own way in Central Europe'.[26] This clearly was the case for the time being.

When the British military attaché saw the Austrian Chief of Staff, General Jansa, in July 1937 he was told that the government was 'making headway against the disloyal elements', and that the internal 'situation had improved to an extent which he, personally, would not have dared to hope for two years ago'. The improved economic situation was a big factor in favour of the government. The general was convinced that Austria had nothing to fear from Germany as long as the Rome–Berlin axis lasted as Germany 'would not ignore Italian susceptibilities in this respect'.

In September Mussolini travelled to Berlin, where Hitler impressed him with German military might and the pact between the two countries was confirmed. But even then the Italian Foreign Minister, Count Ciano, assured the Austrian Minister in Rome that, as a result of the visit, 'there had been no change of any kind as regards Italian policy towards Austria'; the Political Director of the Austrian Foreign Office even informed Selby 'that this might be regarded as very reassuring'. When Selby left Vienna soon after he too considered 'the internal situation improved out of all comparison with that which I found here upon my arrival. Austria has just passed through the most peaceful summer she has been able to enjoy for four years past.' Under the influence of economic progress 'the Nazi agitation within Austria has seemed to have been robbed of much of its impetus', and many Austrian authorities believed 'it would be to-day a negligible quantity but for the influence of continuing pressure from Germany'. Schuschnigg, Selby stated, was 'held in high esteem in almost all quarters' and enjoyed the full confidence of the armed forces. An 'Austrian tradition' had developed and found expression in many ways, for example in the increasing encouragement of the Habsburg cause and the Habsburg tradition; the National Socialist menace aroused in many Austrians older memories of the Prussian menace. In short, 'in these last four years Austria has given proof, under the greatest tests ... that she has a soul of her own.'[27] The Austrian Chief of Staff and the departing British Minister were equally optimistic about the future, and yet within only six months their optimism proved totally unfounded. What they failed to perceive was that the Rome-Berlin axis would allow Hitler to pursue on his own terms his fundamental aim – the union of Austria with Germany. Austria's independence was not assured, but endangered by the new axis.

The revival of the Habsburg tradition and the possibility of a restoration were also discussed in the Foreign Office. In 1934 E. H. Carr wrote a memorandum, 'The Prospects of a Hapsburg Restoration', in which he argued that 'the failure to create any kind of Austrian patriotism' constituted 'an obvious danger to the existing balance of power'; therefore 'the idea has naturally cropped up of endeavouring to supply this want by restoring the old personal loyalty to the house of Hapsburg ... as a sentimental barrier against union with a non-Hapsburg Germany.' Carr found this argument quite unconvincing, for the Habsburgs of those days ruled an empire of 55 million inhabitants, and the Austrians then 'were immune against any strong tendency to gravitate towards Germany. ... Nothing can restore this state of affairs.' A revived Habsburg Empire consisting of the small present-day Austria, or even of Austria and Hungary, under Italian tutelage, 'would no doubt appeal to the remnants of the old aristocracy and to a few survivors of an older generation', but such a restoration would not 'really be popular with the Austrian people as a whole, or could be regarded ultimately as a satisfactory alternative to union with the great German State'. It was doubtful too whether a restoration 'would have any real durability: it would certainly have none unless it included Hungary, and unless it held out hopes of further territorial accretions in future.' Vansittart considered this 'a very good and useful memorandum'.

At the beginning of 1935 Selby reported there was hardly any doubt 'that the sympathies of the majority of those in power today in Austria are distinctly favourable to a legitimist restoration', but the wiser among them were aware of the international difficulties which stood in the way, and the government spokesmen always protested that the question was not actual. He also mentioned that the deputy mayor of Vienna had 'staggered' the French Minister by claiming that large sections of the working class would welcome a restoration. An artist of his acquaintance with many contacts in these circles confirmed 'that the monarchical idea was not as distasteful as might be thought, since the working classes had been very well treated by the Hapsburgs, and they were now disposed to look back with regret to the "wide liberties" which they enjoyed under the Empire, liberties no longer enjoyed under the present regime.'

Soon after, Selby described the elaborate arrangements made at the ball of the City of Vienna and 'the great reception accorded to the Archduke Eugen' who arrived just before President Miklas – 'a special procession being arranged to accompany him to his seat in the midst of the hall beside the Chancellor, President and other members of the Government'. Members of the Imperial family were well represented at the ball, and received 'a welcome of a very significant character'.[28]

In July 1935 Vansittart addressed the question to the Czechoslovak Minister in London, Jan Masaryk, why his government was opposed to a Habsburg restoration, and Sargent further enquired 'whether his Government feared that a Habsburg monarchy would act as a focus of attraction on the German minority in Czechoslovakia'. This was denied by Masaryk, but he admitted that the Yugoslav and Romanian governments had such fears in respect of their Croatian and Transylvanian minorities. To Sargent it seemed 'a sad confession of failure' that these states, after 16 years of independence, had made so little progress in establishing a new patriotism that they were afraid 'lest the ghost of the old Habsburg dynasty at the Hofburg' might tempt away not only the German minorities, but even the discontented elements among the Slavs. He also pointed out that, if responsible Austrian statesmen now toyed with the idea of restoration, 'it was surely because these statesmen were beginning to feel that since all other methods of giving Austria the will to live apart from Germany had failed, they must needs have recourse to this method, ... simply because there was nothing else to try'. The British and French governments were bound to sympathise with any sincere attempt by Austria to strengthen her independence even though they might not have chosen this particular method. Vansittart minuted that he was not impressed by the arguments of the Little Entente against a return of the Habsburgs; their policy towards Austria 'has been a long and wordy futility', and 'they will eventually regret their obstinacy, for they will drive Austria & Hungary in the German direction'.

A few months later Vansittart explained to the former Hungarian Minister in London that a restoration could only be brought about 'as a result of an amicable arrangement with the Little Entente' and that no progress had been made in that direction. When asked whether Archduke Otto von Habsburg (pretender to the throne) could come privately to England to shoot and be received equally privately by the King, Vansittart replied that any such plan should 'be abandoned, at any rate until the world was in a less troubled condition than it was at present', because the visit 'would in itself give rise to endless comment and suspicion in Europe'.[29]

In June 1936 Selby reported that the legitimists were showing signs of great activity which were alarming the French Minister; their argument was that sympathy with a restoration was 'at its height in the country and that opportunity must not be missed'; a restoration would 'consolidate the country against ambitions of Herr Hitler and defeat his policy'. After the agreement of July 1936, Selby wrote later, the legitimists kept quiet but their agitation revived when the National Socialists tried to exploit the agreement 'to establish their authority in the counsels of the Government', and new adherents were won 'in the most unexpected quarters'. The Annual Report of the Legation for 1937 mentioned successful legitimist meetings in Carinthia as well as a speech of the Archbishop of Salzburg which was 'strongly monarchist in tone'. The principal meeting took place in Vienna in November in honour of the 25th birthday of the Archduke Otto in the presence of many members of the Habsburg family. In his speech the legitimist leader, von Wiesner, claimed that the movement had 1,200,000 adherents, calculated by adding up the membership of the societies which had accepted Otto's patronage and one-third of the population of all the communes which had made him an honorary citizen[30] - a rather odd way of reaching a total. But there can be little doubt that the legitimist movement had grown during these years, even if it was not a mass movement.

The Annual Report for 1937 also mentioned the growing political influence of the Catholic Church; but many of its 'sincerest well-wishers' were perturbed at the effect, for they feared that it did not reflect interest in the Roman Catholic religion but caused 'the responsibility for any mistakes made by the Government to be laid at the door of the Church'.

Another force supporting the government was the official 'Patriotic Front', which all those dependent on the authorities had to join. On a Sunday in October 1936 it held a mass demonstration on a former parade-ground outside Vienna which was attended, according to the official estimate, by 365,000 people. As the Legation reported, 'it had apparently been made quite clear to all available State employees that they were expected to attend', and supporters were brought to Vienna by special trains, revealing 'a capacity for organisation about the existence of which there had previously been some doubt'. The voice of Dollfuss was mobilised through a recording of one of his speeches, and Schuschnigg received 'an enthusiastic reception ... well above the average for an Austrian audience'. He spoke with 'energy and vigour' and looked 'unusually cheerful', but according to the report, 'little that is new has emerged from the events' or from the speeches of the leaders.

In June 1937 Selby recorded the appointments of a prominent nationalist from the Tyrol to the *Volkspolitische Referat* within the Patriotic Front and of the nationalist lawyer, Dr Seyss-Inquart, to examine the question of recruitment to it 'of circles which have hitherto abstained and to make suitable proposals'. These appointments, he wired, were 'intended as a gesture to "national" elements'; they were made by Schuschnigg 'in the hope that the more reasonable of these elements will be induced to co-operate loyally with his organisation' and that the tension with Germany would abate. The Chancellor was making similar advances to the workers who had remained 'solidly socialist', but this would probably require allowing free elections in the official trade unions.[31] It was not realised how dangerous such concessions to the 'national' elements were, and what were the aims of the 'more reasonable' among them? To what extent did they differ from those of the National Socialists?

'National' elements were also present in the army. In July 1934 the British military attaché discussed the situation with Major-General Wiktorin of the War Ministry, who stated frankly that 'the Army was as opposed to the present government as ever'. The senior officers were determined to achieve the disbandment of the Heimwehr and the end of the conflict with Germany; they were not in favour of the Anschluss, but they were stubbornly anti-Italian and would like to 'get rid of all the semi-military formations and set the stage for elections and a return to constitutional government'. According to the general, the army would 'continue to do its duty impartially *vis-à-vis* armed rebellion', but as long as the regime maintained its intransigent attitude to Germany it could 'reckon only on the physical as opposed to the moral and political support of the Army'. The Legation's Annual Report for 1934 added that several army units were strongly influenced by 'the Hitler bacillus' but the same units 'took the field against their Nazi comrades with the most surprising unanimity'; the bulk of opinion among officers and other ranks was 'definitely pan-German as opposed to pure "Hitler"'.

In 1935 Military Intelligence confirmed that in the army a strong desire existed for cooperation with Germany and an 'extreme dislike of Italy' (as might be expected after the Great War and the loss of South Tyrol). In the following year the Chief of the General Staff, General Jansa, told the British military attaché that he had been slow to accept the German view about Soviet Russia, 'but it was only necessary to look at Europe to-day to realise what a menace Russian activities had become'. In consequence of the alliance with Czechoslovakia, Russia was 'within easy striking distance of Vienna, Budapest and Berlin'; Russian air-bases were being established all over eastern Slovakia, and a Russian Intelligence Bureau existed in Bratislava, he had heard 'on reliable authority'. When the attaché suggested that Russian preparations in Slovakia were perhaps exaggerated, Jansa agreed that the Russians had not yet established themselves all that firmly, 'but it was only a question of time – possibly of months – before it would be so.' In his opinion, the stepping-up of compulsory military service in Germany 'was prompted entirely by ... the growing danger of Russian militarism'.[32] Even an Austrian General who had a reputation for being firmly anti-Nazi had fully accepted the National Socialist view of the Soviet menace.

Hatred of Italy was not confined to army officers and was particularly strong in Carinthia and the Tyrol bordering upon

Italy, as the British consul reported frequently from Innsbruck: 'sarcastic and indignant comments on the Italian national character and on the Austrian Government are made by all classes of society.' In Carinthia, a high-ranking official remarked to him that Austria had no future until she 'parted company with the two Romes', that of Fascism and that of the Vatican. He also noticed 'a general feeling of uncertainty', caused by a conviction 'that the patience of the people is being tried too highly by the pro-Italian foreign policy' of the government. In 1936 he mentioned bickering between Slovenes and German Nationalists in Carinthia, but this was 'dwarfed by the hatred of Italy at present prevailing in that province'; timber exporters were unable to obtain payment from their Italian debtors and this caused loud protests, even in the local papers. When Mussolini travelled to Berlin in September 1937 the people of Tyrol 'resented the presence in North Tyrol of one whom they regard as the persecutor of their South Tyrolese brothers'; and a contingent of youths to parade at Innsbruck station in honour of the guest had to be brought from Salzburg because the authorities felt 'that representatives of the Austrian Youth Movement from Tyrol could not be relied upon to behave with sufficient decorum in the presence of Signor Mussolini.' After the onset of the Spanish Civil War, it seemed to the consul as if the flood of anit-communist propaganda might overcome the hostility to Italy in western Austria, 'but the old feeling soon returned'.[33]

The pro-Italian policy of the Austrian government clearly caused much uneasiness even among its own followers and prevented it from gaining support from circles which were not in favour of the Anschluss to a Hitlerite Germany. The consul also noticed that in Innsbruck society 'conversation turns immediately and inevitably to the dangers of communism in Europe' and the strong influence exercised by the Spanish Civil War. He had little doubt that this trend was officially encouraged. The conception of the Austrian government 'as a Central European pillar against Bolshevism' was naturally welcome to official circles: – this, and 'spontaneous fear have combined to canalise local political feeling into one dominant obsession.' A British history student at Vienna University remarked in 1937: 'So long as a change of government is possible overnight officials will try to keep a foot in each camp, and this opens the door to measureless bribery and corruption'. Another evil was the government's 'hopelessly unsocial policy'; hardly any attempt was made 'to win the workers from their sullen resentment or active opposition'.[34] At about the same time Selby's assessment was far more optimistic: 'The success of the Austrian resistance has made a deep impression upon the minds of a large and influential section of Austrian opinion'; it had revived memories of 'the great role played by Austria in the centuries gone by in relation to Germany', as well as the Austrian detestation of Prussia 'and everything to do with Prussia'. The strength of this feeling accounted for much that had happened in Austro-German relations since 1934 and it emerged with growing force in almost all his conversations with Austrians. Quite recently President Miklas had remarked to him: 'It is our influence which should extend to the Rhine. It is Austria which represents German culture. It is Austria which remains the last stronghold of that culture against the advance of Prussia.'[35] This no doubt reflected the mood in government circles and among certain groups supporting the government, but it was somewhat simplistic: the decisive question was how widespread such ideas were.

Certainly widespread and growing was anti-Semitism, among supporters as well as opponents of the government. In October 1934 an order was issued to stop the recruitment of Jews for the Heimwehr. The American Minister, Messersmith, told Selby that he had spoken to Schuschnigg about this and warned him of the danger of following the German example, but Schuschnigg indicated that he 'could not exercise that restraint on the anti-Semitic tendencies of his followers which was desirable', while the Jewish leaders informed Messersmith that they were completely satisfied with the Chancellor's personal attitude.

In 1936 Leopold Kunschak, a leader of the Christian Workers' Association, demanded a solution of the Jewish problem on the basis of social considerations, the Legation reported, and added: 'only two courses are open to us: either we must solve the Jewish question without delay . . . or it will solve itself in a battle of wild instincts.' At the same time, E. H. Carr minuted that Mandl and a few rich Jews had nothing to fear, but the ordinary Jews were 'seriously discriminated against'; the trouble was that 'an anti-Semitic policy will increase the popularity of the regime'. From

Vienna Selby wrote in the same year that he had talked to the Foreign Minister and advised him that the government should use their influence 'to discourage anything in the nature of anti-Semitic pronouncements'. The Foreign Minister replied they would do what they could to restrain the press, but the unfortunate affair of the failure of the Phoenix Insurance Company had contributed to the growth of anti-Semitism – a fact which Selby confirmed.[36]

At the end of 1937 the Legation reported that anti-Semitism was increasing in Vienna; the slogan 'Christians, buy from Christians' was receiving some publicity, and the fact that a Jewish tradesman put his foot through a display window of the German Travel bureau caused 'reprisals'; the windows of many Jewish shops in different parts of Vienna were smashed – presumably by National Socialists. The Annual Report for 1937 recorded that 'a more definite economic anti-Semitism has appeared with the complementary slogan: "Buy from Aryan tradesmen"'. A deputy mayor of Vienna, speaking at a meeting of small traders, declared 'that the Viennese would defend themselves with all their force against the dubious competition of post-war immigrants' and distinguished 'between what he called Viennese anti-Semitism and the National-Socialist brand'. The general atmosphere in Carinthia had become so strongly anti-Semitic that Jews no longer went there for their summer holidays. In short, 'Austria is at present growing gradually a less comfortable and profitable home for the Jews.'

From Innsbruck the British consul wrote that there was no official discrimination against Jews, but their position was 'steadily becoming worse'. The very few Jewish lawyers of Innsbruck 'have been boycotted out of their profession by their colleagues'; a few Jewish doctors maintained themselves 'by working exceedingly hard' and principally treating foreign tourists; 'it is virtually impossible for a Jew to work at a local hospital', and 'Jewish businessmen are suffering from a silent, but effective boycott'. In the schools 'non-Jewish children are not discouraged when they indulge in petty persecution of Jewish children', and a special section of the official *Jungvolk* had been created for Jewish children. 'In theory Jews are treated with an undiscriminating liberalism, in practice there is great anti-Semitic pressure.'[37]

What emerges from the reports is that in provinces such as Carinthia or the Tyrol anti-Semitism was considerably stronger than in Vienna although the Jewish population outside the capital was extremely small. As the Legation's Annual Report put it in 1937, 'many ordinary Austrian town-dwellers' felt an 'inborn dislike for the Jew'. Only a few weeks after these reports were sent to London Austrian anti-Semitism showed itself in its true colours.

Economically the regime had become more stable, and Schuschnigg had gained in political stature. But politically it was still very fragile, unable to win new adherents from either the left or the right. Above all, with the creation of the Rome–Berlin axis, it could no longer reckon on the backing of the Italian dictator, although this was apparently not realised at the time in Vienna.

Notes

1. *The Times*, 26 July, *Manchester Guardian*, 26 July 1934.
2. *Manchester Guardian*, 27 July, Lt.-Col. Mason-MacFarlane to Selby, 31 July, and Drummond to FO, Rome, 26 July 1934: FO 371, file 18354, fo. 106 f., file 18352, fo. 155.
3. Reports by Lt.-Col. Mason-MacFarlane, 19 March, 31 July and 2 August, and Hadow to FO, 27 July 1934: FO 371, file 18366, fo. 67, file 18354, fos. 111, 127, file 18352, fo. 166; *The Times*, 27 July; *Manchester Guardian*, 28 July 1934. The casualty figures are taken from 'Austria. Annual Report, 1934', FO 371, file 19843, fo. 281: they show that the *Schutzkorps* had far heavier casualties than the army or the gendarmerie. For details of the fighting, etc. see Gerhard Jagschitz, *Der Putsch – Die Nationalsozialisten 1934 in Österreich* (Graz and Vienna, 1976), pp. 145–56.
4. *Manchester Guardian*, 31 July, and Simon to MacDonald, 27 July 1934: FO 800, file 291 (Simon Papers).
5. Memorandum by Hadow on the Putsch, s.d., Ian Henderson to Hadow, 18 July, Selby to Simon, 4 and 21 August, minute by Vansittart, 26 July 1934, and a note by Simon, s.d.: FO 371, file 18354, fos. 17, 97, file 18352, fos. 154, 193, FO 120, file 1090.
6. Selby to Sir Samuel Hoare, 28 October 1935; minute by G. Bramwell, 27 October 1936; 'Austria. Annual Report, Economic' for 1936 and 1937; reports by Lt.-Col. K. V. B. Benfield, 30 July, and by Ian Henderson, 21 July 1937; and monthly reports on economic conditions in Austria, 13 August, 9 September, 6

November and 4 December 1937: FO 371, file 19479, fo. 54, file 20362, fo. 309, file 21114, fos. 194, 363, file 21119, fo. 51, file 21115, fo. 232 f., file 21114, fos. 276, 283, 359, 376.

7. Monthly report on economic conditions in Austria, 11 March 1938, and unsigned memorandum, 9 March 1938: FO 371, file 22309, fo. 169, file 22320, fo. 37 f.

8. Selby to FO, 30 January, memoranda by Eden, Runciman and Chamberlain, 24–25 February, and Conclusion of a Cabinet Meeting, 26 February 1936: Cab. 24, vol. 260, Cab. 23, vol. 83, pp. 184–5.

9. Notes for Col. Paget's lecture on 'Austria', 25 January, and unsigned note on conversation with O'Malley, 1 April 1935: WO 190, files 293 and 316.

10. Minutes by Carr, 15 and 27 August, and Selby to Simon, 4 August 1934: FO 371, file 18354, fo. 204, file 18355, fo. 154, file 18354, fo. 85.

11. Selby to Simon, 26 October, and FO wire to Rome, 1 August 1934: FO 371, file 18366, fo. 157 f., file 18367, fo. 34 ff.

12. Selby to Simon, 3 August, minutes by Carr, 8 and 16 August, by Vansittart, 9 August, and R. A. Gallop, 14 August 1934: FO 371, file 18354, fos. 14–18, 120 f.

13. Selby to Simon, 9, 16 and 26 October 1934: FO 371, file 18357, fo. 148, file 18366, fo. 157 f., FO 120, file 1079.

14. 'Austria. Annual Report, 1934': FO 371, file 19483, fo. 282.

15. Selby to Simon, 27 October, Ian Henderson to Selby, 6 November 1934 and 15 July 1935: FO 371, file 18358, fos. 142, 184, file 19482, fo. 57.

16. Report by Carr, 14 October, minute by Sargent, 17 December 1934, and Selby to Simon, 27 April 1935: FO 371, file 18358, fos. 339, 345, file 19478, fo. 220.

17. Selby to Simon, 15 February, with minutes by Carr and Simon, 22–23 February 1935: FO 371, file 19481, fos. 99 f., 103.

18. Ian Henderson to Selby, 13 April, Mack to Hoare, 23 October, Sargent to Selby, 30 October, and Selby to FO, 13 September 1935: FO 371, file 19481, fo. 140 f., file 19482, fo. 121, file 19485, fo. 231 f., FO 120, file 1093.

19. Selby, *Diplomatic Twilight 1930–1940*, pp. 51–2; Sargent to Selby, 14 November 1935: FO 120, file 1103.

20. Selby to Eden, 13, 16 and 19 May, and minute by Vansittart on conversation with Franckenstein, 13 May 1936: FO 120, file 1113, FO 371, file 20361, fos. 111–14, 144 ff.

21. Selby to Sargent, 3 March, Mack to Eden, 14 March, Selby to Eden, 12 October 1936: FO 120, file 1116, FO 371, file 20360, fo. 33 f., file 20362, fo. 277 f.

22. Selby to Eden, 1 January 1937: FO 371, file 21115, fo. 49, p. 23.
23. Selby to FO, 10 July, Mack to Eden, 18 July, and Henderson to Selby, 10 August 1936: FO 371, file 20363, fos. 182 f., 269–75, file 20364, fo. 24 ff. The full text of the agreement of 11 July 1936 in K. Schuschnigg, *Im Kampf gegen Hitler* (Vienna, Munich and Zürich, 1969), pp. 187–90.
24. Connor to Gascoigne at the FO, 27 July 1936: FO 120, file 1108.
25. *The Times*, 13 July; *Manchester Guardian*, 13 July 1936.
26. Selby, *Diplomatic Twilight 1930–1940*, pp. 70–1; Vansittart's minute, 31 March 1937: FO 371, file 21119, fo. 362; *The Times*, 26 April; and Selby to Eden, 4 May 1937: FO 120, file 1126.
27. Report by Lt.-Col. Benfield on conversation with General Jansa, 30 July, Selby to Eden, 5 and 13 October 1937: FO 371, file 21119, fo. 51 f., FO 120, file 1136, FO 371, file 21116, fo. 321 ff., FO 120, file 1129.
28. Memorandum by Carr, 3 April, with Vansittart's minute of 16 April 1934, Selby to Simon, 31 January and 14 February 1935: FO 371, file 18364, fos. 78, 83 f., file 19483, fos. 9, 24, FO 120, file 1096.
29. Minutes by Sargent and Vansittart, 26–28 July and 18 November 1935: FO 371, file 19483, fos. 115 ff., 203f.
30. Selby to FO, 28 June 1936 and 13 February 1937, 'Annual Report on Austria for 1937': FO 371, file 20365, fo. 310, file 21119, fo. 2, file 22320, fo. 181.
31. 'Annual Report on Austria for 1937', Mack to Eden, 21 October 1936, and Selby to FO, 18 June 1937: FO 371, file 22320, fo. 178, file 20362, fo. 295 ff., file 21118, fos. 73, 76.
32. Lt.-Col. Mason-MacFarlane to Selby, 31 July 1934; 'Austria. Annual Report, 1934'; secret Intelligence note, 1 April 1935; and report by Major Benfield, 26 August 1936: FO 371, file 18354, fo. 124 f., file 19483, fo. 281 f., WO 190, file 316, FO 371, file 20364, fo. 16 f.
33. Henderson to Selby, 1 December 1935, 29 January 1936, 3 October and 12 December 1937: FO 371, file 19482, fo. 169 f., FO 120, files 1099, 1109 and 1136, FO 371, file 21116, fo. 407 f.
34. Henderson to Selby, 25 August 1936, and Seiby to Sargent, 11 May 1937: FO 120, files 1120 and 1123.
35. Selby to Eden, 15 March 1937: FO 371, file 21115, fo. 111.
36. Selby to Simon, 27 October 1934, Mack to Eden, 31 March, minute by Carr, 2 April, and Selby to Eden, 23 April 1936: FO 371, file 18358, fo. 142 f., FO 120, file 1117, FO 371, file 20367, fos. 398, 410.
37. Mack to Eden, 21 December 1937, 'Annual Report on Austria for 1937', and Henderson to Palairet, 5 January 1938: FO 371, file 21116, fo. 413 f., file 22320, fos. 177 ff., 107 ff.

8 The Opposition

For five years the authoritarian Austrian regime was able to maintain a precarious balance between the forces opposing it from the left and the right. The greater threat to its existence seemed to come from the right, partly because its strength was spread more evenly over the whole country, party because it was consistently backed by the might of Hitler's Germany, and partly because the measures taken against the right were intermittent and alternated with periods of leniency, especially after the agreement of July 1936. In September 1934 Selby reported that a National Socialist cell had been discovered in the Lower Austrian Medical Association and that it had been completely reorganised; 400 employees of the 'Alpine Montangesellschaft' and its Managing Director were dismissed for their role in the July Putsch; and all professors of known socialist or Nazi leanings were compulsorily retired.

In Vorarlberg, as the British consul wrote from Innsbruck in August, the majority of the people were still National Socialist in sentiment; the centre of their activities was focused on Dornbirn. This applied in particular to business circles which had long been anti-clerical, and to the younger generation of industrialists: 'political sentiment is not here the result of economic depression.' When E. H. Carr had lunch in a small town near Linz in the autumn, he was treated by the waiter 'to the most thoroughgoing Nazi propaganda'. When the man had finished his harangue 'he took out of his pocket with a wink a membership card and badge of the Fatherland Front, and explained that 60 groschen a month was the cheapest form of political insurance he had every heard of'; 80 per cent of the people he knew were National Socialists and all had enrolled in the Fatherland Front.[1] Its colossal membership figures reported from all over Austria obviously included many such prudent people as well as many who joined under pressure, or to obtain jobs and other benefits.

In the spring of 1935 Selby was informed by one of the principal intermediaries between the 'national' opposition and the government that all negotiations between them were suspended because 'the present recognised leader of the Nazis, Herr Leopold', was under police supervision in his house at Krems which he was not permitted to leave. Selby was told that a grave danger of 'a fresh campaign of terrorism' existed, including attempts on the lives of government ministers; the government was 'courting disaster by their attitude', for the National Socialists were allegedly willing to recognise the independence of Austria, 'provided they are allowed a say in the Government of the country consistent with what they believe to be the support behind them', but they were 'being driven to desperation' by the attitude of the government. It was the old story of the 'moderate Nazis', who were willing to treat with the government and recognise Austria's independence, and of the 'extremists' who favoured violence and terrorism and carried out the July Putsch. Who could say what the strength of these factions was, and which one would be supported by Germany?

In the autumn the British consul in Innsbruck stated that 'Carinthians of all ranks remain staunch in their Pan-Germanism' and that 'the inroads made by the National Socialist creed into official circles are remarkable'; the National Socialists of Vorarlberg were equally active and among their leaders were members of the local intelligentsia, including the masters of the Protestant school at Bregenz. In Vienna, medallions commemorating the return of the Saar to Germany were distributed with the legend 'the Saar has proved it, Austria will prove it'. In Upper Austria, however, certain leaders of the underground party in March 1935 'voluntarily decided to cease their political activities and to enter the Patriotic Front'; they advised their sub-leaders to report to the authorities. This was followed to some extent and quantities of arms were surrendered. But, as Selby quite rightly commented, 'it would certainly at present be premature to conclude from it that it represents a definite beginning of the cessation of Nazi activities.' The British military attaché estimated that only 5000 National Socialists were enrolled within Austria in military formations, and another 12,000 in the Austrian Legion in Germany; its camps in Bavaria 'have been more or less broken up and a proportion of the personnel has been enrolled in the Reichswehr.'[2] We know from other sources that other 'legionaries' were trained by the SS at the concentration camp of Dachau; and the figure of only 5000 for the Austrian SA and SS seems to have been an underestimate.

In the spring of 1936 the British consul reported from Innsbruck that the local authorities had discovered repeated attempts to reform the National Socialist political and para-military organisations, which had largely collapsed after the uprising of July 1934; provincial organisations of the SA and the Hitler Youth were uncovered, and in Carinthia one of the SS; a National Socialist Winter Help fund was active in several provinces, almost certainly with German support. The chief activity of the National Socialists was the distribution of leaflets and pamphlets and the 'spreading of alarmist and defamatory rumours'; money was freely given to party members who lost their jobs or were reduced to want for political reasons. In April, the consul added, the authorities seized a whole convoy of arms which were smuggled for the National Socialists from Yugoslavia into Carinthia; the struggle between the National Socialists and the government was 'increasing in intensity' in the Alpine provinces. When the consul visited Vienna in the same month, he mentioned strong sympathies with National Socialism among the garrison and police of Salzburg; anti-government and anti-Italian feelings were 'stronger than ever'. In the autumn he stated that the economic distress in Carinthia 'continued to engender a bitter feeling' against the government; the National Socialist rank and file were holding clandestine meetings, collecting funds for their cause, and undergoing secret military training; desertions had occurred from the ranks of the Heimwehr and the Ostmärkische Sturmscharen.

When Hitler occupied the Rhineland in March 1936, the Legation reported, the National Socialists were 'naturally elated'; many others 'in their heart of hearts are glad to see that their blood brethren have asserted their right to equality, and while not condoning Hitler's method, hope he will nevertheless be successful.' In August Selby wrote of the results of the agreement of July between Austria and Germany: the National Socialists released under the amnesty were received in Linz 'with music and bombarded with flowers, the police available being too weak in numbers to enforce the official prohibition'. Similar scenes occurred in Innsbruck at a meeting of the German-Austrian Alpine Club. Worse was to follow in Vienna on the occasion of the passing of the Olympic torch through Vienna and of a parade of the athletes going to the Olympic games in Berlin: 'a concentrated mass of Nazis had placed themselves between the Burg ... and the main bulk of the athletes'; they constantly interrupted the official speeches making them inaudible, and sang the 'Horst-Wessel Lied' as well as 'Deutschland über Alles'. According to Selby, the demonstrators numbered 5000–6000; they were well organised, 'mostly young men and women of the poorer classes'.[3]

How close were the links between the National Socialists and the German Legation in Vienna emerged in October 1936 on the occasion of a mass demonstration of the 'Patriotic Front'. Hitler's special envoy in Vienna, von Papen, expressed the hope that Schuschnigg would use the occasion to say 'something nice' about the July agreement, and the Austrians expected that he wished to be present, but he left Vienna on one of his frequent shooting trips. When his counsellor asked whether he should attend the ceremony von Papen prevaricated, 'and said – this is the sinister part of the story – that he had better consult Herr Leopold', the leader of the National Socialists recently released from prison. The counsellor did so and was 'advised' not to attend. 'The fact that the German Legation takes advice, if not orders, from Herr Leopold is an interesting illustration of the value of the Austro-German Agreement of 11th July,' the Secretary of the British Legation wrote. The Austrian government were 'particularly annoyed about this incident' because they were for the first time officially represented at the Nuremberg party rally of September, 'although it was known in advance that members of the Austrian Legion would take part in the march past.'

In May 1936 Phipps in Berlin heard 'on excellent authority' that Hitler 'instructed his Munich leaders to have nothing to do with violence in Austria if they valued their lives'; the Austrian problem must be handled very differently, 'he must advance step by step', and there must be no Putsch. The agreement of July clearly was a big step for Hitler in the direction he wanted to move. Even if he had no high opinion of the Austrian National Socialists and their leaders who were for ever quarrelling among themselves, they were certainly extremely useful for putting pressure on the Austrian government and for exploiting the July agreement.

In November the British Legation reported that since the agreement 'the pro-German section of the population has arrogated greater liberty to itself in Styria and elsewhere'; National Socialist demonstrations in Graz, Innsbruck and Salzburg 'have been treated by the police and gendarmerie with the leniency which they used to show towards members of the Heimatschutz'; the French Minister in Vienna was so worried that he brought the reports privately to the government's notice. The incompetent Minister of Security had been replaced, and it remained to be seen whether his successor would do any better.[4]

In 1937 there were many more reports from the consul at Innsbruck about 'illegal' National Socialist activities. Efforts were made to reorganise the SA, and the labour exchange was used to recruit new members and to collect funds for the party. In Innsbruck and Hall the authorities discovered a 'National Socialist Soldiers' Ring' which aimed at 'undermining the loyalty of the Army' and winning adherents among officers and other ranks. In Carinthia, groups of the party and the Hitler Youth 'continue to flourish and seem lately to have received a fresh impetus'. They also did secret military drilling. In many parts swastika fires were lit on the mountains to celebrate Hitler's birthday on 20 April. 'Most western Austrians' supported the efforts of the Hitler government because they were longing to reverse the result of the Great War with regard to the South Tyrol: neither 'Catholicism nor the desire, where this exists, for Austrian independence' could check this ambition.

The National Socialists were for ever comparing 'the alleged plenty in Germany with the poverty existing in Austria, especially in the western provinces'. Although the economic situation had slightly improved even there, their 'pathetic belief that all goes well in Germany, all ill in Austria' remained 'totally unchanged'; the chances of detaching 'nationally-minded' people from their pro-German stance 'are remote'.

When the consul visited Klagenfurt at the end of 1937 the 'local Nazis were most concerned to impress me with what they called the unreliability of rumours that the Austrian Government is gaining ground in the country.' Anti-Semitism was 'keenly fanned', and people who were considered lukewarm in their attitude to Germanism were 'slandered and ostracised' as being of Jewish origin. In Salzburg and the Tyrol, new SA and SS formations were uncovered, as well as branches of the Hitler Youth, and the propaganda efforts were mainly directed at the young. In Carinthia, 'all classes are dissatisfied with the Austrian regime'; the liberal professions 'are in the main devoted adherents of the German Chancellor', and local industrialists 'speak of Herr Hitler with no less affection than the most loyal National Socialist in Germany'. Bitter memories existed of the fighting in July 1934, and confidential decisions of the local authorities were 'at once communicated to the German Consul'. In short, 'there is certainly less loyalty to the Austrian Government in Carinthia than in any other Austrian province', while in the Tyrol the government had the support of the aristocracy, the gentry, the peasants and to a large extent of official circles.[5] Ever since the fighting against the Yugoslavs Carinthia had been a hotbed of German nationalism and here, as elsewhere, nationalism easily merged into National Socialism.

Even among the Vienna workers, an English history student reported in 1937, 'Nazism has made some progress', partly out of a kind of snobbery. The electrical workers at Siemens had '"gone Nazi" to show that they are not "proletarians"'; other social groups mentioned by her as 'largely Nazi' were students, rural doctors and dentists, shopkeepers and unemployed intellectuals. In July, Austrian and German ex-servicemen met at Wels in Upper Austria. The Legation's Annual Report for 1937 recorded that the German veterans were loudly cheered, in contrast with the Austrians, 'and the Nazis generally obtained control of the situation'. The same happened at the winter ski-jumping competition near Klagenfurt, where 'the German participants were loudly cheered by the spectators ... while the Austrian competitors were received with silence or with boos.'[6] Such meetings offered an ideal ground for National Socialist propaganda.

In 1937 the so-called Committee of Seven was formed, three of whom were active National Socialists, to prepare 'the gradual transfer to a legal status of illegal National Socialist circles', as the Austrian Foreign Ministry put it in a statement sent to London. For this task 'it was obviously necessary to grant the Committee of Seven a certain freedom of movement and to allow them contact with members of the illegal movement', and they were therefore allowed to open an office in the Teinfaltstrasse of Vienna. The government was aware that the toleration of this office would lead to many misinterpretations but accepted this disadvantage 'as part of the bargain, since otherwise every thread leading to National Socialism in Austria would have been severed, which would have been undesirable on grounds of interior and external policy.' According to the Austrian Foreign Minister, the government was very glad this office existed, 'for it enabled the police (who had a *poste d'observation* on the other side of the street) to supervise with ease the activities and the visitors'. One member of the committee was Dr Leopold Tavs, a subordinate to the National Socialist leader Captain Leopold; both were under police observation, a task made easier by the fact that 'the latter's yellow car, supplied by Germany, made itself conveniently conspicious.'

Within the 'illegal' National Socialist movement, however, strong opposition developed to this 'legal' course and the committee's negotiations with the government. Some members of the committee were received by the government and 'took notice' of (but did not recognise) the independence of Austria. Leopold countered the opposition by removing the Gau leader of Vienna and his subordinates from their posts, and open conflict broke out between the factions. When the police raided the office in the Teinfaltstrasse early in 1938 they discovered in Tavs' drawer, as *The Times* reported, a detailed 'plan of action for 1938' which 'allotted to the German Army, SS and SA their respective parts in an attack on Austria'. The plan accused Schuschnigg of not fulfilling the agreement of July 1936 so that its fulfilment would have to be enforced against him. Germany was to demand 'the integral fulfilment' of the agreement, the resignation of the Austrian government and the appointment of a Chancellor 'capable and willing to fulfil inter-state treaties'. If the government declined to accept these demands, the German forces were to be moved to the frontier and the National Socialist Party was to be given complete toleration.[7]

Tavs, who described himself as the *Gauleiter* of Vienna, was arrested on a charge of treason and declared the document was his personal property – a claim which was accepted by the authorities. When the government was criticised for not doing enough for 'pacification' it could now produce this plan to point out what the 'Pacification Committee' had been hatching. The Austrian government stressed that its readiness 'to win the "national opposition" to positive collaboration remains unaltered', but any serious collaboration with 'national' circles 'is now as previously only possible if these abstain from any illegal activity.' The Foreign Minister, Dr Guido Schmidt, informed the British Minister that they hoped 'the German Government will realise that the Austrian Government cannot tolerate this state of things and that a new and better *modus vivendi* will be arrived at.' The Tavs affair, he claimed, was causing the government no alarm: 'on the contrary, they rather welcomed it as means of clearing atmosphere and of proving that National Socialists did not keep 1936 agreement which they are always accusing Austria of breaking.' Schmidt believed 'that only Tavs and Leopold and possibly some unimportant Germans are responsible for treasonable documents; he does not believe German Government knew or approved of it', the Legation wired to London. Schmidt also thought that the 'moderate National Socialists' would now withdraw their support from the 'extremists': 'no dangerous developments will result from this incident', and Germany 'will not make it an excuse for violent action'. An official of the Foreign Office, however, minuted: 'Dr Schmidt is remarkably optimistic – even for him – over this incident.' And Vansittart added: 'I do not think the optimism in this telegram will long be justified, unless we quickly make it clear again that we are interested in Austria. I hope we may be able to do so early next week.'[8] The Austrian optimism was certainly not shared by the Foreign Office officials, but they had been very sceptical of Austria's chances of survival for a considerable time.

A curious footnote to the affair was the information that Leopold had met 'an Englishman Fascist' named Spranklin in the Tyrol, and told him of an impending German intervention in

Austria – information regarded by Dr Schmidt 'as nonsense'. Soon after, the Special Branch of the Metropolitan Police identified the man as Philip John Spranklin, a frequent speaker for the British Union of Fascists.[9] But it was never established what his role was and why Leopold met him in the Tyrol to give him this highly confidential information. Spranklin may, of course, have been an agent either for the Germans or for the Italians, with whom the BUF had contacts.

Time and again efforts were made by the government to conciliate the 'national' opposition, to negotiate with it or to achieve some compromise – efforts which were rather pointless because all its members, whether 'moderate' or 'extremist', desired the Anschluss and were loyal to Hitler. But no such efforts were made towards the other large and solid bloc of opposition, the socialists, although their leaders indicated their willingness to help in the fight against National Socialism. After the ruthless crushing of the revolt of February 1934 relations became even more embittered and the attainment of a compromise between the government and the left seemed almost hopeless. To the Heimwehr supporters of the government the 'Reds' were the real enemy, and not the National Socialists; their goal was fascism on the Italian model and this precluded any concession to the socialists, or even any clemency towards the prisoners of the revolt.

To promote clemency was the aim of the Labour Party and the British trade unions. As soon as the fighting in Vienna had come to an end Arthur Henderson and Walter Citrine, the Secretaries of the Labour Party and the TUC, respectively, called at the Foreign Office with that aim in view. They were assured by the Foreign Secretary that the British Minister in Vienna had been instructed to express 'the earnest hope that a policy of clemency and appeasement would be followed', but this made no impression on the Austrian government. In the autumn of 1934 British efforts concentrated on the person of the former mayor of Vienna, Dr Seitz, who was being kept in detention by the government, but obviously had committed no crime. In September Henderson forwarded a letter from Frau Seitz to the Foreign Office asking for support to obtain her husband's release. Sargent minuted that the Austrian government ought to realise 'that this continued detention without trial has excited a great deal of unfavourable comment in English political circles and is likely to be the subject of embarrassing questions in Parliament and elsewhere.' Vansittart thought that the first opportunity should be used 'of speaking unofficially but earnestly to the Austrian Minister on the subject'; as Franckenstein was 'not a very upstanding or outstanding person', the speaking would have to be in 'earnest', otherwise 'his government will get but little of it'.[10]

On 4 October 1934 Sir John Simon saw Franckenstein and told him that 'he would be well advised to warn his Government of the effects which the continued detention of Dr. Seitz is likely to produce in British political circles.' Simon disclaimed any intention of interfering officially in Austrian affairs, but urged him 'to report to his Government that this was an obstacle to wider and more general sympathy with Austria in this country'; Franckenstein 'took all this in very good part and promised to make a report of it.' Simon also wrote privately to Selby and informed Henderson that he had spoken strongly to Franckenstein and pointed out 'how desirable it would be to clear up that situation by appropriate action'; he would 'keep up all the pressure' he could. A few days later Simon received a large delegation from the Labour Party, including its Chairman, W. A. Robinson, as well as Attlee and Morrison, and the TUC with its Chairman, W. Keen, and Ernest Bevin, to discuss the situation of the Austrian Socialists. He told the delegates that the British Minister in Vienna acting on instructions had suggested to Schuschnigg 'the expediency of broadening the basis of the popular support of his Government', and that similar representations had been made by the French Minister. The information available to the Foreign Office was that the Austrian Socialists had 'reformed their secret organisation and have kept the bulk of their stores of arms intact'; the party leaders showed no signs of coming to terms with the government; a few of the rank and file had gone over to the National Socialists, and many more to the communists, but 'the majority maintain their allegiance to the Socialist party.' In 1936 Citrine again wrote to the Foreign Office about the political prisoners in Austria, 42 of whom had been awaiting trial for more than twelve months; the date of their trial had been fixed four times and postponed each time; some of them had gone on hunger strike in protest. His

letter was forwarded to the British Legation in Vienna but there
is no record of any action taken. It was quite clear, as Vansittart
wrote in the autumn of 1934, that the Austrian government
'unfortunately' did not intend to adopt a conciliatory policy
towards the socialists.[11]

In the summer of 1934 an application was received from the
Labour Party for a visa to be granted to Julius Deutsch, leader of
the dissolved Republican Defence League, who had been invited
to the centenary commemoration of the trial of the Tolpuddle
Martyrs as the president of the Workers' Sports Federation and
intended to give some lectures on Austrian Socialism after the
celebration. The Home Office asked the Foreign Office whether
the condition that Deutsch would not engage in any political
activities should be attached to the visa. E. H. Carr thought that
there was no need to incur the odium of this condition: 'the
Austrian question and the fate of the Austrian Socialists does not
really arouse interest here, except in a quite narrow circle', and
there would be no 'enthusiasm for Dr Deutsch and his lectures'.
Vansittart, however, disagreed:

> Deutsch is apparently a Communist.... I see no particular reason
> why he should be admitted at all, except of course the obvious
> apprehension as to giving offence to the Labour Party.... We have
> no interest in having these old far off things raked up in regard to
> Austria now.... We shall not make our influence more acceptable in
> Austria by allowing Dr Deutsch in to give inflammatory, even if
> partially unsuccessful, lectures.

He suggested allowing Deutsch in for a few days, 'but no more,
or perhaps one day at each end. Like that we should have granted
the most essential part of the request of the Labour Party, and
should not have to enter into any stipulation or arguments about
the lectures, for which there wd. not be time, or anyhow not
much time.' Simon agreed and the Home Office was informed
accordingly. A few days later Vansittart saw Franckenstein who
objected to the grant of a visa, and explained that, if the Labour
Party's request had been refused, 'no doubt a considerable stir
would have been caused, and this stir might have been made the
occasion for anti-Austrian utterances in certain quarters.'
Deutsch would probably make a speech or two, but in the very
short time at his disposal 'he would not be able to make many
speeches'. He would have wished to stay much longer, but 'his

permit was only valid for a few days': even from the Austrian point of view 'it was obviously much better' to grant the request.[12] By 'these old far off things' which Deutsch might 'rake up' Vansittart seems to have meant the February revolt, which was then six months old, and its savage repression. The allegation that Deutsch 'is apparently a Communist' was equally strange and showed the built-in bias of the most senior Foreign Office official. It was a very discreditable episode.

The British Legation soon sent reports on the underground left-wing movement. As early as April 1934 'those in close touch with Socialist relief work' informed Selby of active communist propaganda in Vienna and of the activity of 'terrorist squads' consisting of men 'won over by despair and propaganda against the former Socialist leaders' by the communists. A few weeks later he reported on 'the growth of genuine Communism – or of revolutionary Socialism hardly distinguishable from the latter – among the rank and file of former Socialists'. The members were young men 'filled with a bitter hatred which makes them impatient both of the recognised Socialist leaders now in exile in Czechoslovakia, and also of the comparatively moderate tenets which made of "pink" Socialist Vienna an opponent of "red" Moscow.' Thus communism, Selby continued, apparently found a footing in Austria 'as a result of the uprooting of the very Socialism with which Austrians of other political opinions' mistakenly confounded it.

In August 1934 a memorandum by the First Secretary of the Legation stated that, instead of the 'relatively innocuous Austrian Socialism of yesteryear' the government was now faced by 'a dangerously interlaced mixture of revolutionary Marxist doctrines, preached by Dr Bauer' and allegedly 'backed by Soviet skill and gold'. Fortunately, the rank-and-file socialists were 'forced by prudence and economic want to look for a compromise even with the present Government', if the latter were only wise enough to release the arrested moderate socialist leaders and to temper 'Fascist justice with Austrian mercy and common sense'. But 'the sands are running out of the glass' and the moderate leaders might not be able much longer 'to keep their followers from seceding to Dr Bauer and Dr Deutsch', who sided with the Revolutionary Socialists. From Moscow the British ambassador even wired that Bauer was visiting Moscow to negotiate with the

Comintern about possible cooperation.[13] The Legation was clearly well informed about the differences in the Socialist Party – probably through its contacts with some of the moderate leaders whose names were mentioned in the memorandum.

By October 1934 the Legation was able to report on the 'underground propaganda' carried on by the Revolutionary Socialists. According to one of their leaders, they believed 'they can gradually rebuild their Party', but their activities were tempered by the fear that 'they might be paving the way for a Nazi victory', if they weakened the government. The Legation also reported that the matrices of the *Arbeiter-Zeitung* were smuggled from Brno to Vienna and that 20,000 copies a week were printed at a 'friendly press'. One edition had been seized by the authorities but arrangements were made for the next issue on another press. When the agreement between Germany and Austria was signed in July 1936 the Legation reported that the 'combined Revolutionary Socialist and Communist Party [sic]' was 'highly incensed'.

In reality there never was such a party, but the two parties, although they cooperated at times, remained quite separate, and they had strong ideological differences. The Legation's Annual Report for 1937 mentioned more correctly an 'acute division' between the two parties, the communists favouring cooperation with the official trade unions of the regime so as to win influence in them, and the Revolutionary Socialists being 'more dogmatic or more cautious'; they desired 'to keep a very careful control over any tendency which might lead towards reconciliation between the extreme Left and the Government'. In any case, many socialists occupied minor posts in the official unions and worked inside them with the aim of winning free elections in the future. Strong socialist opposition to the government was also reported from Carinthia, 'especially among the artisans'.[14] Otherwise the reports contain no information on the socialists outside Vienna. There was no British consul in either Styria or Upper Austria, and this may account for the lack of information.

In September 1934 Vansittart noted that Schuschnigg, as he had told some journalists, 'was ready to make peace with the Socialists as soon as emigré Socialist propaganda ceased', but had immediately added that propaganda and weapons were being smuggled from Czechoslovakia into Austria. As this propaganda continued throughout his years as Chancellor, it was obviously out of the question 'that success can attend Dr Schuschnigg's policy', as Vansittart observed. Vansittart also feared 'that the Socialist reaction' to Schuschnigg's policy might be 'that if they are to be bullied anyhow, they may as well suffer at the hands of the big bully, i.e. Nazi Germany, as of the little one'.[15] But in this assumption he was to be proved wrong. The Austrian socialists knew full well that their persecution under Hitler would be of an entirely different order from what it was under Schuschnigg, and they were to prove this during the critical weeks of March 1938.

Notes

1. Selby to Simon, 18 September, Ian Henderson to Selby, 17 August, and report by E. H. Carr, 14 October 1934: FO 120, file 1079, FO 371, file 18355, fo. 97, file 18358, fo. 341.
2. Selby to Simon, 4 March and 24 April, Henderson to Selby, 1 December, and memorandum by Major Benfield, 28 October 1935: FO 371, file 19481, fos. 140 f., 201 f., file 19482, fo. 171 f., file 19485, fo. 25 f.
3. Ian Henderson to Selby, 5 April, 1 May, 17 June and 27 November, Mack to Eden, 16 March, Selby to Eden, 13 April and 3 August 1936: FO 371, file 20361, fos. 66, 94, 199, file 20362, fos. 81, 335, file 20363, fo. 304 ff., FO 120, file 1107.
4. Mack to Eden, 23 October, Phipps to FO, 13 May, and Mack to Eden, 6 November 1936: FO 120, file 1108, FO 371, file 20362, fo. 117, file 20362, fo. 325 f. The new Minister of Security was Odo Neustädter-Stürmer, like his predecessor a protagonist of the Heimwehr.
5. Henderson to Selby, 19 November 1936, 8 March, 16 May, 21 July, 14 September, 13 October, 28 November and 12 December 1937: FO 371, file 20364, fo. 89, file 21115, fos. 132 ff., 161 f., 232 f., file 21116, fos. 275 ff., 406 ff., file 21118, fo. 182 f., FO 120, file 1132.
6. Selby to Sargent, 11 May 1937, 'Austria. Annual Report for 1937' and M. Palairet to Eden, 14 February 1938: FO 120, file 1123, FO 371, file 22320, fo. 176, file 22311, fo. 162.
7. Austrian Foreign Ministry to Franckenstein, 27 January, Palairet to Eden, 29 January 1938: FO 371, file 22310, fos. 200 f., 215; *The Times*, 14 February 1938; Carsten, *Fascist Movements in Austria*, pp. 305 f., 316 f.

8. Austrian Foreign Ministry to Franckenstein, 27 January, and Palairet to Eden, 29 January 1938, with minutes by J. Nicholls, 31 January, and Vansittart, 4 February 1938: FO 371, file 22310, fos. 201 ff., 217, 191 ff.

9. Palairet to Eden, 29 January, and Special Branch to Home Office, 7 March 1938: FO 371, file 22310, fo. 195, file 22319, fo. 186.

10. *Manchester Guardian*, 19 February 1934; Henderson to Simon, 27 September, with minutes by Sargent and Vansittart, 29–30 September 1934: FO 371, file 18368, fo. 51 ff.

11. Simon to Selby, 4 October, and to Henderson, 5 October, minute by Vansittart, 11 September 1934; Citrine to Eden, 3 February 1936: FO 371, file 18368, fos. 37, 77–80, FO 800, file 291, fos. 379, 391 f., FO 120, file 1109.

12. E.W. Cooper, Home Office, to Carr, 14 August, with minutes by Carr and Vansittart, 14–15 August, Carr to Cooper, 22 August, and minute by Vansittart, 30 August 1934: FO 371, file 18368, fos. 160 ff., 164, 167 f. In 1834 the Tolpuddle Martyrs were sentenced to seven years' deportation for swearing men into a Lodge.

13. Selby to Simon, 27 April and 28 May, memorandum by Hadow, 18 August, and Chilston to FO, Moscow, 2 August 1934: DBFP, 2nd series, vi, no. 411, p. 665, FO 371, file 18351, fo. 373, file 18355, fo. 76, file 18354, fo. 11.

14. Memorandum by Hadow, 30 October 1934, Mack to Eden, 18 July 1936, 'Annual Report on Austria for 1937', and Henderson to Mack, 28 November 1937: FO 371, file 18368, fo. 97, file 20363, fo. 269, file 22320, fo. 170 f., file 21118, fo. 183.

15. Vansittart to Simon, 11 September 1934: FO 800, file 291, fo. 379 f. (Simon Papers).

9   The End of Austrian Independence

On 4 February 1938 von Neurath was replaced as German
Foreign Minister by von Ribbentrop and von Papen, Hitler's
special envoy, was recalled from Vienna. At the same time drastic
changes were introduced in the command structure of the
German army. The Commander-in-Chief was dismissed, Hitler
himself assumed the new post of Supreme Commander of the
Armed Forces, and generals loyal to him were appointed to the
key posts in the High Command on the three armed forces and
that of the army. A few days later the new British Minister in
Vienna, Michael Palairet, wired to London that the Austrian
government was more perturbed by the appointment of von
Ribbentrop, who 'may wish to begin his career in Berlin by some
dramatic coup', than by the military changes, 'as they do not
think the Army, even before the changes, would have resisted
[the] Chancellor, however distasteful his orders might have been.'
Military circles in Vienna were 'greatly relieved by [the] retention
of General Beck as Chief of Staff' because he had assured them
that 'he will oppose any military adventure in Austria'. In May
1937 Beck had indeed written a memorandum opposing military
intervention in Austria; but how and when did he inform the
Austrians of his attitude?

A few days later (11 February), Palairet was told 'in strictest
confidence' by the Foreign Minister, Dr Schmidt, that he and
Schuschnigg were going to meet Hitler at Berchtesgaden the
next day. When Palairet asked whether 'disagreeable surprises in
shape of unacceptable demands might not be sprung upon
them', Schmidt denied this: it was settled in advance that the
meeting should in no circumstances make the situation any
worse. He did not know what line the discussion would take, but

he thought the 'result would be general affirmation of agreement of July 11th [1936] and determination to make it work well. Austria would not accept anything she did not want.' He foresaw 'intense dissatisfaction in Nazi circles'. Palairet suspected that the same would apply to the supporters of the government. Although he did not share Schmidt's 'confident optimism', he was certain that Schuschnigg would not have accepted the invitation if he anticipated any danger to Austrian independence. The French Minister in Vienna looked on the meeting as a 'decidedly risky venture which may however turn out well'; the Austrians hoped to obtain a German disavowal of illegal activities in Austria, and in return a National Socialist might be appointed to a ministerial post; a 'peremptory enquiry' had come from Hitler whether they intended to keep the agreement of 11 July or not; if they refused the invitation no German Minister would be sent to Vienna for the time being.[1]

After his return from the fateful meeting Schmidt admitted to Palairet that it 'had been extremely difficult'. The Austrian concessions were far-reaching: the appointment of Seyss-Inquart as Minister of the Interior and Public Security, the admission of National Socialists to the 'Patriotic Front' as long as they recognised the Austrian Constitution, an amnesty for imprisoned National Socialists, and the reinstatement of dismissed National Socialist officials. When Palairet asked whether the first two concessions were not dangerous and a 'first step to complete Pacification', Schmidt replied no: Seyss-Inquart was honestly in favour of Austrian independence and a practising Catholic. Originally, Hitler had asked for much more and the heads of the German armed forces had been present; Hitler undertook to recognise the Austrian Constitution and to suppress all illegal propaganda in Austria. But Schmidt's optimism was 'decidedly shattered' and he admitted that the situation was critical. He remarked that Britain and France would do nothing to save Austria and 'Italy could do no more than show displeasure at any German move'; in any case, Austria could not be 'saved by foreign bayonets'.

Palairet also learned that the meeting at Berchtesgaden had been 'threatening in character' and that Schuschnigg could neither refuse to go nor to accept Hitler's demands, which would have meant 'a worse state of things than before the agreement'.

Palairet considered Schuschnigg's position 'seriously weakened'. But when he met the Chancellor at a party, Schuschnigg claimed 'that he was not alarmed and that a breathing space had been secured'; he had been met by threats and only yielded the minimum. Hitler had mentioned to him that Lord Halifax, the Lord President of the Council, completely approved of Germany's attitude towards Austria and Czechoslovakia – a claim immediately denied by Palairet.

The Vienna correspondent of *The Times* believed that the new agreement would lead to Schuschnigg's fall and was 'the beginning of the end'. The correspondent sent this warning: 'Any liberty given to the Austrian Nazis to canvass and demonstrate in the same way as the Austrian Monarchists ... would, in the opinion of the Austrian Government's supporters and of anti-Nazis generally, be very difficult to keep within bounds.' But a first leader of *The Times* stated rather differently that it seemed unnecessary

> to quarrel with an agreement with which the Führer, the Duce, and Herr von Schuschnigg are all apparently content.... The two principal negotiators at Berchtesgaden are rather to be regarded as deserving the congratulations of their respective peoples upon an achievement which is thought to safeguard the requirements of both.'2

A leader of the *Manchester Guardian* was more sceptical: 'The German attitude towards Austria has always been plain; Austria is geographically and racially a part of the Greater Germany, and must sooner or later be incorporated in it.' At best Germany might admit 'that the union might as well come later, and that it would be as well not to use methods to hasten it which might have unfortunate results elsewhere.' Early in 1938, the paper wrote, Austro-German relations had become very tense, especially when compromising documents were discovered during the police raid on the National Socialist office in Vienna; Italy grew nervous and made friendly representations in Berlin: 'The "peaceful penetration" of Austria by the Nazis, which has proved so successful lately, must cause Signor Mussolini only slightly less anxiety than it does Dr Schuschnigg.' The paper's Vienna correspondent reported that Hitler had 'only demanded a "little" thing – the inclusion of Dr Seyss-Inquart in the Cabinet as Minister of Public Security', which meant 'handing over the police to the Nazis, which, in turn, would have meant the recognition of illegal Nazi associations'; Hitler had also said that, if the demand were rejected, 'there would be trouble in Austria'. A compromise might still be possible, but 'a sword is hanging once more over unfortunate Austria.'

The control of the police was also considered 'the crux of the matter' by the Foreign Office. On 15 February a meeting was held in the Foreign Secretary's room in which Eden, Vansittart, Cadogan, Sargent and Ingram took part, and a telegram was drafted which suggested a compromise, by which Seyss-Inquart would become Minister of the Interior without control of the police; the text was approved by Prime Minister Chamberlain and sent to Vienna on the same day. Palairet wired on that day that the Austrian government had decided to accept the terms of the agreement; their reply had to be given by the evening, and 'they really had no alternative'. The French Minister believed it was impossible to urge rejection of the terms 'since France has nothing to offer Austria'; Schuschnigg had told him 'the day of Berchtesgaden was [the] worst in his life; Herr Hitler had talked like a madman and had openly declared his intention of absorbing Austria.' Apparently Schuschnigg had 'complete confidence in Seyss-Inquart but German insistence on his appointment seems to show that he is really Nazi as we learn from other sources.' Schuschnigg's position, Palairet thought, was 'very seriously shaken since he cannot rely on whole-hearted support of any section of Austrians', but it was extremely unlikely that he would resign.[3]

As to the person of the new Minister of the Interior, the Legation reported that Schuschnigg was '*literally* correct in saying he is not a convinced Nazi', but this was an example of the 'juggling with words' for which he was well known among his friends; the Austrians described Seyss-Inquart as '*national-gesinnt*' (holding nationalist opinions) and he had 'behind him the support and hopes of the entire serious-minded "nationalist" Austrian movement', except only 'the irresponsible "Putsch"-loving extremist youth'; he would work for the closest possible cooperation with Germany, 'and that he is therefore "Hitler's man" is equally sure.' In the Austrian provinces his appointment would have 'an immense effect'.

On 19 February the Political Director of the Austrian Foreign Ministry told a member of the Legation that Schuschnigg had conceded the minimum at Berchtesgaden. Hitler's demands had included the assimilation of Austria's financial and economic system to the German one – and thus went further than a customs union – as well as the 'assimilation' of the Austrian army to the German one. If Schuschnigg had not made concessions, Hitler might have sent troops into Austria 'to restore order'; the National Socialists joining the 'Patriotic Front would be treated on a par with the other groups in it', such as Legitimists and workers, and facilities for meetings would probably be reduced to a minimum for all. When asked how the police had taken Seyss-Inquart's first speech to them in which he addressed them as 'deutsche Menschen' (German men), he answered that the feeling among the police 'was bad, especially in the provinces'; 45 National Socialists arrested on account of their demonstration at the ski-jumping competition near Klagenfurt had all been released and were 'cocking snooks at those who had arrested them'. The Political Director added it could not be in the 'British interest that Germany should be allowed to absorb Austria, which would inevitably lead to the absorption of Bohemia and to a subsequent domination of the Balkans, and bring her down to the Mediterranean.'

On the same day Schuschnigg informed the French Minister that the 'Patriotic Front' would in future include three groups – nationalists, Legitimists and workers – and all would have to accept the 'Corporative Christian Constitution'. He felt greatly encouraged by the attitude of the workers and thought that, if a plebiscite could be held, it would give him a large majority. But in Palairet's opinion this was 'of course' not practicable and people in Vienna were 'greatly discouraged and alarmed'.[4] It was the first time that the idea of a plebiscite was mentioned.

In London meanwhile the Austrian chargé d'affaires visited the Foreign Office and told Sargent that he had been instructed not to mention the 'extreme pressure to which Schuschnigg had been subjected by Hitler'; this was symptomatic of the change of regime at the Ballhausplatz, and he feared this 'would be the last time the Austrian Legation in London would be able to discuss matters with the Foreign Office on the old friendly and confident basis'. In future he and Franckenstein would 'speak more or less as the mouthpieces of the German Government', and he felt inclined to blame the British government for not giving Schuschnigg any support. Sargent replied that they had only been told of the Berchtesgaden meeting the day before the event, although it had been under consideration for at least a week previously.

On 19 February Sargent wrote: 'I think we must start on the assumption that Austria is lost, in spite of Schuschnigg's brave words'; Hitler's growing conviction since the visit by Lord Halifax 'that we could be counted upon not to interfere with the *peaceful* penetration of Austria has, I have little doubt, been one of the factors which has encouraged Hitler to go ahead, ... so as to present us with a *fait accompli.*' The only factor which might alter the situation to some extent 'would be if Italy were to join with us, but of that there is no sign.' A warning, as suggested by the French, would be useless: 'The most we would have done would be to give empty encouragement to Schuschnigg and his friends to continue the useless struggle, in the false hope that we were going to really see them through.'

When the British Cabinet discussed the Austrian situation on the same day its conclusions were equally pessimistic. Chamberlain stated: 'Herr Hitler has treated the Austrian Chancellor in a most brutal manner, summoning him to Berchtesgaden, confronting him with his Generals and, as it was rumoured, movements of troops and threats of the consequences of a refusal.' Mussolini had gone on a skiing trip and when Schuschnigg appealed to him he could get no answer but was informed that Mussolini had tried to persuade Hitler by telephone 'to adopt an attitude of moderation, but without success': he, Schuschnigg, should 'make the best terms he could'. Europe, so Chamberlain continued, 'had received another lesson as to the methods by which Germany would pursue her aims. It was difficult to believe that this effort was the last, or that the eventual result would not be the absorption of Austria and probably some action in Czechoslovakia.'[5] Hitler's aims were clearly recognised, but what was Britain prepared to do?

From Vienna *The Times* reported 'signs of restlessness' among the National Socialists; they were 'smashing Jewish shop windows, damaging telephone boxes (which are maintained by a Jewish concern), disturbing monarchist meetings, and the like.' The threat underlying these actions was that, if Austria did not comply with the latest German demands, they would 'open a new era of real terrorism', like that of 1934. The former editor of *The Times*, Wickham Steed, received information from Vienna that leading Catholic authorities were trying to organise 'united resistance to the Nazification of Austria'; they were insisting on a reconciliation of the government with the moderate socialists and the trade unions, but this was opposed by Schuschnigg and by Bishop Hudal in Rome who had strong sympathies with National Socialism. At the Vatican, the British Minister was told that Berchtesgaden was 'a disaster', the elements of which were 'German arrogance, Italian folly and Anglo-French weakness': now the National Socialists would have things more or less their own way in Austria.

In Vienna Palairet gathered that the Austrian government was unlikely to appeal to the powers for protection; it believed that the powers realised the danger and hoped that the conversations taking place between London, Paris and Rome 'will render Austrian independence less precarious; without support from outside it may be destroyed at any moment'. The 'Patriotic Front', however, was convinced that an immediate plebiscite would strengthen the Austrian position and obtain a large anti-Nazi majority, Palairet wired on 23 February. A Foreign Office official immediately minuted that the idea 'is quite impracticable'; and another added his agreement and a warning: 'At no time and in no circumstances would the Germans permit a plebiscite to be held, if they could help it, under conditions in which the Austrian population would be able to give a free and objective opinion.' Vansittart also thought that 'Germany would no doubt oppose a plebiscite, & probably disregard its results. But a successful plebiscite is about the only remaining way in which the Austrian Govt. could strengthen its position.' If they rejected it as impracticable, there was no more to be said.[6]

On 24 February Schuschnigg addressed the Austrian Parliament, giving figures of Austria's economic progress and admitting that 'no miracles' had been achieved. 'His whole speech,' Palairet reported, 'was in fact an affirmation of Austria's right and determination to remain independent', as recognised by Germany in the agreement of July 1936. 'The thunders of applause which greeted the words "Thus far and no farther" showed that they were interpreted as an affirmation that no more concessions could be made to Germany.' Outside the house, large crowds demonstrated for 'Austria'. Palairet added:

> No one, I think, could listen to such a speech unmoved, nor fail to feel that the man who made it was not only determined to preserve his country's integrity and independence, but was convinced of his power to do so. I believe that his calm assurance will have a considerable effect both at home and abroad, and it appears to me that this great speech may secure his real popularity in this country.[7]

But the mood in Vienna, The *Manchester Guardian* reported, remained pessimistic; neutral observers feared 'that the influence of Dr Seyss-Inquart in the Government will have a corroding effect on the regime and will clandestinely introduce National Socialism into the country'. Yet the leaders of the 'Patriotic Front' were still convinced 'that, in spite of the presence of a Nazi representative in the Government in such an important post, the future of Austria is assured – or, at least, valuable time has been gained.'

More ominously, from 19 February onwards the British press reported National Socialist demonstrations in many parts of Austria. In Linz, the National Socialists released from prison on 18 February were given 'an unproarious welcome'; they arrived 'in flower-decked motor cars and were greeted with the Storm troopers' song and cries of "Heil Hitler".... The police did not interfere.' On the following days there were large demonstrations in Graz. According to the *Manchester Guardian*:

> Nazi Storm Troops in full uniform marched through the streets and drove in lorries with huge Swastika flags. They gave the salute and shouted Nazi slogans. 'Whom have we to thank for our freedom?' asked the crowd. 'Adolf Hitler', was the answer, given by thousands of people demonstrating in front of Graz Cathedral, the town hall and the palace of the Styrian bishop.[8]

On 27 February the paper's correspondent reported from Graz that a visitor 'would imagine he has entered a German Nazi city. The majority of the people in the streets this afternoon wore the Swastika emblem, some of them just metal Swastika badges, others the official German party sign. Young boys greeted each other with the Hitler greeting and some of them were singing the "Horst Wessel" song.' People wearing swastikas and others with 'Patriotic Front' badges 'walked peacefully next to each other in the streets and even talked with each other. It is certainly not a revolutionary atmosphere.' Over the town hall a large swastika flag was flying, hoisted with the approval of the mayor. Graz 'had become a sea of Swastika-red,' another British correspondent recorded. But when he began to wonder how the local National Socialists could suddenly be so strong, he was informed by a party member that the SA had received strong reinforcements from Innsbruck, Klagenfurt and Salzburg: 'Graz was to be made the breach in Austria's defences.' From Vienna police reinforcements and troops were sent to preserve order. In Vienna too, *The Times* wrote, many thousands of demonstrators 'marched round the city with torches, shouting for Hitler and for union with Germany'. A speaker who addressed the crowd shouted 'We have won after all', and referred to 'the end of a long period of suffering and depression'.[9] The President of the Austrian National Bank, however, wrote to a business friend in London that 'Schuschnigg was holding his own and was not going to surrender to German domination'; the press reports about German penetration were 'greatly exaggerated', and Seyss-Inquart was a 'patriotic Austrian'. In the opinion of the British diplomat, commenting on this letter, the events in Graz were mainly due to 'youthful exuberance' and were distorted and 'sensationalized' by reports in the British newspapers.[10]

The British government remained sceptical. On 26 February the Secretary of State for Dominion Affairs sent out a circular 'that there can be little doubt that the effective independence of Austria has been materially prejudiced by the concessions secured by Herr Hitler from the Austrian Chancellor, and that the country is on the high road to becoming a vassal state of Germany'. Much would depend on the interpretation of the 'agreement' by Hitler, but if Schuschnigg should make any attempt to whittle down his concessions, 'there is a risk that he might expose himself to a vigorous counterstroke at the hands of the Führer.' The French government had suggested a vigorous joint *démarche* in Berlin, but after careful consideration the British government concluded 'that any such *démarche* might do more harm than good.' Indeed, the French Foreign Minister, Yvon Delbos, told the British ambassador at dinner that, after the seizure of Austria, Hitler would undoubtedly attack Czechoslovakia, and 'in that case France will faithfully and unhesitatingly carry out her engagements with the latter. This means war, in which France will be fighting for her existence, and Great Britain will not be able to stand aside.' All this, Delbos urged, could be averted 'by firm language at Berlin, without any trace of threats, while there is still time.'[11] But this advice was rejected.

On 23 February *The Times* reported from Vienna that the socialist workers were 'deeply depressed' by the Berchtesgaden agreement as well as by the resignation of Eden (on 20 February) and saw in this 'signs of the general trend away from democracy and towards the general prestige of the dictatorships', so that they had no hope for their own cause. But Schuschnigg's speech in Parliament 'had an effect on them which could hardly have been forseen by even the greatest optimists,' Palairet wrote. The newly-appointed State Secretary for Workers' Protection, Adolf Watzek, gave an interview in which he stated that the entire working class were 'determined to devote themselves to the cause of a self-subsisting, sovereign and independent Austria. . . . I can honestly declare that the storm of approval from workers circles came perfectly freely and spontaneously without any kind of pressure.' A Foreign Office official added the comment that these were 'the so-called Bolshevik workers'.

On 3 March Schuschnigg received a delegation of fourteen workers from the local factories and they submitted to him four demands: the right to freedom of speech and to political equality with the National Socialists within the 'Patriotic Front'; free elections in the official trade unions; the publication of a daily paper; and guarantees of a 'social course' in matters of wages, holidays and social insurance. Schuschnigg adopted a friendly attitude but made his acceptance dependent on negotiations; he permitted the delegates to report to a larger meeting of workers' representatives. A few days later 200 of them met, representing, according to *The Times*, 4000 factories and workshops: 'it was the first unhindered Socialist meeting since the suppression of the party in February 1934.' The discussion proved that the workers and employees 'were ready to join in the struggle to defend the independence of Austria'. They felt 'that the clock stands at five minutes to 12', that the regime would be unable to withstand the National Socialists and needed the support of the anti-Nazi workers in its struggle. As Palairet reported, 'there was general agreement . . . that it was impossible to get the workers to support the Schuschnigg regime unconditionally. "Slaves cannot fight; only free men", was one of the expressions used.' If the government argued that it could not make concessions for fear of Germany, it was useless for the workers to act, 'since there was no independence left to fight for'.[12]

The British Minister hoped that Schuschnigg would lose no time reaching an agreement with the workers: 'he will have to move quickly if he is to check a drift of the workers to the ranks of the Nazis.' The peasants were too scattered to make their voice heard, and so far the workers had not been allowed to raise theirs. 'The result has been that the vocalism has been confined to the Nazis and the bourgeoisie in the towns', and in Graz and Linz the National Socialists had it all their own way. In Vienna, a British correspondent saw the socialist badge of the three arrows for the first time in five years openly worn in the streets, and here and there the salute of 'Freedom' was given. At first the police were instructed to order anyone wearing the three arrows to remove the badge, but later they tolerated it – with sour faces: 'It was the beginning of the rebirth of political liberty.'

On 10 March the correspondent of the *Manchester Guardian* observed 'the workers marching through the streets of Vienna shouting 'Freedom, Austria' and giving the salute with their clenched fists. He also saw 'the unusual sight' of factory workers wearing the badge of the 'Patriotic Front': 'the sudden gathering of the workers in support of the Government' was a most remarkable fact, but the negotiations between the government and the workers' representatives were not yet completed.[13]

On 9 March Schuschnigg was given a tremendous reception in Innsbruck and announced to a large, cheering crowd in front of the town hall that on the following Sunday a plebiscite would be held on the question whether Austria should be free and German, Christian and social, independent and united. After the speech, many thousands of peasants, workers and members of youth organisations marched through the streets cheering and urging the hoisting of the Austrian colours. The local National Socialists also marched, shouting 'Heil Hitler' and 'One people, one Reich,' *The Times* reported. From Vienna Palairet telephoned that Schuschnigg felt obliged to ascertain 'where he stands and whether Berchtesgaden agreement is to be kept or not'; for the words and actions of Seyss-Inquart went far beyond its terms; he was objecting to the plebiscite 'and if he is backed by Herr Hitler the situation may at any moment become dangerous.' The Austrian Foreign Minister told Palairet that the plebiscite was no concern of Hitler's, but he replied that this was not the German view. Nevertheless Palairet thought 'that the risk is worth taking. [The] Chancellor would lose his authority if the present atmosphere of alarm and uncertainty were to continue'. If he gained a large majority he intended 'to put down all illegal activities with a firm hand'. From Berlin, however, the British ambassador telephoned that Schuschnigg's action seemed 'precipitous and unwise'; German opinion was 'uncompromisingly hostile', and it would be 'difficult for Herr Hitler not to yield this time to extremist advice'.[14] Apparently, Sir Nevile Henderson assumed that Hitler was prone to listen to advice, whether 'extremist' or not.

On 6 March the Vienna correspondent of *The Times*, Douglas Reed, returned from Linz, where he had gone to report on a speech by Seyss-Inquart to National Socialist delegates from Upper Austria. He was much perturbed by what he had seen. He found the streets lined by 'supposedly illegal' stormtroopers, the police scarcely in evidence, and Seyss-Inquart in the company of a German emissary. The local National Socialists were 'very bellicose' and the atmosphere was 'most ominous'. Two Austrian soldiers who refused to stand up at the playing of Hitler's favourite march 'were actually hurtled out of a café'. The crowd was estimated by the police at 30,000 and by the National Socialists at 35,000. According to the *Manchester Guardian*, the large majority were boys between the ages of 10 and 18. The SA and SS men appeared in uniform, and the Hitler Youth in white shirts and stockings.[15]

On the day after the announcement of the plebiscite Palairet wired that the 'Nazis seem far from pleased'. The government anticipated that they would abstain but that the figures in favour would be satisfactory; the chief danger was that they would create disturbances on Sunday and try to intimidate would-be voters. *The Times* correspondent reported 'organised demonstrations of Nazis' against the plebiscite which were causing 'pandemonium'. In Graz, a clash between demonstrators and counter-demonstrators resulted in seven people being injured, two of them seriously. Later the National Socialists again marched through Graz shouting 'Down with Schuschnigg' and distributed leaflets with the slogan 'Schuschnigg has broken the Berchtesgaden agreement' and 'Schuschnigg must go'. The police did not interfere.

On 11 March the British consul in Munich reported 'general mobilization in Bavaria and troops pouring towards Austrian frontier'. In Vienna, Seyss-Inquart and Glaise-Horstenau, a 'nationalist' member of the government, presented an ultimatum to Schuschnigg which demanded the abandonment of the plebiscite; if this were refused, the National Socialists would abstain and 'could not be restrained from causing serious disturbances during voting'. An answer was requested by 1 p.m. on the same day. Schuschnigg, as Palairet wired, refused to accept the ultimatum or to call off the plebiscite. He suggested a compromise by which a second plebiscite was to be held later on the basis of a regular voters' list; meanwhile on Sunday voters could vote 'yes' to his policy but 'no' to Schuschnigg, so as to make it clear that the issue was not a personal one of his remaining in office.

Two hours later there was another telegram that, if the Chancellor gave way 'it will be the end of Austrian independence: if he holds firm he is faced by threat of armed action by Germany when disturbances take place (or rather are engineered) during the plebiscite'. Glaise-Horstenau had gone to see Hitler who 'raved like a madman for an hour' and totally rejected the plan of a plebiscite. In the early afternoon there was a telephone message that Schuschnigg agreed to cancel the plebiscite 'under threat of civil war and absolutely certain menace of military invasion' to avoid bloodshed. He asked for 'immediate advice' by the British government what he should do. Hitler, however, insisted that Schuschnigg must resign and be replaced by Seyss-Inquart, with only one hour to reach a decision.[16]

Schuschnigg's request for immediate advice from the British government reached London in the afternoon of 11 March and Lord Halifax consulted the Prime Minister. He then replied 'that His Majesty's Government could not take the responsibility of advising the Chancellor to take any course of action which might expose his country to dangers against which His Majesty's Government are unable to guarantee protection.' In other words, Britain would not do anything to preserve Austria's independence. On the next day the course taken was approved by the British Cabinet, and Chamberlain stated that Schuschnigg had not asked for advice before announcing the plebiscite 'which has caused so much trouble'. He added that 'the manner in which the German action in Austria has been brought about was most distressing and shocking to the world and was a typical illustration of power politics'; it would make 'international appeasement much more difficult'.[17] What Chamberlain objected to was the *manner* of Hitler's action, not the action as such, because it would interfere with the general policy of appeasement which he seemed determined to continue, in spite of Hitler's policy.

When Seyss-Inquart and Glaise-Horstenau returned to Schuschnigg in the afternoon of 11 March he 'offered every guarantee that [the] plebiscite would be freely carried out as a genuine expression of opinion'. But this offer was rejected, and Seyss-Inquart declared he would resign and thus destroy the basis of the Berchtesgaden agreement unless the plebiscite was cancelled by 3 p.m. This was followed by a German ultimatum brought by air from Berlin demanding Schuschnigg's resignation and his replacement by Seyss-Inquart. The Austrian Legion was to march into the country and keep order in Vienna, and the National Socialist Party was to be legalised. Schuschnigg's reply was to be given before 7.30 that evening, and he informed London that 'if he yields any semblance of Austrian independence is gone.' President Miklas, however, refused to accept the ultimatum and German troops were ordered to cross the frontier. Seyss-Inquart announced on the radio that the German army was marching in and that there would be no resistance.

Within an hour of his speech the National Socialist units marched in Vienna. 'Thousands of voices shouting "Heil

Hitler!" "Heil Victory!" and "One people, one Reich!" filled the air, exhilarating to the masses of Nazis, threatening and nerve-racking to the other masses of people who are sitting in their homes wondering what the morrow will bring,' *The Times* correspondent recorded. In Vienna, 'the Nazis are in full control, commanding the obedience of the police.' In the evening an official statement was issued that, 'under the pressure of external political conditions and the threat of military occupation by the German Reich', the President had entrusted Seyss-Inquart with carrying on the government 'at the demand of Germany'.[18] It was made absolutely clear by this statement and the despatches of the British Minister that Schuschnigg's resignation and Seyss-Inquart's appointment were due to Hitler's ultimatum, that Germany dictated the course of events, that the German army was used to enforce Hitler's will, and that the two members of the Austrian government who effected this change were no more than Hitler's stooges.

It was left to Nevile Henderson, the British ambassador in Berlin, to state that 'Dr Schuschnigg has let us all down badly by his rash decision without consulting members of his Government', and this had enabled the two ministers 'to assume technical authorship of ultimatum'. When Henderson saw Göring and the latter accused Schuschnigg of having broken the Berchtesgaden agreement, Henderson 'reluctantly agreed that Dr Schuschnigg had acted with precipitate folly'. As instructed from London, Henderson made a strong protest, but Göring simply claimed – against his better knowledge – that the occupation of Austria 'was being undertaken at direct request of Seyss-Inquart who feared Communist trouble particularly in Wiener Neustadt'. The German troops would be withdrawn as soon as the situation was stable and then a 'free election would be held without any intimidation whatever'. Unless Britain was prepared to use force Henderson recommended that his government should insist on this undertaking being carried out: 'the best thing to work for' was 'independence on lines of pre-war Bavaria'.

This, however, was not the line adopted by the British government. Lord Halifax saw the new German Foreign Minister, von Ribbentrop, on the afternoon of the fateful day and told him Germany had committed 'an exhibition of naked force' and public opinion would 'inevitably ask when the facts were known what there was to prevent the German Government from seeking to apply in similar fashion naked force to the solution of their problems in Czechoslovakia or to any other in which they thought it might be useful'; the British people had never denied that there was an Austrian problem, 'but they would violently resent ... the method by which it had been chosen to solve it.' A leader of *The Times* declared: 'This, the latest and worst demonstration of the methods of German foreign policy, can only deepen in this country the suspicions and indignation aroused by the manner in which the Berchtesgaden agreement was negotiated'; it dealt 'a blow to the policy of appeasement by leaving it more than doubtful whether appeasement is possible in a continent exposed to the visitations of arbitrary force ... and a British protest in the strongest terms has already been presented.'

The tone of the *Manchester Guardian* was considerably sharper. Under the headline 'The Naked Fist' a leader stated that, 'under the double threat of war and civil war, of a German invasion and a Nazi rebellion', Hitler had forced Schuschnigg to resign: 'This is invasion of an independent State as brutal as that of Japan's into China or Italy's into Abyssinia. If it is not also war it is only because Dr Schuschnigg preferred surrender to bloodshed. This, then, is Hitler's policy; this is the naked fist.'[19]

From Vienna Palairet expressly denied Henderson's assertion that Schuschnigg had acted 'precipitous and unwise', for he had played the card of the plebiscite

> in the hope of saving the independence of Austria. ... He considered rightly or wrongly that plebiscite must be taken at once to meet threat against Austrian independence which his Minister of the Interior was undermining under German guidance. His tactics may have been mistaken but his motives have throughout been un-selfseeking and patriotic.

If the British or the French government still had any hope of concerted action with Italy (this was one of the suggestions made by Paris) any such idea was doomed to disappointment. On 12 March Count Ciano told the British ambassador: 'there is nothing we can do, we cannot force the people to be independent if they do not wish to be so'; the revolution in Austria was a *fait accompli* and was carried out 'with greatest enthusiasm not only in Graz but also in Vienna and even Innsbruck', without any loss of life; it 'might be compared to what had happened when Fascist march on Rome took place.' When the ambassador interjected that only 30 per cent of the Austrians 'were really Nazi supporters and without outside aid *coup* would never have taken place', Ciano countered that the 30 per cent 'were enthusiastic, well organised and young', while the 70 per cent 'were much older men without any strong views and divided amongst themselves'. In the Foreign Office, Sargent minuted:

> If we hoped before to be able to weaken the Rome–Berlin axis by coming to an agreement with Italy, I fear that these hopes have been diminished almost to vanishing point by the appearance of German troops on the Italian frontier. So long as Germany remains, in the eyes of Italy, the strongest and most dangerous power in Europe, so long is she bound to associate with Germany in the interests of self-preservation.

If Italy ever thought that Britain was stronger and more dangerous than Germany, she might change her policy, but there was no 'possibility of this happening in the forseeable future'.[20]

On 13 March Palairet reported that all public offices, in Vienna as well as in the provinces, had been taken over, 'without, so far as I can ascertain, any incident whatsoever'. The military and air displays of the previous day 'had the desired effect and even population of Vienna which seemed apathetic and depressed yesterday morning had reached high eminence of enthusiasm by the evening. ... Nazification of Austria is proceeding very rapidly.' On the following day he telephoned: 'It is impossible to deny enthusiasm with which both the new régime and last night's announcement of incorporation in the Reich has been received here.' In his opinion, Hitler was 'justified in claiming that his action has been welcomed by Austrian population'. The British military attaché in Berlin, who knew Austria from many years' service, also commented on the vast throngs and the enthusiasm which he had observed in Vienna, far exceeding that of many earlier demonstrations by the Social Democrats, Heimwehr, Patriotic Front or the Church which he had seen. 'Austria as a whole appears not only satisfied, but to a great extent enthusiastic.' People holding different views 'were avoiding making themselves conspicuous', but the success of the inevitable *Gleichschaltung* seemed guaranteed by 'the number of keen supporters of fusion with Germany'. The German troops were well received everywhere and there was much fraternisation. The whole operation was carried out in a 'smooth and efficient way', but 'mechanised march discipline on the road was definitely very poor', and he had seen about 50 of the older light tanks broken down by the roadside; otherwise the columns made good time and the bearing of the troops was 'very soldierly'.

These accounts were outdone by *The Times* correspondent who reported on Hitler's reception:

> No adjective suffices to describe the jubilation which greeted him in Linz ... or that which awaited him in Vienna. ... This triumphant welcome was shared by the army he had sent into Austria; flowers were strewn in the path of the rumbling tractors and armoured cars. If any Austrians were against him on Friday, they either hid their faces or were completely converted yesterday and to-day.

The scene in Vienna had completely changed from the easygoing atmosphere beloved by visitors 'and become more like that of a militarized nation which National-Socialist Germany offers'.[21]

From Innsbruck the British consul wrote that during the night of 11/12 March, the National Socialist Party 'took over the public administration in this consular district with speed, precision and thoroughness'. In Salzburg the Austrian commanding officer placed himself under the orders of the arriving German general. In Innsbruck the Austrian Chief-of-Staff was cooperating with the Germans. SS Death's Head units from Dachau were 'welcomed by a boisterous crowd' which consisted partly of visitors from Munich; all leading officials were at once arrested, as were the leaders of the monarchists; clerks and typists in public offices who were not National Socialists were dismissed, but the Innsbruck police 'has gone over as a body to the new regime', under the command of a well-known National Socialist officer. SA and SS units were instructed not to be provocative and had on the whole obeyed these orders, but SS men had torn down and broken crucifixes they found in public offices.[22]

On 15 March *The Times* reported on the 'tumultuous welcome' Hitler received in Vienna: 'There are no signs of a people bowing unwillingly to a foreign yoke' and Vienna 'resembled a town which has just received news of a great victory'; every inhabitant seemed to be wearing a swastika. As Hitler reached the outskirts of the city, Cardinal Innitzer ordered the ringing of the church bells, the *Manchester Guardian* recounted. Later the Cardinal had an interview with Hitler which was stated to have been friendly, and it was understood that Innitzer would issue a proclamation to the people.

At the end of March a statement of the Austrian bishops was indeed read out in all Catholic churches,

> in view of the great and historical nature of the hours through which the people of Austria are now passing and in the consciousness that the centuries-old longing of the people to be united in one great Reich of the Germans has found its fulfilment.

The bishops acknowledged that the National Socialist movement provided 'in an outstanding manner for the German people ... in the spheres of popular and economic construction and social policy', especially for the poorest groups; they were convinced that the movement banished 'the danger of Bolshevism with its all-destroying godlessness'. Therefore on the day when the official plebiscite took place it was their 'natural national duty ... to profess our loyalty as Germans to the German Reich', and they expected 'all faithful Christians' to fulful their duty to the nation.[23] And this after years of a violent campaign of the German National Socialists against the Catholic Church.

As early as 14 March a Foreign Office official wrote: 'As Austria now has become a province of Germany and the President has resigned, we shall presumably before long be faced with a demand for the withdrawal of our Legation, that is for our recognition of Austria's demise.' To him it seemed advisable 'to accept the *fait accompli*', nothing could be gained by a refusal, and it would 'only make our relations with Germany worse than they are already.' If the question of Austria was not brought directly before the League, no British obligation to the League seemed to exist 'which would prevent us from taking this inglorious but realistic line.'

Only eight days later it was decided to withdraw the Legation and its staff from Vienna and to replace it by a consulate, and the

British consul in Munich was transferred to Vienna. The British Minister had been asked to report in person to the Foreign Office immediately after the occupation so as to avoid a 'possible German demand for your recall'. He did not return to Vienna. When a member of the German embassy in London called at the Foreign Office and expressed his hope that the events in Austria would not 'affect unfavourably the prospects of reconciliation between our two countries', Cadogan, the new Permanent Under-Secretary of State, replied that he fully shared this feeling: 'It was indeed unfortunate that all this should have occurred at a moment when conditions appeared favourable for the improvement of relations'; but it was a fact that the events 'had aroused a measure of indignation in this country, that the attitude to Anglo-German *rapprochement* would be found to have changed, and that it was no use thinking that we stood exactly where we did a week ago.'[24] The improvement of Anglo-German relations remained the overriding interest.

Not only was the Legation quickly withdrawn from Vienna, but in the same month the Treasury enquired what the Bank of England should do about the gold held for the Austrian National Bank which the latter had instructed them to transfer to the Bank of International Settlement, presumably for German account: unless the Bank of England received an indemnity from the government they would have to carry out the instruction, and the Treasury had no power to grant such an indemnity. In the Foreign Office Sargent minuted that the gold was at the free disposal of the Austrian National Bank and not pledged as a security for Austrian loans; the Bank of England would have to satisfy itself that the instructions came from the Austrian National Bank and not from any German authority; the fact that the British government had not yet recognised the annexation of Austria, but had only declared their intention of doing so, did not affect the issue, and the instructions would have to be carried out, although the Austrian National Bank had been taken over by the Germans.[25]

Soon numerous and detailed reports reached London about the persecution of Jews and the political enemies of the new regime. Even Henderson in Berlin telephoned to London that numerous arrests had been made all over Austria and 'it is feared that a policy of vengeance may be pursued against Dr

Schuschnigg and his supporters'. German 'Nazi Extremists' had taken control and all 'Austrians, even Austrian Nazis, are being pushed into the background', but 'moderate elements' wanted to urge on Hitler a policy of 'generous toleration' and 'of allowing Austrians some say in the Government of their own country'. The saga of the 'moderates' and 'extremists' who were supposed to gain Hitler's ear was still running strong.

The horror of the persecution of Jews and other 'enemies' of the new regime emerged even from the deprecating reports of the British Legation. On 15 March the chargé d'affaires wrote: 'Jewish cars and property have been seized and many Jewish houses searched. I hear that many Jews have been detained.' Cars belonging to Legitimists and supporters of Schuschnigg had also been confiscated and many members of both groups as well as many socialists had been arrested; there were rumours of executions but he was unable to confirm this. A few days later he reported that the Jews were treated as they were in Germany and there were 'many stories of acts of brutality committed against them'; arrests were said 'to run into thousands of various classes'; no doubt 'unofficial Austrian bands' were active. That the looting was perpetrated by 'unofficial bands' was the official German version, but this the report did not mention.

The British consul reported that a former RAF captain, now a hotel proprietor in Vienna, was arrested by two SA men carrying rifles but released after some hours following consular intervention. The arrest had been made on the ground that, as a Jew, he had no right to hoist the swastika flag on his hotel. In fact, he had not been near it and was not responsible for raising the flag. He was then told not to return to the hotel which had been confiscated and was now run by the National Socialist Party. As he had a British passport he was able to leave Vienna with his family. Another British citizen preparing to leave by air was stopped and directed 'to proceed to one of the buildings of the airport, where he was not merely searched in an insulting manner, but was stripped even to his socks.'[26] These were British citizens who were protected by their passports: the fate of the many thousands of Austrians can easily be imagined.

On 16 March *The Times* carried a story of what happened to them when they reached the Swiss frontier. Even before they arrived there, they had been taken off the train, conveyed to police headquarters in Innsbruck and strip-searched for any contraband. At the frontier there 'stood a young man with a thick book in his hand containing many thousands of printed names and descriptions and a thumb index'; he then compared the name of each fugitive with his papers to see if he was on the wanted list – 'a living proof of the extraordinary efficiency of the parent National-Socialist Reich'. On the following day *The Times* mentioned that many Jewish professional men had received visits from SA men who took away all the money and jewellery they could find; many cafés were putting up notices saying 'Jewish customers not desired', and the elimination of Jews from their posts was 'rapidly and ruthlessly carried through'.

According to the *Manchester Guardian*, three kinds of shops now existed in Vienna: those declaring 'this shop is Aryan', those labelled 'non-Aryan' or simply with the word 'Jude' on the windows, and those with notices 'This shop has been taken over by the Nazi trading organisation' or 'This shop is now under Aryan control'. On 19 March the paper stated that 'the terror in Austria has become unbearable'. Since the return of the Austrian Legion from Germany the situation had further deteriorated; the legionaries arrived with lists of their enemies, 'and their revenge is terrible'. The terror had first been directed at activists of the 'Patriotic Front', but was now intensified against socialists and communists as well as monarchists, and arrests were estimated to exceed 10,000. On the following day reports were published that Jews were taken from their flats to clean off the patriotic slogans daubed on the walls during the plebiscite campaign; other Jews were forced to wash the streets or the cars of SA leaders.

On 26 March *The Times* recorded that SS guards in 'their new uniforms' had turned the synagogue and house of the Jewish community 'into a Jew-baiting establishment'; Jews were forced to put on top-hats and liturgical scarfs 'as if for a religious ceremony' and were then made to sweep the street. Jews who did not know of the SS occupation were allowed in and later ejected: 'their treatment could only be guessed by their wry faces and the limping gait.' The correspondent of the *Daily Telegraph* watched how, for the amusement of the crowd, Jews were brought out of the house 'and forced to sweep the streets of the rubbish which grinning storm-troopers kept throwing out of the windows.'[27]

The Times also reported that three times in four days the activities of unauthorised plunderers were denounced by the National Socialist Party as well as the police. Severe punishments were threatened to all those who did not report these 'collections', whether they were the victims or their 'visitors'. An official communiqué claimed that communists disguised as stormtroopers were responsible for robbing Jewish flats; any intereference with private enterprises was to be avoided if possible. These orders meant, as the correspondent thought, that the authorities recognised 'that the reckless pace set by local anti-Semites in the first few days threatens Austrian economics with complete chaos.' It was impossible for Jews to leave Austria legally for the time being because the Gestapo was 'engaged in a systematic investigation of the entire Jewish community', and the frontiers were watched so closely that an illegal crossing was extremely difficult.[28] The loot and plunder was to benefit the Third Reich, and not individual National Socialists, eager to line their own pockets.

From Vienna Lord Cecil received a letter describing the events in detail: 'Yesterday morning came lorries manned by Nazis with fixed bayonets on rifles to all Jewish provision shops. The owners of the shops were compelled to hand over all the goods free, and further to hand over the business to an Aryan, and then were sent away.' Jews were stopped in the streets and their money was confiscated. In the Jewish quarter of Vienna, 'drunken National Socialists stormed the temples, drove out the Jews, who were then by other groups bloodily assaulted. The most holy books of our Law were then torn to pieces and trodden under foot, and all the gold and silver vessels ravished.' An official of the Foreign Office, however, thought that this picture of conditions in Vienna was 'rather highly coloured'; but he had to admit that 'the sober facts are unpleasant enough', as shown by the press reports.[29] He also wrote: 'there will be many Jews anxious to get out of Austria when the frontier is opened again.... The refugee problem may then become more acute.'

On 19 March another Foreign Office official, P. Nichols, minuted that he hoped 'we shall use what influence we have with the Home Office in favour of interpreting the existing regulations regarding the entry of aliens as widely as is compatible with the general interest. We may yet stand to gain by stretching points at this moment in favour of the unfortunate Jews fleeing from Nazi terrorism' – a point he made 'on grounds both of humanity and our own self-interest'. A meeting on the admission of refugees was held at the Home Office at which its representatives stressed that 'they cannot tolerate a continuance of uncontrolled immigration' from Austria or Germany; they were in favour of introducing a visa system to avoid 'that refugees will be turned back from the ports at the end of their journey'. The purpose was not 'that no more refugees should be admitted, but only that they should be more carefully scrutinised in order to ensure that they will not become a liability.' It was also pointed out that the influx 'may be used as a cover for the introduction of enemy agents' – a claim made repeatedly, but for which no proof was ever furnished. The Home Office officials realised 'that they will be shot at for restricting the entry of Austrian – and German – refugees', but 'considerations of national interest' were paramount. It was in vain that Nichols again wrote that 'it will be in our own best *self-interest* (& quite apart from the humanitarian aspect) to give as generous an interpretation as possible to our regulations'. He was the only official to make this crucial point.[30] On 15 March Dr Ernest Jones flew to Vienna to rescue Sigmund Freud, and the Legation was instructed to help him at the special request of the Lord Privy Seal, the Earl de la Warr.[31]

That there was 'considerable anxiety' in Britain about the 'position of Jews and Socialists in Austria' emerged during a debate in the House of Commons on 22 March. Arthur Henderson asked the Home Secretary, Sir Samuel Hoare, why some Austrian refugees had been refused permission to land a week earlier. The Home Secretary replied that of the six Austrians concerned four had been admitted, one was not a refugee, and the sixth had previously been refused permission to settle in Britain. Later he declared that he was anxious to maintain the traditional policy of offering asylum to refugees, who were forced to leave their country for political, religious or social reasons, but objections existed to 'any policy of indiscriminate admission. Such a policy would not only create difficulties from the police point of view, but would have grave economic results in aggravating the unemployment problem, the housing problem and other social problems.' Admission would not be refused to persons 'whose work in the world of science or the arts or business and industry might be advantageous to this country'; but it must be remembered that even in the professions there was a 'danger of overcrowding' and it was 'essential to avoid creating an impression that the door is open to immigrants of all kinds.' When Aneurin Bevan pressed him that poor people who had to leave Austria or Germany on account of persecution should also be admitted, Hoare only added: 'I shall give the most sympathetic consideration that I can to every case.'

On the same day another Labour MP, Sir Josiah Wedgwood, asked leave to introduce a Bill to amend the Aliens Act and to relax the conditions for the entry of refugees for six months, even if they were destitute, and provided many details of the terror reigning in Vienna, and of the 'public humiliation and degradation' of innocent people. But he was opposed by a Conservative MP, Sir George Davies, who declared that 'drug traffickers, white slave traffickers, people with criminal records' might easily slip in, and the motion was lost by 210 to 142 votes. The policy of the Home Office with regard to the admission of refugees from the Continent remained restrictive, and in fact a mere 1317 Austrians were given leave to land between 1 and 29 March 1938, while 61 were refused entry.[32] A more liberal policy was only adopted after the terrible German pogroms of November 1938, and there can be no doubt that Britain greatly benefited from the more generous policy.

Notes

1. Wires by Palairet to FO, 7, 11 and 12 February 1938: FO 371, file 22310, fos. 227, 235, 249. In general see Alan Bullock, *Hitler – A Study in Tyranny*, rev. edn (London, 1973), pp. 420 ff. For Beck's memorandum of May 1937, see K. J. Müller, *General Ludwig Beck* (Boppard am Rhein, 1980), pp. 493 ff.
2. Palairet to FO, 14–15 February 1938: FO 371, file 22310, fo. 255 f., file 22311, fo. 4; *The Times*, 14 February 1938.
3. *Manchester Guardian*, 13–15 February; minute by E. M. B. Ingram, 15 February, and Palairet to FO, 15 February 1938: FO 371, file 22311, fos. 1 ff., 20.
4. Minute by P.H. Hadow, 16 February (emphasis in the original), Palairet to Eden, 19 February, and wire to FO, 19 February 1938: FO 371, file 22311, fo. 142, file 22312, fo. 231 f., file 22311, fo. 192.

5. Minutes by Sargent, 16 and 19 February (emphasis in the original), and Conclusions of a Cabinet meeting, 19 February 1938: FO 371, file 22311, fo. 64, file 22312, fo. 6, Cab. 23, vol. 92, pp. 178, 183.

6. *The Times*, 15 February; minute by Vansittart, 19 February, W.G.Osborne to Eden, 18 February, Palairet to FO, 23 February, with minutes of 23–24 February and Vansittart's minute of 4 March 1938: FO 371, file 22312, fos. 85, 109, 111 ff., 115.

7. Palairet to Secretary of State, 25 February 1938: FO 371, file 22313, fo. 24 ff.

8. *Manchester Guardian*, 19 and 21 February; *The Times*, 19 and 26 February 1938; Gordon Brook-Shepherd, *Anschluss – The Rape of Austria* (London, 1963), p. 105.

9. Gedye, *Fallen Bastions*, p. 251; *The Times*, 21 February; *Manchester Guardian*, 21 and 28 February 1938.

10. Minute by Hadow, 3 March 1938, on letter from Kienböck, s.d.: FO 371, file 22313, fo. 170.

11. Circular to Dominion governments, 26 February, and Phipps to FO, Paris 4 March 1938: FO 371, file 22313, fos. 80 f., 157.

12. *The Times* and the *Manchester Guardian* of 9 March carried brief accounts of the meeting; more detailed Palairet to Halifax, 9 March 1938: FO 371, file 22318, fos. 39–42. The four demands listed vary somewhat in these reports and in Schuschnigg, *Im Kampf gegen Hitler*, p. 175, and Joseph Buttinger, *Am Beispiel Österreichs* (Cologne, 1953), p. 510, but the discrepancies are slight. The Watzek interview in Palairet to Halifax, 7 March, with a minute of 15 March 1938: FO 371, file 22316, fo. 13 ff.

13. Palairet to Halifax, 9 March 1938: FO 371, file 22318, fo. 42 f.; *Manchester Guardian*, 11 March 1938; Gedye, *Fallen Bastions*, p. 284.

14. *The Times*, 10 March; Palairet to Halifax, 9 March, and Henderson to Halifax, 11 March 1938: DBFP, 3rd series, i, 1949, nos. 2 and 14, pp. 1 f., 8; Gedye, *Fallen Bastions*, pp. 275–6.

15. Palairet to FO, 7 March: FO 371, file 22313, fo 168; *The Times*, 7 March; *Manchester Guardian*, 7 March 1938.

16. *The Times*, 11 March; Palairet to FO, 10–11 March 1938: DBFP, 3rd series, i, nos. 7, 13, 17, 19 and 20, pp. 4, 7, 9 f.; Gedye, *Fallen Bastions*, pp. 289–90.

17. Conclusions of a Cabinet meeting, 12 March, 1938: Cab. 23, vol. 92, pp. 346–9.

18. Palairet to FO, 11 March: DBFP, 3rd series, i, nos. 21, 30, 35, 38, pp. 11, 15, 17 f.; *The Times*, 12 March 1938.

19. Henderson to FO, Berlin, 12 March, and Halifax to Henderson,

11 March 1938: DBFP, 3rd series, i, nos. 44, 46, 48, pp. 22–5; *The Times*, 12 March; *Manchester Guardian*, 12 March 1938. For the decisive hours in Vienna, see Bullock, *Hitler – A Study in Tyranny*, pp. 428–31.

20. Palairet to Halifax, 13 March, Earl of Perth to Halifax, 12 March, Chamberlain's circular to Dominion governments, 12 March, and Sargent's minute, 14 March 1938: DBFP, 3rd series, i, nos. 53, 65, pp. 27, 38; FO 371, file 22318, fo. 25 f., file 22315, fo. 25.

21. Palairet to FO 13–14 March, and Col. Mason-MacFarlane to Henderson, 16 March 1938: DBFP, 3rd series, i, nos. 66, 76, pp. 38, 43; FO 371, file 22318, fos. 9–12; *The Times*, 14 March 1938.

22. Ian Henderson to Palairet, 13 March 1938: FO 371, file 22318, fos. 139–43.

23. *Manchester Guardian*, 16 March; Mack to Halifax, 28 March 1938: FO 371, file 22319, fo. 283 f.

24. Minute by A.M. Noble, 14 March, FO to Palairet, 13 March, FO to Mack, 22 March, and minute by Cadogan, 15 March 1938: FO 371, file 22317, fo. 29, file 22315, fo. 197, file 22319, fo. 85, file 22318, fo. 123.

25. Minute by S. D. Waley, Treasury, S. D., with minute by Sargent, 21 March 1938: FO 371, file 22309, fo. 202 f.

26. Henderson to Halifax, 16 March, Mack to FO, 15 and 19 March, J. W. Taylor to Halifax, 14 March, and Commander O. Locker Lampson to Halifax, 16 March 1938: DBFP, 3rd series, i, no. 88, p. 59f.; FO 371, file 22316, fo. 133, file 22318, fo. 50, file 22321, fos. 273 f., 319. For a question on this asked in the House of Commons, see *Parliamentary Debates*, 5th series, 1938, vol. 333, col. 382.

27. *The Times*, 16, 17 and 26 March; *Manchester Guardian*, 18, 19, 21 and 26 March 1938; Gedye, *Fallen Bastions*, p. 310.

28. *The Times*, 17 and 21 March 1938.

29. Unsigned letter from Vienna, 15 March 1938, sent by Cecil to FO, with a minute by A. M. Noble, 25 March: FO 371, file 22319, fo. 42 ff.

30. Minutes by P. Nichols and A. M. Noble, 19–21 March 1938 (emphasis in the original): FO 371, file 22317, fo. 214 ff. For Home Office policy with regard to the refugees, see A. J. Sherman, *Island Refuge – Britain and Refugees from the Third Reich* (London, 1973), esp. pp. 73, 88, 179 ff.

31. FO to Mack, 15 March 1938: FO 371, file 22321, fo. 290.

32. Halifax to Palairet, 12 March 1938: FO 371, file 22317, fo. 146; *Parliamentary Debates*, 5th series, vol. 333, cols. 990 ff., 1003–10, 2157.

10 Conclusion

The records of the Foreign Office and other British government departments as well as those of the Legation in Vienna amply illustrate the history of the First Austrian Republic; they are very detailed, not only on foreign policy but equally on internal political, social and economic developments and contain much that is not known from other sources. During the early years after the collapse of the Habsburg Monarchy, the reports are to a large extent concerned with the appalling social and economic conditions, with the alleged danger of Bolshevism spreading into Austria from Hungary, and with the armed para-military associations which grew up to combat this danger but were illegal under the terms of the Treaty of St Germain. It was soon recognised that, with the collapse of the Hungarian Soviet Republic in August 1919, the Bolshevik danger receded and that the strong Austrian Social Democratic Party provided an effective barrier against this supposed danger. But there remained the fateful division between town and country, between 'red' Vienna and the provinces, and with it the continued existence of the Heimwehren which were supported by the right-wing provincial governments of Carinthia, Styria, Vorarlberg and the Tyrol.

For some time the British diplomats hoped that Schober, as the 'strong' man of the government, would bring about the disarmament of the rival para-military associations, but these hopes were doomed to disappointment. After July 1927 the Heimwehren became a real menace to the Republican order and came increasingly under the influence of the victorious fascist government to the south.

What may have saved the Republic for the time being was the

fact that they never managed to establish a unified leadership, that their provincial leaders constantly quarrelled with each other, and that none of them was of the calibre to carry out a successful *coup d'état*. Indeed, it seems miraculous that a movement so disunited and so barren of ideas and able leaders was able to play such a major part in politics for many years. That the Austrian government was able to resist all the demands for disarmament shows that a small country, entirely dependent on outside financial help, could successfully defy far more powerful countries even if their demands were perfectly legitimate. If the para-military associations had been dissolved, or only effectively disarmed, the whole history of the first Republic might have been different, and it seems at least possible that a stronger consensus might have developed between the government and the socialist opposition.

It is well known that for some years after 1918 Austria wholly depended on imports of food and coal and on foreign financial aid. It is less well known how much the British diplomats and authorities, especially Sir Thomas Cuninghame, the military attaché, and private British organisations achieved in organising this aid. The best-known general history of Austria, by Professor Erich Zöllner, lists the countries contributing to the relief efforts for Austria, but does not mention Britain. The records of the Society of Friends give a vivid picture of how much was done for Austria and how many young men and women worked selflessly in Vienna and elsewhere. Strong sympathy was aroused in Britain, especially for the suffering children, and British help matched that rendered by the United States and by the Scandinavian countries: efforts which then received ample acknowledgement from the Austrian authorities. More might have been done earlier, and more certainly could have been done in the 1930s, when the German boycott of Austrian trade once more jeopardised the very existence of Austria. The British Cabinet papers show how pitiful the British record was during the world economic crisis, when 'velour hats' was all that the Board of Trade felt able to offer as an aid to Austrian exports and soon after imposed a special duty on this very item. All the efforts of the Foreign Office to gain concessions for Austrian exports proved in vain against the opposition of the Board of Trade.

After Hitler became the German Chancellor and pursued

ruthlessly his policy of trying to compel Austria to surrender, the prevailing opinion in the Foreign Office and elsewhere in Britain was that Austria was a 'lost cause', that British diplomacy was backing 'the wrong horse': an opinion that was reinforced by Dollfuss's suppression of 'red' Vienna and the Socialists. The basis of the new 'authoritarian' regime was extremely narrow, and the regime was constantly threatened from inside and out. Time and again it sought a compromise or tried to negotiate with some allegedly 'moderate' Nationalists or National Socialists; but an attempt to do so with the political left was only undertaken when the clock showed 'five minutes to twelve'. By then it was much too late. It could be argued that a successful attempt of that kind undertaken not in 1938, but years earlier might have provided a more stable basis for the regime. It would certainly have been opposed by Mussolini, but after 1935 Mussolini did precious little for Austria. His empire-building in Africa met with opposition from the Western powers and made him rely more and more on the support and friendship of the other great 'Duce', who was violently hostile to an independent Austria. Whether a reconciliation with the left was practical politics, and what its results might have been, is a question which the historian cannot answer. All he can say is: it might have been worth trying. The attempts to obtain from the so-called 'moderate' right recognition of Austria's independence were bound to fail as long as the German dictator remained firmly opposed to it.

The events of February/March 1938 gave British policy a severe jolt – but one not sufficient to abandon the government's policy of appeasement. This policy was seen by Hitler as a sign of British weakness and decay. It did not deter him from pursuing his preconceived aims with even greater determination. These aims were clearly analysed in the Foreign Office, but the recognition did not lead to a change of policy. For the time being 'appeasement' remained the order of the day.

There is another important question which cannot be answered from the evidence available. How strong was the longing for union with Germany which the reports mentioned so often, and to what extent was it due to the suffering of the people? That the leaders of the beleaguered socialists hoped to find succour from the much stronger German socialist parties which were strongly represented in the government of Germany is only natural. Otto Bauer and other leaders remained committed to the Anschluss throughout their lives, but it does not seem that the idea found an equally strong echo among the masses of the working class.

The true protagonists of the Anschluss were the German Nationalists or Pan-Germans who were above all a party of the urban intelligentsia and the white-collar workers. In 1919 they polled 18 per cent of the total vote, but less than 13 per cent in 1923 – a considerable decline – the time of acute economic crisis and severe inflation which in theory should have strengthened their case. At the same time the Christian Social Party, which was markedly lukewarm towards a possible union with Germany, grew from 36 to 45 per cent of the total vote. If these figures have any relevance to the question they seem to indicate that propaganda for the Anschluss was not an issue which swayed the masses. In the later 1920s German nationalism in Austria seemed to be a dead cause.* The reports mention on several occasions that there was quite a different tendency which counteracted the idea of union with Germany: the widespread dislike of Prussia and North German Protestantism, and who could deny that in a 'Greater Germany' the north and the Protestants would still have been the dominating factor? After 1933, of course, the issue changed completely, and the protagonists of the Anschluss were the National Socialists, while their opponents also opposed a union with Hitler's Germany. Among the defenders of the authoritarian regime, on the other hand, there began to develop an Austrian patriotism, basically conservative and Catholic, but in the end penetrating to the socialist workers – and this was to bear fruit in later years.

The British reports provide a detailed picture of political life in Austria, of the political parties and their leaders, among whom Otto Bauer and Karl Renner figure very prominently, as do Ignaz Seipel and Johann Schober. In general, though with some

---

* In May 1931 Vansittart believed 'that a political "Anschluss" has lost some of its attractiveness ... while even in Austria it is at the moment less to the fore.' The German Ambassador in London, von Neurath, had recently told him 'that 90 per cent of political Germany was now against the "Anschluss", seeing the accretion of Socialists and Catholics — and nothing else — that Austria would bring to the already well-stocked Reichstag' (Vansittart's memorandum of May 1931: FO 371, file 15205, fo. 338, p. 14).

exceptions, the reports are sympathetic and without a strong bias; and the same applies to the later accounts of Dollfuss and Schuschnigg. The records show how close the contacts were between the British Ministers in Vienna and the members of the Austrian government and senior civil servants who supplied the Legation with confidential information. Unfortunately, however, any one Minister was posted to Vienna at most for a few years, and many of them for a much shorter time. If there were far too frequent changes of Austrian governments, the same applied to the British diplomats in Vienna. When a serious crisis occurred – as in 1927 or in 1938 – the British Minister was as a rule new to his post, which did little to facilitate his task. The records also describe in great detail the economic disabilities from which the Austrian Republic suffered: the near-famine conditions of the early 1920s, the collapse of all the leading banks in the late 1920s and early 1930s, which was not due to the aftermath of the Great War, but largely to mismanagement and corruption. During the world economic crisis of the 1930s Austria once more suffered from declining trade and severe unemployment, which especially affected the young who began to listen to the siren song from across the frontier. Among them, and among other social groups, anti-Semitic propaganda which had a long tradition in Austria found a ready echo. This applied above all to the university students and to the 'intelligentsia' of town and country, whose ideology was traditionally German Nationalist or even Pan-German.

The reports show how fragile was the political structure of the first Austrian Republic, with government and opposition separated by a wide gulf, with strong para-military associations violently opposed to each other, with the outbreak of civil war as an ever-present threat, and with the terrible riots of July 1927 and their bloody repression. It is true that similar weaknesses bedevilled the history of the Weimar Republic; but in Austria polarisation and confrontation were more clearly marked, and much more clearly based on deep social conflicts. After 1920 the Social Democrats, in contrast with Germany, went into permanent opposition, and the deep division between town and country made the outbreak of civil war much more likely. When civil war did break out in 1934 it only lasted a few days – in February as well as in July. But the authoritarian regime was not really strengthened by its victories and remained uneasily balanced between the strong opposition forces of the right and of the left. It tried to cope with the ever-growing threat from Germany by making concessions to the 'national opposition' and finally succumbed, having been left in the lurch by the western powers and by fascist Italy.

Yet from the chaos of the Second World War a new Austria was to arise, far more stable and prosperous than the first Republic had ever been, and no longer dependent on the hand-outs of the great powers. No one looking at the history of the years 1918–38 could have expected this 'miracle'. The idea of the Anschluss is dead and buried, it would seem for good: one of the lasting achievements brought about by Adolf Hitler.

Bibliography

Unpublished sources

Haus-, Hof- und Staatsarchiv, Vienna: Nachlass Otto Bauer, box 261.

Imperial War Museum: Papers of G. E. R. Gedye, GERG 10 and 15.

Labour Party Archives: Labour Party International Advisory Committee, Memos no. 263.

Public Record Office

Cab. 23, vols 78, 92, 93.
Cab. 24, files 229, 237–45, 247–51, 253–7, 259–65, 267–75.
FO 120 (Legation Vienna), vols 924–1137.
FO 371, files 3133–39, 3507–62, 4355, 4625–55, 5738–88, 7333–60, 8537–54, 9645–57, 10660–62, 11211–15, 12074–81, 12849–51, 13563–67, 14304–12, 15150–65, 15888–93, 16626–48, 18342–68, 19478–85, 20359–68, 21113–20, 22309–21.
FO 800, file 272 (Sargent Papers), files 280–4 (Henderson Papers), files 287–89, 291 (Simon Papers).
WO 155, files 21 and 22.
WO 190, files 73, 83, 90, 107, 128, 137, 148, 167, 191, 192, 204, 206, 210, 213, 288, 293, 316, 319, 418, 443, 444, 605.

Society of Friends Library

Friends' Council for International Service, Central Europe Committee, Minutes 1921–25.

Minutes of the Vienna Sub-Committee & Austria Committee, 1925–27.
Friends' Emergency and War Victims Relief Committee, Minutes of the Austria and Hungary Sub-Committee, 1920–22.
Papers relating to Friends' Relief Mission in Austria, box 4, parcel 2, folders 2, 4 and 8.
Box 4, parcel 3, folders 1 and 3a.
Box 5, parcel 3, folder 1.
The Friend, new series, vols lix, 919, xx, 1920, xxi, 1921.

Published sources

Akten zur deutschen auswärtigen Politik 1918–1945, series C 1933–37, vol. I 2 (Göttingen, 1971).
Documents on British Foreign Policy 1919–39, 1st series, vols vi and xii (London, 1956 and 1962).
Series IA, vol. vii (London, 1975).
2nd series, vols v and vi (London, 1956–57).
3rd series, vol. i (London, 1949).
Parliamentary debates, 5th series, vol. 333, House of Commons (London, 1938).
Manchester Guardian, 1927, 1928, 1931, 1933, 1934, 1936 and 1938.
The Times, 1919, 1925, 1927, 1928, 1931, 1933, 1934, 1936, 1937 and 1938.

Secondary authorities

Borkenau, Franz, *Austria and After* (London, 1938).
Brook-Shepherd, Gordon, *Anschluss – The Rape of Austria* (London, 1963).
Bullock, Alan, *Hitler – A Study in Tyranny*, rev. edn (London, 1973).
Buttinger, Joseph, *Am Beispiel Österreichs* (Cologne, 1953).
Carsten, F. L., *Fascist Movements in Austria – From Schönerer to Hitler* (London and Beverly Hills, 1977).
——*Revolution in Central Europe 1918–1919* (London, 1972).
Dockrill, Michael L. and Goold, J. Douglas, *Peace without*

Promise – Britain and the Peace Conference 1919–1923 (London, 1981).

Gedye, G. E. R., *Fallen Bastions – The Central European Tragedy* (London, 1939).

Goldinger, Walter, *Geschichte der Republik Österreich* (Vienna, 1962).

Gulick, Charles A., *Austria from Habsburg to Hitler* (Berkeley and Los Angeles, 1948).

Jagschitz, Gerhard, *Der Putsch – Die Nationalsozialisten 1934 in Österreich* (Graz, Vienna and Cologne, 1976).

Pulzer, Peter G. J., *The Rise of Political Anti-Semitism in Germany and Austria* (New York, London and Sidney, 1964).

Schuschnigg, Kurt, *Im Kampf gegen Hitler – Die Überwindung der Anschlussidee* (Vienna, Munich and Zürich, 1969).

Selby, Sir Walford, *Diplomatic Twilight 1930–1940* (London, 1953).

Sherman, A.J., *Island Refuge – Britain and Refugees from the Third Reich 1933–1939* (London, 1973).

Stadler, Karl R., *The Birth of the Austrian Republic 1918–1921* (Leiden, 1966).

Vanry, Frank (Franz Weinreb), *Der Zaungast – Lebenserinnerungen*, Materialien zur Arbeiterbewegung Nr. 27 (Vienna, 1983).

Weinberg, Gerhard L., *The Foreign Policy of Hitler's Germany – Diplomatic Revolution in Europe 1933–1936* (Chicago and London, 1970).

Zöllner, Erich, *Geschichte Österreichs – Von den Anfängen bis zur Gegenwart* (Vienna, 1961).

Austrian Chancellors, 1918–38

Karl Renner, November 1918 – June 1920
Michael Mayr, June 1920 – June 1921
Johann Schober, June 1921 – May 1922
Ignaz Seipel, May 1922 – November 1924
Rudolf Ramek, November 1924 – October 1926
Ignaz Seipel, October 1926 – May 1929
Ernst Streeruwitz, May – September 1929
Johann Schober, September 1929 – September 1930
Carl Vaugoin, September – November 1930
Otto Ender, December 1930 – June 1931
Karl Buresch, June 1931 – May 1932
Engelbert Dollfuss, May 1932 – July 1934
Kurt von Schuschnigg, July 1934 – March 1938

Index